T0380404

DIGITAL PRODUCT MANAGEMENT

Focusing on operational excellence, this book will take readers through the practicalities of product development, market launch, and ongoing product support. Building on the strategic foundation from Volume 1, *Digital Product Management: Strategic Planning and Market Opportunity*, this volume emphasizes executing product strategies in real-world contexts.

The book covers key methodologies such as agile development, product lifecycle management, and data-driven decision-making. Topics include marketing strategies, sales channel management, customer engagement, and optimizing digital experiences. It also delves into product analytics, customer retention, and feature adoption. With chapters on building a product operating model and scaling product operations, the volume emphasizes how organizations can drive continuous improvement and ensure alignment across teams. Ethical leadership and continuous innovation are also explored, highlighting the critical role of ethics in digital product management.

This book is an essential resource for product managers looking to refine their skills in execution, cross-functional collaboration, and operational growth as well as for professionals aiming to combine strategy with practical delivery. It is particularly useful for those responsible for managing the development, launch, and support of digital products, ensuring products not only meet market needs but also evolve with customer expectations.

Boon Kee Lee is a senior lecturer in the Department of Information Systems and Analytics, School of Computing, National University of Singapore. He has 30 years of consulting experience in product management and software development. His research interest is digital product management and digital ethics.

DIGITAL PRODUCT MANAGEMENT

Managing Product Development, Launch and Support

Boon Kee Lee

CRC Press
Taylor & Francis Group
Boca Raton London New York

CRC Press is an imprint of the
Taylor & Francis Group, an **informa** business

Designed cover image: Getty Images

First edition published 2025
by CRC Press
2385 NW Executive Center Drive, Suite 320, Boca Raton FL 33431

and by CRC Press
4 Park Square, Milton Park, Abingdon, Oxon, OX14 4RN

CRC Press is an imprint of Taylor & Francis Group, LLC

© 2025 Boon Kee Lee

Library of Congress Cataloging-in-Publication Data
Names: Lee, Boon Kee, author.
Title: Digital product management : managing product development, launch and support / Boon Kee Lee.
Description: First edition. | Boca Raton, FL : CRC Press, 2025. | Includes bibliographical references and index.
Identifiers: LCCN 2024054227 (print) | LCCN 2024054228 (ebook) | ISBN 9781041013228 (hardback) | ISBN 9781041013211 (paperback) | ISBN 9781003614180 (ebook)
Subjects: LCSH: Management–Technological innovations. | Digital media–Management. | Digital electronics–Management.
Classification: LCC HD30.2 .L436 2025 (print) | LCC HD30.2 (ebook) | DDC 658.4/038–dc23/eng/20250204
LC record available at https://lccn.loc.gov/2024054227
LC ebook record available at https://lccn.loc.gov/2024054228

ISBN: 978-1-041-01322-8 (hbk)
ISBN: 978-1-041-01321-1 (pbk)
ISBN: 978-1-003-614180 (ebk)

DOI: 10.1201/9781003614180

Typeset in Sabon
by Newgen Publishing UK

CONTENTS

1

DIGITAL PRODUCT MANAGEMENT OVERVIEW

1.1 Introduction

In this opening chapter of *Digital Product Management: Managing Product Development, Launch, and Support,* we reintroduce the digital product management (DPM) landscape and offer readers a comprehensive view of how product management responsibilities extend beyond strategic planning and market opportunity. Volume 1 of this series detailed how product managers are primarily responsible for creating value through product strategy, market opportunity analysis, and product planning. Volume 2 now focuses on the operational aspects: how products are developed, launched, and continuously supported in the market. We explore how modern product managers must orchestrate the entire product lifecycle, ensuring products remain relevant and valuable long after their initial launch.

1.2 The Digital Product Management Framework

The DPM framework revolves around five core process groups, as shown in Figure 1.1.

1. Product Opportunity

The first process group focuses on defining and establishing a product's strategic vision. Product managers create a clear and actionable product strategy, evaluating market opportunities, and identifying customer needs. By shaping product positioning, pricing strategies, and go-to-market plans, product managers align the product's development with overall business goals. This stage lays the groundwork for long-term success, as product

DOI: 10.1201/9781003614180-1

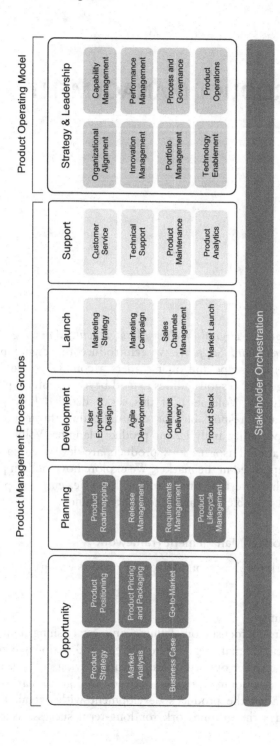

FIGURE 1.1 Digital Product Management Framework.

managers work to ensure that their product is addressing a genuine market gap and is well-positioned for profitability.

Key Activities:

- **Product Strategy:** Develop a product vision and realistic plans to shape the product's direction.
- **Market Analysis:** Assess market trends, target customer segments, and unmet needs.
- **Business Case:** Justify new products or strategic shifts through well-structured business cases.
- **Product Positioning:** Define how customers should perceive the product in the marketplace.
- **Product Pricing and Packaging:** Optimize financial returns and customer value with tailored pricing strategies.
- **Go-to-Market Strategy:** Plan the effective introduction of the product to the market.

2. Product Planning

Product Planning is the next step, where product managers turn the vision into actionable steps by developing roadmaps and planning product releases. They work with cross-functional teams to prioritize requirements and align releases with market conditions. Although this stage is carried out before the market launch, planning is iterative, and adjustments must be made throughout the product lifecycle.

Key Activities:

- **Product Roadmapping:** Create a roadmap that outlines the product's vision and direction over time.
- **Release Management:** Plan and communicate product releases to market and stakeholders.
- **Requirements Management:** Identify, analyse, and prioritize product requirements in alignment with business goals.
- **Product Lifecycle Management:** Adapt product iterations in response to fast-paced market changes.

3. Product Development

Product Development involves the actual design and creation of the product, with a strong emphasis on customer experience. Modern Agile methodologies are employed to deliver the product in iterative cycles, while maintaining a focus on User Experience (UX), continuous delivery, and refining the product stack. Development is a continuous process that extends across all stages of the product life cycle, ensuring the product evolves to meet changing customer needs.

Key Activities:

- **UX Design:** Prioritize customer interactions and touchpoints for a seamless user experience.
- **Agile Development:** Utilize Agile methods to develop the product iteratively in collaboration with customers and teams.
- **Continuous Delivery:** Deliver product updates frequently and with accuracy through short, iterative cycles.
- **Product Stack:** Assess and optimize the technology and resources supporting the product's development.

4. Product Launch

In the Product Launch phase, product managers ensure the product's introduction to the market is well-executed. This includes developing a robust marketing strategy, managing sales channels, and ensuring the right audience is targeted. The product launch can extend beyond the initial release, as new updates and product expansions may require re-launch activities throughout the lifecycle.

Key Activities:

- **Marketing Strategy:** Develop strategies that effectively communicate the product's value to acquire customers.
- **Marketing Campaign:** Create multichannel campaigns to meet specific business goals and reach intended audiences.
- **Sales Channels Management:** Build and manage a sales distribution strategy to maximize reach.
- **Market Launch:** Plan and execute the successful market introduction of the product.

5. Product Support

Product Support is essential for the ongoing success of a product, as it involves managing customer service, technical support, product maintenance, and product analytics. This stage is critical to ensuring the product continues to perform well and adapt to changing customer needs. Product managers oversee these areas to improve customer satisfaction and drive continuous product improvement.

Key Activities:

- **Customer Service:** Enhance customer experience by proactively resolving issues and offering valuable support.
- **Technical Support:** Create structures for addressing technical challenges faced by users.

- **Product Maintenance:** Continuously update and refine the product to stay in line with customer demands and technological advances.
- **Product Analytics:** Track product usage and performance metrics to identify opportunities for improvement and growth.

This framework reflects the product manager's journey from conceptualizing and strategizing a product, through development and market launch, to providing continuous support. Each core process group builds on the previous one, enabling product managers to deliver products that meet market needs, maintain a competitive edge, and ensure long-term success.

Volume 1 covered the first two process groups – *Product Opportunity* and *Product Planning* – which laid the groundwork for a strategic approach to product management. These two areas are largely within the direct responsibility of product managers. Now, Volume 2 explores the latter three process groups – *Product Development, Launch, and Support* – where the product manager's role expands to include cross-functional collaboration with development, marketing, sales, customer support, and more.

1.3 Product Operating Model (POM)

A **Product Operating Model (POM)** serves as the organizational backbone that ensures a product's successful journey from inception through to market launch and beyond. It defines the key components, roles, and processes that enable product managers to align their product vision with the business's broader strategic goals. The **POM** offers a structured approach to manage product development, delivery, and support, helping to bridge the gap between strategy and execution. It ensures that all product-related activities are carried out efficiently, cohesively, and in line with customer needs and market demands.

The **POM** focuses on enhancing collaboration across departments, managing innovation, and scaling product management efforts to meet business growth. By establishing clear roles and responsibilities, it creates accountability and facilitates seamless communication across teams. Below are the key components of the POM:

1.3.1 *Key Components of the Product Operating Model*

1 **Organizational Alignment:** Ensures that product goals are aligned with business strategy, enabling cross-functional collaboration and cohesive decision-making. This alignment ensures that the product management team works towards shared objectives with sales, marketing, and other departments.

2 **Innovation Management:** Focuses on fostering creativity and implementing structured processes to bring innovative products and features to market. Innovation management ensures that the company stays ahead in the market by continuously evolving its product offerings.

3 **Portfolio Management:** Manages the company's entire product portfolio, including resource allocation, balancing short-term projects with long-term goals, and ensuring that all products are delivering optimal value. This allows companies to make informed decisions about which products to prioritize, expand, or retire.

4 **Technology Enablement:** Establishes the tools and technology required to support product development and delivery. This includes the tech stack, digital platforms, and automation tools that help scale product development efforts and improve time-to-market.

5 **Capability Management:** Focuses on developing the skills, processes, and frameworks needed to support successful product management. By identifying and nurturing the right talent, companies can ensure that product teams are equipped to deliver on their objectives.

6 **Performance Management:** Tracks and evaluates product and team performance against key performance indicators (KPIs). This includes assessing product profitability, customer satisfaction, and market impact, ensuring that the product continuously meets business goals.

7 **Process and Governance:** Defines structured processes and governance frameworks that ensure consistency and quality across product development, planning, and support. This involves establishing best practices, setting up project management frameworks, and ensuring compliance with internal policies.

1.3.2 Why a Product Operating Model Is Crucial

Without a structured POM, product development efforts can be misaligned with business goals, and resources may be wasted. A well-defined POM ensures that product teams can operate efficiently, meet deadlines, and adapt to market changes without losing sight of their strategic objectives.

Example: Amazon's Product Operating Model
Amazon's POM is a prime example of how companies align product management with overall business strategy. The tech giant's model focuses heavily on customer experience, technology enablement, and innovation management, all while maintaining tight performance management. By continuously refining its **POM, Amazon** ensures it delivers high-quality products that are scalable and adaptable to the ever-evolving market landscape.

This **POM** framework provides the foundation for driving product success, enhancing team collaboration, and ensuring that strategic goals are translated into actionable outcomes across the product lifecycle.

1.4   From Strategy to Execution

In DPM, a seamless transition from strategy to execution is critical. The gap between conceptualizing a product and delivering it to the customer can be fraught with challenges, making a well-structured plan vital to success. Product managers are responsible not only for the high-level strategy but also for ensuring that development teams, marketing teams, and customer support teams have the tools, information, and motivation needed to bring the product to life. A robust POM is crucial here.

Volume 2 will explore how to bridge these stages, focusing on agile product development, continuous delivery, and how to maintain an ongoing customer focus throughout the product's lifecycle.

1.4.1   Modern Agile Methods and UX Design

One of the foundational elements of the modern DPM process is *Agile development*. Agile offers a flexible, iterative approach to product development that encourages frequent reassessment and adaptation. Agile methodologies are critical in aligning customer needs, UX design, and rapid iteration to ensure a product is both functional and user-friendly.

UX design, on the other hand, plays an essential role in ensuring customer satisfaction. No matter how well a product is developed, it must meet customer expectations in terms of usability, accessibility, and experience. A product that lacks a strong UX is unlikely to succeed in the marketplace. In this volume, we'll delve into how product managers can work with UX designers to enhance the overall product experience.

1.4.2   Marketing Strategy and Campaigns

Launching a product successfully requires more than a great idea – it demands a robust marketing strategy. Product managers must work closely with marketing teams to craft messaging that resonates with target audiences, identify the right channels to reach these customers, and measure the effectiveness of their campaigns. We will explore marketing tactics that go beyond traditional advertising, including omnichannel engagement, the PESO model (Paid, Earned, Shared, and Owned), and customer-centric marketing.

1.4.3   Product Launch and Support

A product launch marks a pivotal moment in the product lifecycle, but the work doesn't stop there. The post-launch phase is equally critical, requiring product managers to maintain engagement with their customers, ensure smooth operation, and continuously gather feedback for product improvements. This volume will also cover *Product Support*, which includes customer service, technical support, and ongoing product maintenance. Product managers need to work closely with support teams to ensure customer satisfaction while iterating on product improvements based on real-world feedback.

1.4.4 Continuous Improvement and Scaling

With the product live and functioning, a product manager's job shifts to ensuring the product scales effectively and continues to evolve. This requires a mindset of continuous improvement – adapting to customer feedback, evolving market demands, and technological advancements. Scaling strategies will be covered in detail, helping product managers guide the product through its growth stages and ensure long-term viability.

1.5 Product Case Scenario: A Mobile Car-Sharing Platform

This Product Case Scenario contains essential information about **QuikDrive's** car-sharing service to car owners and car renters which operates in shopping malls, residential estates, office buildings, bus and rail stations, hotels and airports in Singapore. This product will be used throughout the book to illustrate key concepts around managing digital products and services.

1.5.1 Introduction

With the rising costs of car ownership in Singapore, more citizens are turning to car-sharing platforms as a flexible, cost-effective alternative. **QuikDrive**, a Singapore-based company, offers a car-sharing solution through its mobile app and website, connecting car owners with renters and managing the rental process. This case study explores **QuikDrive's** innovative approach to car-sharing, its implementation, and its future potential to transform the transportation landscape in Singapore. Figure 1.2 shows the **QuikDrive** platform in the form of a website and mobile app, that brings car owners and renters together, manages rental bookings, and collects payment.

1.5.2 Background

Car ownership in Singapore is prohibitively expensive due to the high cost of obtaining a **Certificate of Entitlement (COE)**, which is required to own a car. With an average sedan costing more than **S$100,000**, many Singaporeans are seeking alternatives to ownership. Car-sharing has emerged as a popular solution, providing individuals with the flexibility and convenience of driving without the long-term financial burden of owning a vehicle.

```
QuikDrive

A platform which
brings car owners and
renters together,
manages rental
bookings and collects
payment.
─────────────────
Offers a pay-per-use service
to renters

Operates in shopping malls,
residential estates, office
buildings, bus and rail
stations, hotels and
airports.
```

FIGURE 1.2   Case Scenario: A Mobile Car-Sharing Platform.

QuikDrive entered the market with a platform designed to empower car owners to monetize their unused vehicles and provide renters with an affordable, convenient car-sharing option. By offering both a website and mobile app, **QuikDrive** simplifies the process for both owners and renters, facilitating vehicle rentals, payments, and insurance coverage.

1.5.3   Challenges in Current Market

Car-sharing platforms are not without their challenges. Current offerings often face issues such as:

- **Complicated user interfaces,** which make the process of renting or leasing cars cumbersome.
- **Unclear rental terms** that leave both car owners and renters uncertain about their rights and obligations.
- **Limited rental options and locations,** which can reduce the convenience of accessing vehicles for renters.
- **Lack of trust between owners and renters,** leading to concerns over the condition of the car and payment security.
- **High subscription fees** for some platforms, which can deter potential users, particularly renters who only occasionally need access to a car.

These issues have highlighted the need for a more streamlined, flexible, and user-friendly approach, which **QuikDrive** aims to address through its new platform.

1.5.4 Product Innovative Approach

QuikDrive differentiates itself from other car-sharing platforms with a variety of innovative features designed to enhance both the car owner and renter experiences.

For Car Owners:

1 **Convenient Lease Scheduling**: Car owners can easily plan when renters can use their vehicles through a flexible scheduling system.
2 **Car Return Location Selection**: Owners can set specific return locations, adding convenience and control over where the car will be dropped off.
3 **Renter Profile Verification**: Car owners can verify renters' identities and driving credentials, building trust, and reducing risks.
4 **Insurance Coverage**: QuikDrive simplifies the process of insuring cars against damages while in use by renters.
5 **Late Return Compensation**: Owners receive compensation if renters return cars late, offering peace of mind and ensuring fairness.

For Renters:

1 **Multiple Rental Options**: Renters can choose from various vehicle types based on their needs.
2 **Accessible Rental Locations**: Convenient pick-up and drop-off locations ensure that renters can access cars easily across Singapore.
3 **Digital Key**: Renters can lock and unlock cars via their smartphones, eliminating the need to exchange physical keys.
4 **Virtual Cash Cards**: The platform integrates virtual cash cards, making payments seamless for road tolls and other charges.
5 **No Subscription Fees**: QuikDrive removes the barrier of membership fees, making car-sharing more accessible for casual users.

These features allow **QuikDrive** to stand out by addressing both the logistical and psychological concerns of car owners and renters, ensuring a smooth and secure experience for all parties involved.

1.5.5 Strategic Implementation

QuikDrive's strategic implementation focuses on three core objectives:

1 **Improving the Customer Experience:**
  • The platform's integration of both web and mobile technologies simplifies the car-sharing process, providing users with a seamless

experience. Renters can quickly book cars and manage their rentals on the go through the mobile app, while car owners can manage availability, view bookings, and communicate with renters easily.

2 **Increasing Adoption Rates:**
   - By eliminating membership subscription fees and automating the sign-up process, **QuikDrive** reduces the friction of entry for new users. The streamlined onboarding process includes automatic driver's licence and credit card verification, making it faster and easier for users to begin renting or leasing vehicles.

3 **Leveraging Data Analytics and Machine Learning:**
   - **QuikDrive** plans to implement data analytics and machine learning to monitor real-time operations, predict user preferences, and optimize vehicle availability. By analysing user behaviour and demand patterns, **QuikDrive** can ensure that cars are available when and where they are most needed, improving operational efficiency and reducing downtime for owners.

1.5.6 Future Prospects

As Singapore continues to focus on sustainability and reducing the environmental impact of vehicle ownership, car-sharing platforms like **QuikDrive** are positioned for growth. By offering a cost-effective, convenient alternative to owning a car, **QuikDrive** has the potential to expand its user base and transform urban mobility in Singapore.

Key future prospects include the following:

1 **Expansion into New Markets:** QuikDrive can scale its platform to other densely populated urban areas across Southeast Asia, where similar car ownership challenges exist.

2 **Integration with Public Transportation:** Collaborating with public transportation systems could provide users with a multi-modal transport solution, allowing them to seamlessly switch between public and private transport based on their needs.

3 **Electric Vehicle Integration:** As Singapore shifts towards more sustainable transportation solutions, **QuikDrive** can integrate electric vehicles (**EVs**) into its platform, catering to eco-conscious users and supporting the government's goal of reducing carbon emissions.

By continuing to innovate and adapt to the needs of its users, **QuikDrive** is well-positioned to grow and evolve, driving forward the future of car-sharing in Singapore and beyond.

1.5.7   QuikDrive's Conclusion

QuikDrive represents a forward-thinking solution to the challenges of car ownership in Singapore. By offering a flexible, convenient platform for both car owners and renters, the company has created an innovative model that simplifies car-sharing and enhances user trust. Through its strategic implementation of technology, **QuikDrive** is poised to disrupt the traditional car rental market and expand its reach, transforming urban mobility in Singapore. The future of **QuikDrive** looks promising as it explores new opportunities for growth, integration, and sustainability.

1.6   Conclusion

This chapter sets the foundation for the entire volume. While Volume 1 focused on strategy, Volume 2 takes a deeper dive into executing on that strategy. You will learn how to lead product development, orchestrate successful product launches, and build the frameworks necessary to sustain and scale digital products in today's fast-moving digital economy.

In the chapters ahead, we will delve deeper into each process, explore real-world examples, and give actionable insights that will empower you to manage the lifecycle of your digital products effectively. The conclusion of this volume bridges the gap to future challenges, highlighting the importance of adaptability, ethical leadership, and ongoing product evolution in today's dynamic market.

2

LEADING PRODUCT DEVELOPMENT

2.1 Introduction

In today's digital landscape, building successful products requires more than just technical expertise – it demands a deep understanding of user needs and the ability to iterate rapidly. **User Experience (UX) Design** and **Agile Development** are two cornerstones of this process. UX Design ensures that users have a positive, intuitive experience when interacting with a product, while Agile Development provides the framework for delivering that product in a flexible, iterative manner. This chapter explores the best practices in user interface (UI) Design and the principles of Agile Development, offering real-world examples to illustrate how these methodologies can be applied effectively.

2.2 Designing and Building Successful Products

A successful product is one that is designed and built not only meets business goals but also delivers a seamless and satisfying experience to users. To achieve this, product managers can leverage a framework that integrates three powerful methodologies: **Design Thinking, Lean Startup,** and **Agile Methodology**. These approaches ensure that products are designed with the user in mind, validated through feedback, and iterated swiftly to minimize the risk of failure.

Figure 2.1 shows the three key approaches in designing and building successful products, while Figure 2.2 shows an adapted framework based on Gartner's Design Thinking + Lean Startup + Agile Diagram.

DOI: 10.1201/9781003614180-2

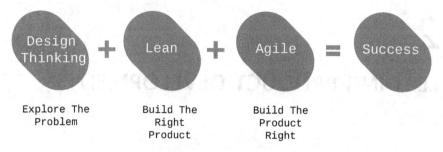

FIGURE 2.1   Designing and Building Successful Products.

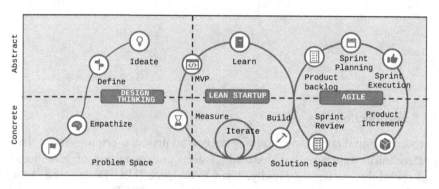

FIGURE 2.2   Design Thinking + Lean Startup + Agile.

1. Design Thinking – Exploring the Problem

Design Thinking focuses on deeply understanding the problem from the user's perspective. This human-centred approach begins with **empathy**, which helps product teams understand the true needs and pain points of users before defining and ideating solutions. The stages of Design Thinking are:

- **Empathize:** Observe and understand users' needs and challenges.
- **Define:** Clearly articulate the problem based on user insights.
- **Ideate:** Brainstorm solutions that address the problem creatively.
- **Prototype:** Develop mock-ups or models of the solution for testing.
- **Test:** Continuously test prototypes to gather feedback for improvement.

Examples:

- **Airbnb** applied Design Thinking when creating their user-friendly platform for both hosts and guests. The team deeply empathized with people's frustrations over the traditional hotel experience and created a platform that addresses those pain points by enabling unique, personalized stays in homes worldwide. This approach has helped Airbnb grow into one of the most successful platforms globally.

- **GovTech Singapore,** which designed the **TraceTogether** app during the COVID-19 pandemic, used the principles of Design Thinking. The team empathized with the public's concerns about privacy while recognizing the need for contact tracing. They iterated on the app design to strike a balance between privacy (using randomized IDs) and public safety, continuously improving the app based on feedback.

2. Lean Startup – Building the Right Product

Lean Startup methodology focuses on building products that solve real user problems with minimal wasted effort. The cycle of **Build, Measure, Learn** ensures that teams quickly test ideas and iterate based on real feedback, reducing the risk of building products that users don't need.

- **Build:** Create a Minimum Viable Product (MVP) that addresses core user needs.
- **Measure:** Gather data from users to evaluate the MVP's effectiveness.
- **Learn:** Use feedback to iterate and improve the product continuously.

Examples:

- **Dropbox** followed the Lean Startup model by releasing an explainer video before building a fully functional product. This video served as an MVP, gauging interest from potential customers before the company invested in development.
- **Carousell,** a popular online marketplace based in Singapore, followed a Lean Startup approach when it launched its platform. Initially, Carousell focused on building a simple MVP that allowed users to list and sell items quickly. As the platform grew, they continuously gathered user feedback and expanded features, such as integrating more secure payment methods and improving the UI.

3. Agile Method – Building the Product Right

Agile methodology emphasizes flexibility, collaboration, and iterative development. Product teams work in **sprints** – short, focused periods of development – followed by reviews and adjustments. Agile fosters continuous feedback loops, ensuring that the product evolves in alignment with user needs.

- **Sprint Planning:** Define work for the sprint based on the product backlog.
- **Product Backlog:** This is a prioritized list of tasks, features, and fixes that the development team will work on in future sprints. It is dynamic and continually updated based on feedback and new requirements.

- **Sprint Implementation**: Teams focus on implementing the planned features during the sprint. Daily stand-ups allow team members to track progress and address roadblocks.
- **Sprint Review**: Assess the completed work and gather feedback from stakeholders.
- **Sprint Retrospective**: Reflect on the sprint's process to improve future iterations.
- **Product Increment**: At the end of each sprint, the team delivers a potentially shippable product increment that adds value to the user.

Examples:

- **Spotify** uses Agile methodologies across its product teams, allowing them to release small, incremental improvements to its platform regularly. This enables Spotify to quickly adapt to user needs, such as when they rolled out personalized playlists like "Discover Weekly", which were developed and iterated based on continuous user feedback.
- **Grab** (the Southeast Asian super-app) adopts Agile practices across its various services, including transportation, food delivery, and financial services. Grab runs multiple sprints in parallel for different products, such as its payment platform **GrabPay**, allowing teams to continuously improve based on user feedback. Each sprint focuses on specific improvements, such as faster transactions or better UI Design for mobile users.

2.3 User Experience (UX) Design

2.3.1 The Three Lenses of Design Thinking

The Design Thinking process integrates three crucial lenses – **Desirability**, **Feasibility**, and **Viability** – to guide teams in developing solutions that not only meet user needs but are also technologically feasible and economically viable. These lenses ensure that the product is both user-centred and sustainable from a business and technical standpoint. By focusing first on **Desirability**, Design Thinking encourages empathy for the user, followed by a practical evaluation of technical and business considerations. Figure 2.3 depicts the three lenses of Design Thinking.

1 Desirability: Meeting People's Needs
Design Thinking starts by exploring the **Desirability** of a product – how well it meets the needs, desires, and behaviours of the target users. The focus is on deeply understanding the end user through empathy, rather than assuming

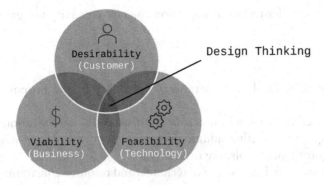

FIGURE 2.3 Three Lenses of Design Thinking.

what the organization thinks the users need. This lens helps teams stay grounded in the real-world experiences and aspirations of their customers.

- **Key Actions:**
  - Observe user behaviour and gather insights through interviews, surveys, or observational studies.
  - Identify what users truly want, addressing their pain points and dreams.
  - Ideate solutions from the perspective of the end user, ensuring that the product is desirable and fulfils a genuine need.
- **Example:**
  - When **Airbnb** was first created, its founders empathized with users who were frustrated by the high cost and impersonal nature of hotels. By listening to travellers who wanted authentic, affordable stays in local homes, Airbnb developed a solution that met these users' needs, rather than what the hospitality industry assumed people wanted.

2. Feasibility: Being Technologically Possible

Once the team has ideated solutions that meet the users' needs, the next step is to evaluate the **Feasibility** of these solutions – whether they are technologically possible with the current resources, time, and tools available. While in theory any solution could be feasible with unlimited resources, real-world constraints must be considered to ensure the product can be realistically built.

At this stage, teams focus on whether they have the right skills, tools, and infrastructure to implement the solution, or if they need to iterate and adjust the idea to fit within the organization's technical capabilities. However, teams should be careful not to let technical limitations dictate creativity too early in the process.

- **Key Actions:**
  - Assess the technological and operational feasibility of the proposed solutions.
  - Determine whether the solution can be built using the organization's current resources or whether additional resources, such as hiring new talent or acquiring new tools, are necessary.
  - Iterate on the solution if needed to fit technical and resource constraints.

- **Example:**
  - Tesla pushed the boundaries of **Feasibility** by developing electric vehicles that were both technologically advanced and capable of mass production. The feasibility of Tesla's solution was challenged by resource constraints early on, particularly around battery technology and production costs. However, by iterating on their solution and scaling their technology, Tesla managed to make electric vehicles feasible for the mass market.

3. Viability: Generating Profits

Lastly, the **Viability** lens focuses on ensuring that the product can generate profits and sustain the organization's financial goals. A solution that is desirable to users and feasible from a technological standpoint is not enough – companies also need to ensure that the solution is financially viable. This means that the solution should have the potential to generate revenue and be profitable in the long term. Even non-profit organizations must consider viability, as they need to ensure their solutions are financially sustainable.

Design Thinking reverses the traditional approach, where organizations often start with feasibility or viability and then try to find a problem to fit their solution. Instead, teams should begin with **Desirability**, ensuring the product meets user needs, and then evaluate the technical and financial aspects afterwards.

- **Key Actions:**
  - Evaluate the product's revenue potential, cost structure, and long-term profitability.
  - Determine if the market size and demand are large enough to support the product.
  - Adjust the business model if necessary to ensure the solution is financially sustainable.

- **Example:**
  - **Netflix** initially began as a DVD rental service but realized that their long-term profitability would be higher with a streaming service that

could reach a broader audience and reduce distribution costs. By transitioning to a digital platform, Netflix ensured that its solution was not only desirable and feasible but also financially viable.

By integrating **Desirability**, **Feasibility**, and **Viability**, product teams can ensure that their solutions are holistic, user-centred, and sustainable. The key to successful product development lies in starting with empathy for the user, followed by careful consideration of what is technologically possible and financially sound. This approach prevents the common pitfall of developing solutions that might be technically impressive or profitable but fail to meet the real needs of users. Ultimately, the three lenses of Design Thinking provide a structured yet flexible approach to innovation, ensuring that products deliver real value to both users and the business.

2.3.2 Double Diamond Design Process

One of the most powerful techniques within Design Thinking is the **Double Diamond Design Process**, which structures the product development journey into two phases: **divergence** (exploring a wide range of ideas) and **convergence** (narrowing down to the most viable solutions). Figure 2.4 depicts the Double Diamond Design Process.

1. First Diamond: Discover and Define (Divergence)
In this phase, the team works to understand the problem space by exploring many possibilities before narrowing down the focus.

- **Discover:** Teams research user needs, behaviours, and pain points. This could include interviews, observations, and data collection.
- **Define:** Based on the insights gained, the team narrows down the information to define the problem clearly.

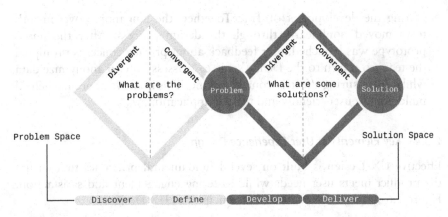

FIGURE 2.4 Double Diamond Design Process.

2. Second Diamond: Develop and Deliver (Convergence)

Once the problem is defined, the team starts brainstorming and iterating on potential solutions.

- **Develop**: Ideate and prototype solutions that address the problem.
- **Deliver**: Test, iterate, and refine the prototype until it meets user expectations.

Example of the Double Diamond in Action:

- **Singapore Airlines** used the Double Diamond process when redesigning its customer service experience. In the Discover phase, the airline gathered passenger feedback on pain points such as long wait times or confusing booking systems. In the Define phase, these insights were used to focus on improving specific touchpoints in the customer journey. In the Develop phase, new solutions such as streamlined mobile check-in or more personalized customer service were prototyped. Finally, the Deliver phase involved testing these features with actual customers before rolling them out widely.

2.3.3 The Nonlinear Aspect of Design Thinking

A hallmark of Design Thinking is its nonlinear, iterative approach. Unlike traditional, linear processes, Design Thinking allows teams to move back and forth between stages based on new insights. For example, after testing a prototype, the team may discover new user behaviours that lead them back to the **Define** or **Ideate** stages to reframe the problem or generate new ideas. This flexibility encourages innovation and responsiveness to user feedback. Figure 2.5 depicts the nonlinear process in Design Thinking.

Example:

- During the development of **TraceTogether**, the Singapore government's team moved nonlinearly through the design process. After the initial prototype was launched, user feedback about privacy concerns prompted the team to return to the Define stage to reassess how to anonymize data while still ensuring effective contact tracing. This iterative approach helped build a more user-friendly and trusted application.

2.3.4 Key Elements of User Experience Design

Effective UX Design is built on several fundamental principles that ensure the product meets user needs while fostering engagement and satisfaction. Figure 2.6 shows four fundamental principles of UX Design.

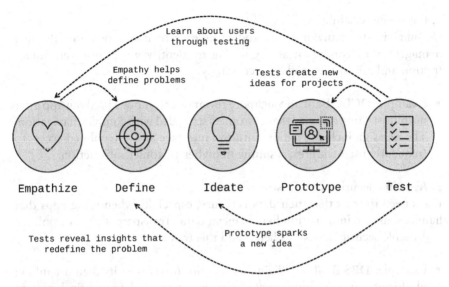

FIGURE 2.5 A Nonlinear Process in Design Thinking.

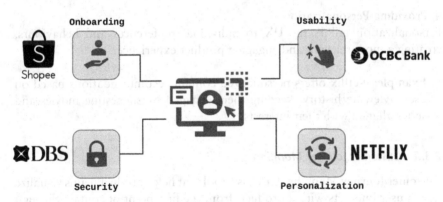

FIGURE 2.6 Fundamental User Experience Design Principles.

1. Efficient Onboarding Experience

First impressions matter. A well-designed onboarding experience should introduce users to the product's value quickly and guide them through the key features in an intuitive way.

- **Example: Shopee,** a leading e-commerce platform in Singapore, offers a simple onboarding experience where new users are immediately introduced to promotions and a tutorial on how to navigate the app, resulting in higher retention rates.

2. Improving Usability

Usability is about making the product as easy to use as possible. Product managers must conduct usability testing to identify where users encounter friction and adjust the product accordingly.

- **Example: OCBC Bank** in Singapore revamped its mobile banking app after usability testing revealed that customers struggled with complex navigation. The redesign included a more intuitive interface and streamlined access to frequently used features, resulting in higher customer satisfaction.

3. Assuring Security and Trustworthiness

Users need to trust that their data is secure, especially when using apps that handle sensitive information like financial data. Transparent privacy policies and visible security measures help build this trust.

- **Example: DBS Bank** highlights its security features in its digital banking platforms, such as multi-factor authentication and biometric login, to reassure customers that their transactions are safe.

4. Providing Personalization

Personalization tailors the UX to individual preferences and behaviours, creating a more relevant and engaging product experience.

- **Example: Netflix** offers personalized content recommendations based on users' viewing history, keeping them engaged by suggesting movies and series aligned with their interests.

2.3.5 Customer Journey Mapping

Customer Journey Mapping (CJM) is a tool that helps product teams visualize how a user interacts with a product, from the first point of contact through the final interaction. This tool is invaluable for understanding the UX from start to finish and identifying areas for improvement. Figure 2.7 shows a Customer Journey Map for a user renting a car on a car-sharing platform.
Steps to Create a CJM:

1 **Identify Customer Personas**: Define the key personas who interact with the product. Each persona will have unique behaviours and pain points.
2 **Uncover Customer Pain Points**: Pinpoint areas where users experience frustration or confusion.
3 **Determine Moments of Truth**: Identify the critical interactions that determine whether a user continues using the product or abandons it.

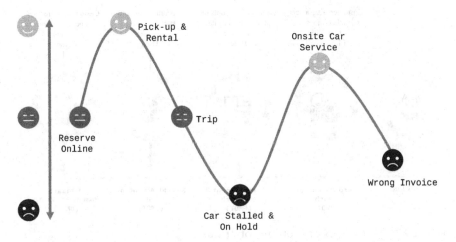

FIGURE 2.7 Customer Journey Map.

4 **Create the Customer Journey Map**: Visualize the entire journey, mapping out touchpoints, emotions, and pain points to find opportunities for improvement.

Example:
• **Disney** used Customer Journey Mapping when developing its **MagicBands** system. By mapping out the customer journey, Disney identified long wait times at park entrances and payment points as major pain points. The MagicBands, which integrate entry, payments, and ride access, addressed these issues, improving the overall UX.

2.3.6 Moments of Truth

Moments of Truth refer to the critical points in the customer journey where a customer forms a strong impression – positive or negative – about a brand, product, or service. These are moments that have a disproportionate impact on the customer's overall experience and can shape their long-term relationship with the company.

There are four types of **Moments of Truth** commonly identified in a Customer Journey Map (CJM), as depicted in Figure 2.8.

1 **Zero Moment of Truth (ZMOT)**:
   • This occurs before the customer buys the product or service. It's the moment when a potential customer recognizes their needs and is researching, reading reviews, or comparing different options to fulfil their needs.

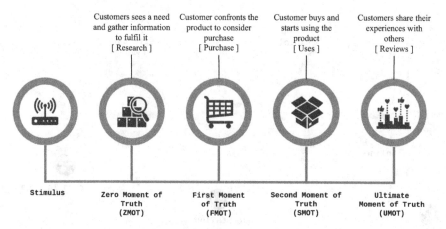

Customers sees a need and gather information to fulfil it [Research]

Customer confronts the product to consider purchase [Purchase]

Customer buys and starts using the product [Uses]

Customers share their experiences with others [Reviews]

Stimulus

Zero Moment of Truth (ZMOT)

First Moment of Truth (FMOT)

Second Moment of Truth (SMOT)

Ultimate Moment of Truth (UMOT)

FIGURE 2.8   Four Types of Moments of Truth.

- **Example**: A customer considering a vacation in Singapore might search for hotel reviews on TripAdvisor, check user ratings on Google Maps, or browse Instagram photos tagged at different resorts. Their decision is influenced by the impressions they gather before making a booking.

2 **First Moment of Truth (FMOT)**:
   - This occurs when the customer first confronts the product or service, often during the purchase or when encountering the product in-store or online.
   - **Example**: When a customer first lands on the checkout page of an e-commerce website like **Lazada** or **Shopee**, the design, ease of use, and clarity of information in this step significantly affect whether they complete the purchase or abandon the cart. A confusing or difficult checkout process can lead to frustration, turning this into a negative Moment of Truth.

3 **Second Moment of Truth (SMOT)**:
   - This happens when the customer buys and starts using the product or service. It's when customers decide if the product delivers on the promises made during the earlier stages.
   - **Example**: A customer purchasing a smartphone from **Samsung** experiences the SMOT when they first unbox and use the device. The ease of setup, interface design, and initial performance all play a crucial role in shaping their perception of the product. A smooth, intuitive experience strengthens their satisfaction, while glitches or poor design lead to disappointment.

4 **Ultimate Moment of Truth (UMOT)**:
   - This occurs when customers share their experiences with others. Whether through reviews, social media, or word-of-mouth, customers' feedback plays a significant role in influencing other potential customers' decisions.

- **Example: Grab,** the Southeast Asian ride-hailing service, relies heavily on user-generated feedback. Customers leaving a ride will often provide a rating and review of their driver and overall experience. Positive reviews increase Grab's credibility and attract new users, while negative reviews can impact customer retention and acquisition.

Examples of Moments of Truth in Customer Journeys

1. Airline Customer Journey: Booking and Travel Experience
For an airline, the customer journey can include multiple touchpoints, from searching for flights online to the in-flight experience. Here's how **Singapore Airlines** identifies Moments of Truth in its journey:

- **ZMOT:** A potential customer researches flight options and reads reviews about Singapore Airlines' punctuality, customer service, and amenities. Positive reviews about its premium services can influence the decision to book with them.
- **FMOT:** When the customer visits the airline's website to book a flight, the ease of navigation, transparency of pricing, and options for seat selection are critical. If the booking process is smooth, this can enhance the customer's confidence in their choice.
- **SMOT:** Once the customer boards the flight, they experience the service, comfort, and amenities promised during the booking stage. Singapore Airlines is known for delivering exceptional service here, and meeting or exceeding expectations can lead to customer loyalty.
- **UMOT:** After the flight, the customer shares their experience on social media, leaving reviews on platforms like Google, TripAdvisor, or the airline's app. Positive reviews can influence future passengers' decisions.

2. E-Commerce Journey: Online Shopping with Shopee
In an online shopping experience, **Shopee** identifies several Moments of Truth that are crucial to converting and retaining customers.

- **ZMOT:** A customer searching for a specific product might check prices and reviews across multiple platforms. Positive feedback about Shopee's discounts and shipping reliability influences the customer's decision to visit the platform.
- **FMOT:** When the customer finds the desired product on Shopee, the product description, price, and seller ratings determine whether they proceed to add the item to the cart. A clear, well-organized product page with accurate descriptions creates a positive first impression.
- **SMOT:** After placing the order, the customer's experience with delivery, unboxing, and the product quality determines their satisfaction. If Shopee delivers on time and the product meets expectations, this reinforces a positive experience.

- **UMOT**: After receiving the product, the customer might leave a review or share their experience on social media. Positive reviews contribute to Shopee's reputation and influence new shoppers to trust the platform.

3. Hospitality Journey: Hotel Stay with Marina Bay Sands
The customer journey at **Marina Bay Sands,** a luxury hotel in Singapore, involves several critical touchpoints where Moments of Truth define the guest's perception.

- **ZMOT**: A traveller reads reviews and looks at photos on TripAdvisor and Google to decide whether to book a stay. Positive reviews about the infinity pool and luxurious amenities are often deciding factors.
- **FMOT**: Upon arrival, the guest's experience during check-in is key. Friendly staff, quick service, and a smooth check-in process contribute to a positive first impression of the hotel.
- **SMOT**: The quality of the room, the views, and the hotel services experienced during the stay reinforce the guest's expectations. Marina Bay Sands is known for offering premium experiences that align with guest expectations, contributing to its positive reputation.
- **UMOT**: After their stay, many guests post pictures of the infinity pool and their room views on Instagram or write reviews on travel sites. These shared experiences serve as powerful recommendations for future guests.

Utilizing Moments of Truth for Product Management
For product managers, identifying and optimizing these **Moments of Truth** are crucial for creating a positive, memorable customer experience. Here's how they can leverage Moments of Truth:

1 **Optimize Key Touchpoints**: Product managers should focus on enhancing critical interactions during each Moment of Truth. For instance, improving onboarding processes at the FMOT can dramatically increase user retention.
2 **Feedback Loops**: Use customer feedback gathered after key moments, particularly the UMOT, to refine product offerings and fix pain points. Customer reviews and social media sentiment provide invaluable data on how well the product is performing at each stage.
3 **Proactive Customer Support**: By identifying where things can go wrong (such as during the SMOT when customers are using the product), product managers can implement proactive support to reduce negative experiences and prevent churn.
4 **Driving Advocacy**: Encourage satisfied customers to share their experiences during the UMOT. Positive reviews, testimonials, and social sharing can help attract new customers and fuel the flywheel effect of growth.

By understanding and optimizing **Moments of Truth,** product managers can ensure that their customers have a seamless experience that builds trust, increases satisfaction, and turns users into advocates.

2.3.7 CJM in Car-Sharing Platform Case Scenario

Let's use the Car-sharing Platform product case scenario to explore how Customer Journey Mapping is used to enhance the customer experience, by accounting for a wide range of eventualities during the customers' engagement with the product and services. People value their convenience and comfort and want to go places on their own terms and at their own pace. This is why the car-sharing business is becoming so popular today.

If you're offering a car-sharing car-rental service, like QuikDrive, how would you know if your customers are satisfied and have a positive experience with your service? And how would you know exactly what problems they face during their car rental customer journey?

To answer these questions, you can make use of customer personas and a Customer Journey Map. The Customer Journey Map is an Agile method and a way of mapping the experiences of your customers – as represented by customer personas. Doing so involves imagining the customer's experiences throughout their entire journey with the product. This allows you to anticipate all eventualities, and identify opportunities to solve problems and improve the customer experience.

In this segment, you'll see how to create a Customer Journey Map, by following one of QuikDrive's customer personas, Laura, on her road trip. Through Laura's experience of using QuikDrive, you will explore the potential pain points and learn about the moments of truth. These are the points in a customer's journey with a brand or service when a key event occurs and the customer forms an opinion about that brand or service.

We begin our Customer Journey Mapping exercise by identifying the customer persona, Laura, as depicted in Figure 2.9. She's 26 years old, does not own a car, is budget-conscious, and is also environmentally conscious.

FIGURE 2.9 A Car Renter Persona.

Let's take a look at Laura's three-part journey of using QuikDrive's car-rental service.

You can see these positive as well as negative experiences plotted on the Customer Journey Map, as shown in Figure 2.10.

Part 1 of the Journey

As we go through Laura's journey, we'll plot her experience on the Customer Journey Map. In Part 1 of the journey, we will look at Laura's experience of finding and reserving a car.

Laura's journey begins when she needs to rent a car for a road trip to attend a friend's wedding in Johor Bahru, a Malaysian city, north of Singapore – where Laura lives.

To find a car for her planned road trip, she searches online for car-rental options and quickly finds QuikDrive. She's excited to see that QuikDrive offers sporty, electric cars for rental. She downloads the QuikDrive mobile app and signs up for a new user account.

Next, she checks for the nearest available car and finds one located very close by, in her housing estate. It's a sporty, red-hot hybrid, which matches her new bridesmaid dress. Because she's environmentally conscious, she's glad to be able to find a car with hybrid technology. She immediately reserves the car for the day of the wedding.

The search was quick, as was downloading the mobile app, and signing up was a breeze. She quickly found the car she wanted and it was located close to where she lives, so Laura is feeling positive towards her QuikDrive experience so far.

Part 2 of the Journey

In Part 2 of the journey, we will look at Laura's journey of using QuikDrive's rental car on the day of the road trip.

Laura wakes up early on the wedding day to get ready to pick up the rental car for the road trip to Johor Bahru. Laura then uses the QuikDrive mobile app to locate the car, but is disappointed there's no GPS-guided location feature; only the address is provided. Luckily, in this case, it's not a big problem because the car is located in her housing estate.

Laura only takes about 15 minutes to find the car and when she does, she's unhappy to discover the beautiful red car completely covered in bird poop.

She proceeds to unlock the car with the digital key function on the QuikDrive app – a feature that allows customers to use their phones as a means of unlocking the car they've rented. The simple and effective feature represents a satisfying experience for Laura, so we'll plot it as a positive point on the Customer Journey Map.

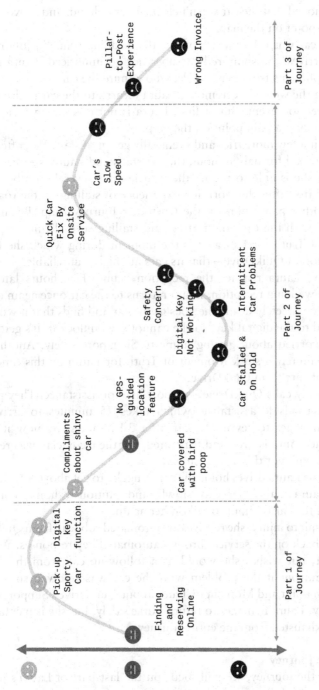

FIGURE 2.10 Laura's Customer Journey Map.

Laura then drives the car to a nearby petrol kiosk for a quick car wash. She feels annoyed that the car wasn't cleaned beforehand, and so we will plot an unhappy point on the map.

After the car wash, Laura sets off for the wedding venue in Johor Bahru. When she arrives, the shiny red car does not go unnoticed. Laura receives several compliments from her friends, who admire the car.

Following the wedding ceremony, Laura returns to the car to drive to the wedding reception event. But at first, Laura is not able to start the engine. Here, we will plot a pain point on the map.

She gives it a few more tries and eventually gets it to start. But, after barely being on the road for half an hour, the car stalls and Laura is forced to pull over. Again, she is able to restart the vehicle after several tries but is now feeling frustrated after the worrying experience of stalling on the road. This deserves another pain point on the Customer Journey Map. By this time, the problem with the car not starting and stalling several times represents a Moment of Truth for Laura. It is the moment during which she forms a lasting opinion of QuikDrive – that its cars are highly unreliable.

Eventually, Laura reaches the reception venue. Five hours later, after enjoying the wedding reception, Laura returns to the car once again and this time finds it completely dead. She goes to the car and finds that it would not even respond to the digital key, so she cannot even unlock it. It's getting late and she is worried about getting home to Singapore safely. Another pain point and definitely a stark Moment of Truth for Laura by this time about the quality of cars from QuikDrive.

She promptly calls QuikDrive's support line for assistance. They promise to send out roadside assistance, which takes 45 minutes to arrive. The technician manages to revive the car after 30 minutes. By now it is past midnight, and Laura is tired and frustrated, but the technician was relatively quick, so we will plot this as a positive point.

However, as Laura drives home the car struggles to get above 80 kilometres per hour. Laura makes her way slowly and cautiously home, constantly worried that the car is about to fail on her again.

To add insult to injury, she receives an automated robocall from QuikDrive, seeking feedback on the service through automated key responses. What she does not get, but wishes she would, is a follow-up call from the Support Centre to find out if the problem with the car was resolved successfully. Another pain point and Moment of Truth about QuikDrive's Support Centre.

Eventually, Laura manages to return home safely, but she is mentally and physically exhausted from the entire journey.

Part 3 of the Journey
In Part 3 of the journey, we will focus on the last part of Laura's journey, where she tries to follow up with QuikDrive.

The next day, Laura tries calling QuikDrive to request a refund, due to the bad experience she had the day before.

However, her request goes from pillar-to-post, as she is cycled through various customer representatives, many of whom repeatedly make operational mistakes. Laura gets nowhere with her refund request. So, we will plot another pain point on the map.

And then, a week later Laura receives a credit card charge, which includes a late fee. This turns out to be someone else's invoice, accidentally sent to her account. Another pain point.

After a wild goose chase and a mix-up of communications by QuikDrive's agents, a week goes by and Laura is still unable to get a satisfactory resolution. Yes, you guessed it – another Moment of Truth for Laura about QuikDrive's customer agents!

Sadly, the story ends with QuikDrive losing a customer, as Laura resolved never to use the service again.

Lessons from Laura's Journey
Let's review Laura's Customer Journey Map, as shown in Figure 2.10.

From left to right, we see how Laura's experience started out as a positive one. She hoped for a painless sign-up and reservation process, and that is what she got.

Locating and picking-up the car was a positive experience. However, when she had to detour to have the car cleaned, her journey took a minor dip. The trip to the venue was a neutral experience for Laura.

But from there, with the ongoing engine troubles, things started taking a turn for the worse. The efficient on-site car service marks a momentary return to a positive experience, but from there it is downhill again.

And then with the bad experiences after Laura gets home and tries to get a refund, resolve issues with QuikDrive's agents, the incorrect invoice, and poor communications, the pain points pile up and Laura decides to cancel her membership.

Moments of Truth
We have seen how each of the pain points in Laura's journey marks a Moment of Truth for her – the multiple car stalling incidents and the poor attitude and unresponsiveness of the customer service agents have helped form a bad impression about QuikDrive's rental car as well as service and support quality.

The Customer Journey Map can be used to create a table that captures the various pain points, touchpoints, engagement channels, and experiences that emerge from the journey, as shown in Table 2.1.

Such tables are used by product managers to analyse customer experiences and determine ideas for improvement.

TABLE 2.1 Customer Journey Map Table

Timeline	Step 1	Step 2	Step 3	Step 4	Step 5	Step 6
Pain point	Renting a car	Picking up the rental car, only to discover that it was dirty	Car dying twice before reaching the wedding venue	Stranded in an unsafe area and waiting for QuikDrive's roadside assistance at midnight	Bad customer experience – not helpful in assisting the issue	Wrong invoice being charged and dispute credit card charges
Touchpoint	Sign up for first-time users Proceeding to free-floating zone	Contacting Quikdrive for car wash reimbursement	Called QuikDrive on possible severe electrical problem	Rep sent an unlock signal Getting roadside assistance	Via a call Several messy customer service reps with no awareness of the complete issue	Call QuikDrive to complaint
Channels	Mobile app	Mobile app	Hotline/Mobile app	Hotline/Mobile app	Email/Call/Mobile app	Email/Call/Mobile app
Experience	Obtained the car as reserved	Car was covered in bird poop	Getting dismissed by the customer service who assumed that the car was fine	Getting unsympathetic and borderline rude response, making customer feel like they don't care and stress over the situation	Stressful and annoying to keep getting transferred to different reps and having to explain everything again	The e-mail was mixed up. Hence, did not get the issue right
Ideas for improvement	User-friendly reservation interface; to have a Q&A segment for the commonly asked questions. It would be helpful for first timers	Have a prompter/FAQ stored in the car which can empower customers on what to do when faced with such situations Previous users to take pictures of car condition after use	Be more proactive and get staff to check on the car since it is not in use Have standard protocols on what to do when car is faulty overseas	Train customer service to be more empathetic and understanding Allow for flexibility while considering the customer's circumstances	Keep a single source of contact Need to have a clear record of every issue so that the next agent can follow up	Have a CRM service on the app where the feedback is tagged to one ticket number and one CRM officer. To have a tracking system on the feedback closure to ensure customer feedback is timely addressed

You have seen how to create a Customer Journey Map by identifying the customer persona and uncovering the customer pain points, as well as the moments of truth. This tool is useful for product managers to identify opportunities to improve customer experience.

Now it is your turn. Imagine a customer persona for a product of your choice. Then, use that persona to imagine the possibilities for product improvements, which could lead to a more delightful UX. To do so, think of the ways you could fix the pains of your customers and even enhance the things that went well.

2.3.8 Use Experience Design Summary

UX Design is a critical component of successful product development. By leveraging **Design Thinking**, product managers can ensure their products not only solve user problems but also provide a seamless and engaging experience. Techniques like the **Double Diamond Process** and **Customer Journey Mapping** offer valuable tools for exploring and refining the product experience, helping product teams identify key pain points and opportunities for improvement. As products continue to evolve, focusing on user needs and iterating based on feedback is essential for delivering lasting success.

2.4 Agile Development

Agile Development is a modern approach to managing IT or software development teams and projects, focusing on delivering solutions incrementally and iteratively, rather than all at once. In contrast to traditional project management methods like the **Waterfall** approach, which delivers a complete product only at the end of the development cycle, Agile delivers small, functional increments over time. This allows for continuous feedback, enabling the product to evolve based on user input and changing requirements.

Agile methods focus on flexibility, collaboration, and rapid iteration, making them ideal for dynamic environments where customer needs can shift during the course of development. This approach emphasizes delivering value early and adjusting to feedback, which is key to staying competitive in fast-moving markets.

2.4.1 Agile vs. Traditional Development: A Chair Analogy

One effective analogy to differentiate between traditional and Agile approaches is the "**Building a Chair**" analogy. See Figure 2.11 for the differences in the approach when building a chair using the traditional and the Agile methods.

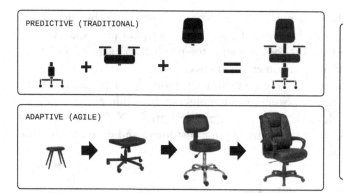

FIGURE 2.11 Building a Chair.

In traditional **Waterfall** development, the process is broken down into sequential phases. The team would develop individual components of the chair – such as the legs, seat, armrests, and backrest – separately, and only assemble them at the end. The customer only gets to use the final chair when all the parts have been completed and put together.

In contrast, Agile would take an **incremental** and **iterative** approach. First, the team might build a **stool** – a simple version of the chair that the customer can test and use right away. Based on user feedback, the stool might evolve into an **open seat with wheels** so the user can move around more easily. Next, based on more feedback, a **backrest** might be added for comfort, followed by **armrests** and additional features like cushioning or lumbar support. The result is a final product that continuously evolves based on what the customer wants at each step, ensuring that the chair meets the user's needs more effectively than if it had been built all at once without any user feedback.

This process embodies the core principle of Agile: **deliver value early, gather feedback, and improve continuously**.

The Challenge of IKIWISI ("I'll Know It When I See It")

A common challenge in software development is that customers often do not fully know what they want until they see a working prototype. This is referred to as the **IKIWISI** phenomenon, meaning "**I'll Know It When I See It**." This happens because software is intangible, and it can be difficult for customers to fully envision the final product from the outset.

In traditional project management, teams gather requirements at the start of the project, build the product over months or even years, and then present the final product to the customer. At that point, customers might say, "Yes, this is what I wanted x months ago, but now our needs have changed," or they may have difficulty articulating feedback because they didn't have a tangible product to react to during the development process. This can lead to costly rework and delays in delivering a product that is relevant to the current business environment.

Agile, on the other hand, addresses this challenge by regularly delivering small, usable increments to customers. This allows them to give feedback in real time, helping developers make adjustments as the product evolves. In today's fast-paced business world, this approach is crucial for keeping up with rapidly changing customer needs.

2.4.2 Paradigm Shift: Fixing Time and Cost, Letting Scope Be Flexible

One of the significant shifts in Agile is in how it approaches **scope, time, and cost.** Figure 2.12 shows the shift in paradigm when product development moves from the traditional approach to the Agile approach.

Traditionally, software projects sought to fix the scope at the beginning and allow time and cost to be flexible. However, this often led to problems such as:

1 **Scope Creep:** When new requirements emerge during the project, it becomes necessary to add features that were not initially anticipated, leading to increased costs and extended timelines.
2 **Cost Overruns:** With scope changes come and cost increases. Teams often need more resources, leading to higher costs, which can erode the expected return on investment (ROI).
3 **Missed Deadlines:** Flexibility with time means that projects may drag on, leading to missed market opportunities and loss of competitive advantage.

Agile turns this on its head. Instead of fixing the scope, **Agile fixes time and cost** while keeping the scope flexible. Teams deliver increments within set

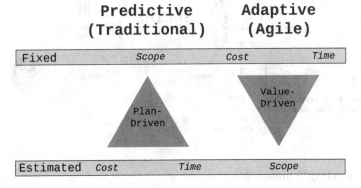

FIGURE 2.12 A Paradigm Shift.

timeframes (sprints), ensuring that the product delivers value early and often. As new insights or requirements emerge, the scope can be adjusted for future iterations.

2.4.3 Agile Methodologies

The **Agile methodology** is an umbrella that includes several specific methods, each with its own approach to managing development. Some of the most commonly used Agile frameworks include:

1. SCRUM

SCRUM is one of the most popular Agile frameworks, particularly in software development. Figure 2.13 shows the SCRUM Framework.

The SCRUM framework structures development into fixed-length iterations called **sprints,** which typically last two to four weeks. During each sprint, teams focus on delivering a usable product increment. The key components of SCRUM include:

- **Product Backlog**: A prioritized list of features, tasks, and fixes the team needs to complete. This is maintained by the **Product Owner**, who decides what the team should work on next.
- **Sprint Planning**: At the start of each sprint, the team selects items from the product backlog to work on during the sprint.

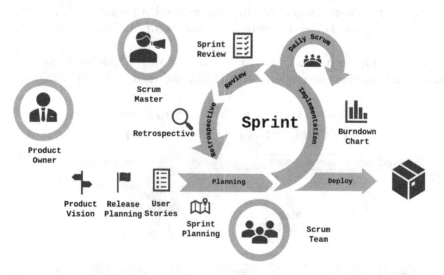

FIGURE 2.13   SCRUM Framework.

- **Daily Stand-Ups**: Short, daily meetings where the team discusses progress, roadblocks, and plans for the day.
- **Sprint Review**: A meeting held at the end of each sprint to review the completed work and gather feedback from stakeholders.
- **Sprint Retrospective**: A meeting where the team reflects on what went well and what can be improved for the next sprint.
- **Product Increment**: The result of the sprint – a potentially shippable product increment that delivers value to the customer.

In a **SCRUM project**, there are three key stakeholders, each playing a crucial role in ensuring the success of the product development process. These stakeholders work closely together to ensure that the product is delivered on time, meets user needs, and is continuously improved through iterative development.

1. Product Owner
The **Product Owner** is responsible for maximizing the value of the product by ensuring that the team works on the highest priority features and delivers meaningful increments with each sprint.

- **Maximizing Value**: The Product Owner focuses on ensuring that the product delivers maximum value to the business and users by managing and prioritizing the work to be done.
- **Managing Requirements**: They own and manage the product backlog, which includes all the features, enhancements, and fixes to be implemented.
- **Defining Priorities**: The Product Owner works with stakeholders to define the priority of each item in the backlog, ensuring the team works on the most valuable features first.

2. SCRUM Master
The **SCRUM Master** acts as a servant-leader and coach for the team, helping them adhere to SCRUM principles and processes while removing obstacles that may hinder progress.

- **Servant-Leader and Coach**: The SCRUM Master supports the team by fostering an environment where the team can be productive and self-organizing, ensuring the team follows the SCRUM framework.
- **Removing Impediments**: A key responsibility of the SCRUM Master is to remove any impediments or roadblocks that might slow down or stop the team's progress.
- **Ensuring Process Adherence**: The SCRUM Master ensures that the SCRUM processes, such as sprint planning, daily stand-ups, and sprint reviews, are understood and enacted by the team.

3. SCRUM Team

The **SCRUM Team** consists of developers who work together to deliver the product increment in each sprint. This group is self-organizing and cross-functional, meaning they have all the skills required to complete the work.

- **Team Size**: The ideal size of a SCRUM Team is seven members, give or take two, ensuring the team is small enough to stay agile and large enough to handle complex work.
- **Self-Organizing**: The team decides how best to accomplish the work assigned during the sprint, and they are empowered to manage their own activities and processes.
- **Cross-Functional**: The team members have diverse skill sets to handle all aspects of product development, including design, coding, testing, and deployment. They take collective responsibility for the success of the project.

Together, these three stakeholders collaborate to ensure that the SCRUM process runs smoothly, with the Product Owner driving the vision, the SCRUM Master guiding the process, and the SCRUM Team delivering high-quality product increments.

Example:

- **Spotify** uses SCRUM to develop features like **Discover Weekly** and **Spotify Wrapped**. Each SCRUM team (or squad) works on a specific part of the product, delivering regular updates through short sprints. This iterative approach allows Spotify to respond quickly to user feedback and continuously improve its product.

2. Kanban

Kanban is a visual framework for managing workflow. It focuses on continuous delivery by visualizing the work in progress (WIP) and limiting the amount of work being done at any given time to improve efficiency.

- **Kanban Board**: A visual tool that displays tasks in various stages, such as "To Do," "In Progress," and "Done." Teams move tasks across the board as they progress.
- **WIP Limits**: Limits the number of tasks that can be in progress at once to prevent bottlenecks.
- **Continuous Flow**: Unlike SCRUM, which works in sprints, Kanban focuses on continuously delivering work without fixed timeframes.

Example:

- **Toyota** famously used Kanban in its manufacturing processes to improve efficiency and eliminate waste. The system later became popular in software development for managing complex workflows and improving the speed of delivery.

3. Lean Software Development

Lean development emphasizes efficiency, eliminating waste, and delivering only what adds value to the customer. It focuses on optimizing the flow of work and continuously improving processes.

Principles of Lean:

- **Eliminate Waste:** Focus on removing anything that doesn't add value to the product or customer.
- **Amplify Learning:** Continuously gather feedback and learn from it to improve.
- **Decide as Late as Possible:** Avoid making decisions before you have enough information.
- **Deliver as Fast as Possible:** Shorten development cycles to deliver faster.
- **Empower the Team:** Give teams the autonomy to make decisions and solve problems.
- **Build Integrity In:** Ensure that the product is built with high quality from the start.

Example:

- **Ericsson** adopted Lean principles to streamline their software development processes, cutting down on waste and ensuring they delivered only what their customers truly needed. This helped the company reduce lead times and improve overall product quality.

2.4.4 Agile Tools and Techniques

Agile methods make use of several tools and techniques to manage development effectively:

- **Personas:** Fictional representations of users based on research to guide product development.
- **User Stories:** Short, simple descriptions of features told from the perspective of the user, such as "As a user, I want to be able to save my playlist so that I can access it later."
- **Epics:** Larger user stories that can be broken down into smaller tasks.
- **Themes:** A collection of related user stories or epics that contribute to a common goal.

- **Storyboards:** Visual representations of user interactions with a product, often used in UX Design.
- **Wireframes:** Visual guides that represent the layout and functionality of a product's UI.

2.4.5 User Interface (UI) Design

UI Design plays a critical role in ensuring that users have a seamless and intuitive experience while interacting with digital products. A well-designed UI simplifies complex tasks, engages users, and enables smooth navigation.

This section highlights the best practices in UI Design, offering a guide for creating user-friendly and functional interfaces.

Best Practices in UI Design

1 **Simplicity**
   - **Keep it simple.** A UI should be easy to navigate without users feeling overwhelmed. The simpler the design, the more intuitive it will be, reducing the need for instructions or training. If tasks are .complex, break them down into manageable steps so users can follow the flow more easily.

Example:

- **Google Search's** UI is a perfect example of simplicity and clarity. Its homepage features nothing but a search bar and a couple of buttons. The minimalistic design ensures users focus on the primary function – searching the web – without distractions. The simplicity also means that users never need instructions on how to use the interface.

2 **Clarity**
   - **Eliminate confusion.** Every element of the UI should be clear, with no room for misinterpretation. Labels, icons, and buttons must be easy to understand, with unambiguous language and design that guides users through the app smoothly.

Example:

- **Apple's iOS Settings** interface is a clear and concise example. The icons and text are simple, and users can easily navigate through various functions without confusion.

3 **Familiarity**

   - **Use recognizable patterns.** Users feel more comfortable when interacting with elements they recognize from other apps or platforms. Familiar icons, buttons, and layouts reduce the learning curve and help users quickly adapt to new interfaces.

Example:
- **Instagram** is an example of using familiar UI elements to create an intuitive experience. The app uses commonly recognized icons for actions like liking (heart), commenting (speech bubble), and messaging (paper aeroplane). This consistency with other platforms ensures that users can quickly understand the app's interface, reducing the learning curve.

4 **Responsiveness**
- **Ensure speed and fluidity.** A responsive interface enhances the UX by reacting quickly to input, without lag or delay. The UI should respond instantly to clicks, taps, or swipes, creating a sense of control for the user.

Example:
- **Amazon's mobile app** is highly responsive, offering quick load times, fast navigation between pages, and a seamless checkout experience, all of which contribute to a smooth and enjoyable shopping process.

5 **Consistency**
- **Maintain uniformity across all screens.** Consistency in UI Design ensures that users understand the behaviour of the interface as they move through the app. Keeping design elements like fonts, buttons, and layouts consistent improves usability and user satisfaction.

Example:
- **Slack** has a consistent design across desktop and mobile platforms. Whether users are switching between the app's mobile or desktop versions, the colour scheme, layout, and function remain the same, making the app familiar regardless of the device.

6 **Flexibility**
- **Account for user mistakes.** People make mistakes, and a good UI Design should allow for easy error recovery. By incorporating undo and redo options, warning messages, and confirmation steps before finalizing actions, designers can create an interface that helps users get back on track easily.

Example:
- **Microsoft Outlook** provides a flexible option for users to recall or resend emails even after they have been sent, giving users a chance to correct mistakes. This feature allows users to recall emails sent to incorrect recipients or make adjustments to emails without causing confusion, significantly reducing errors in communication.

7 **Reusability**
- **Avoid repetitive tasks.** A well-designed UI should remember user data and preferences, minimizing the need for repetitive actions. This improves usability and keeps users engaged with the app without frustration.

Example:
- **Netflix** remembers the user's watch history and automatically suggests content based on their viewing habits. It also resumes playback from where the user left off, eliminating the need for repetitive searching or navigating.

Effective **UI Design** is a critical element in ensuring that digital products are user-friendly, intuitive, and engaging. By following best practices such as simplicity, clarity, responsiveness, and consistency, designers can create interfaces that not only meet user needs but also enhance the overall experience. Real-world examples like Google, Instagram, and Netflix demonstrate how applying these principles leads to successful products that keep users coming back for more.

By keeping the user at the centre of every design decision and continuously refining the interface based on feedback, product teams can build interfaces that are not only functional but also delightful to use.

2.5 Agile Development Summary

Agile development represents a significant paradigm shift from traditional methods by focusing on flexibility, collaboration, and delivering value in small, incremental steps. The key to Agile's success lies in its ability to adjust to changing requirements, gather continuous feedback, and keep the customer at the centre of the development process. With tools like SCRUM and Kanban, and methods such as Lean development, Agile enables teams to respond quickly to the dynamic needs of the business and deliver products that evolve in line with customer expectations. By adopting these principles, organizations can reduce the risk of scope creep, manage costs more effectively, and ensure that they remain competitive in fast-moving markets.

2.6 Conclusion

Incorporating **UX Design** and **Agile Development** into your product development process is essential for creating products that resonate with users and remain competitive in a fast-paced market. UX Design ensures that the product is user-friendly and engaging, while Agile Development allows for continuous iteration and rapid responses to changing requirements. By applying these methodologies, product teams can build solutions that not only meet user needs but also evolve with feedback, ensuring long-term success.

3

DELIVERING DIGITAL PRODUCTS

3.1 Introduction

Delivering digital products in a fast-moving environment requires a robust infrastructure and streamlined processes. **Continuous Delivery** is a software development approach that automates and accelerates the release process, ensuring frequent, reliable updates that deliver value to users. Equally important is the **Product Stack** – the set of tools, applications, and technologies that support the entire product development lifecycle. This chapter explores how teams can implement Continuous Delivery to achieve faster, more reliable releases, and how a well-chosen Product Stack can enhance collaboration, efficiency, and scalability.

3.2 Continuous Delivery

Continuous Delivery (CD) is a software development practice where code changes are automatically prepared for release to production. This approach ensures that software can be reliably released at any time, reducing the time between development and deployment. In this section, we will explore two key concepts in Continuous Delivery: the **Lean Startup Approach** – focusing on the **MVP** (Minimum Viable Product) and continuous iteration – and Continuous Integration, Continuous Delivery, and Continuous Deployment (CI/CD).

DOI: 10.1201/9781003614180-3

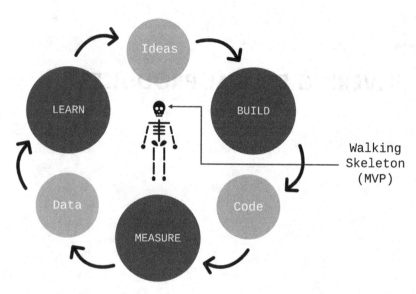

FIGURE 3.1 Lean Startup: Build-Measure-Learn.

3.2.1 Lean Startup Approach: Build-Measure-Learn with MVP

The **Lean Startup Approach,** popularized by Eric Ries, emphasizes rapidly developing products by testing assumptions through continuous iteration. This approach uses the **Build-Measure-Learn** feedback loop to guide development and ensure products are continuously improved based on real user feedback. Figure 3.1 shows the Lean Startup model.

One of the core principles of this approach is starting with an **MVP** and incrementally refining the product.

- **Walking Skeleton (MVP):** The **walking skeleton** is an initial version of the product that contains the minimal, basic functionalities necessary for the system to function end-to-end. It's the bare backbone of the product, designed to show how different parts of the system interact.
- **Backbone:** In the context of agile development, the **backbone** refers to the high-priority functionalities or key components of the system. The walking skeleton adds flesh to this backbone by integrating minimal features that provide immediate value to early adopters.

3.2.2 Story Mapping in Agile Development

A **Story Map** is a visual representation of the product's features, themes, or user stories over time. Figure 3.2 shows the use of a Story Map to build an MVP.

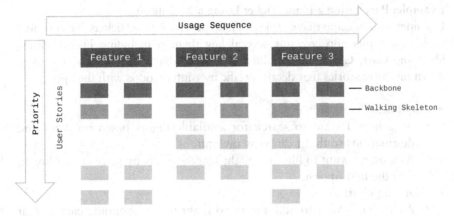

FIGURE 3.2 A Story Map for Building MVP.

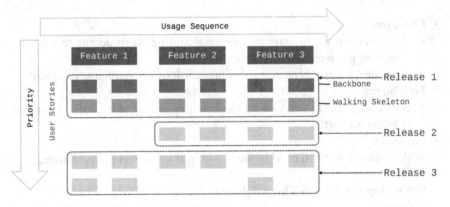

FIGURE 3.3 Horizontal Slicing in Release Planning.

A Story Map helps in prioritizing features, organizing the product backlog, and planning releases. Story Maps help break down complex products into smaller, deliverable increments.

3.2.3 Horizontal Slicing in Release Planning

In agile development, **horizontal slicing** refers to dividing the product into functional layers, or increments, where each slice delivers a working, usable portion of the product. Multiple releases are planned as **swim lanes**, comprising prioritized features and user stories, which are aligned with the backbone of the product, as shown in Figure 3.3.

Example: Purchasing a Plane Ticket Using a Mobile App

Consider a mobile app that enables users to purchase plane tickets. The product backlog for this app contains several key themes, including **Flight Search, Shopping Cart, Checkout, Fulfilment**, and **Post-Sale**. Each theme is broken down into user stories that detail specific user interactions with the app.

- **Flight Search:**
  - As a user, I want to search for available flights based on dates and destinations so that I can view my options.
  - As a user, I want to filter my flight search results by price and airline to find the best option.
- **Shopping Cart:**
  - As a user, I want to add a selected flight to the shopping cart so that I can review my selection.
  - As a user, I want to see the total cost of my selected flight, including taxes and fees.

- **Checkout:**
  - As a user, I want to enter my personal and payment details securely to complete my purchase.
  - As a user, I want to receive a confirmation of my purchase via email.
- **Fulfillment:**
  - As a user, I want to receive an electronic boarding pass so that I can use it at the airport.
- **Post-Sale:**
  - As a user, I want to modify my booking if my travel plans change.

Story Map for Two to Three Releases

- **Release 1:**
  Focuses on the walking skeleton of the system, enabling users to perform basic flight searches and complete a purchase.
  - Flight Search: Search for flights based on dates and destinations.
  - Shopping Cart: Add flight to shopping cart, view total cost.
  - Checkout: Enter payment details, receive confirmation email.
- **Release 2:**
  Expands the backbone by adding more advanced features for customer convenience.
  - Flight Search: Filter by price and airline.
  - Fulfillment: Receive an electronic boarding pass.
- **Release 3:**
  Continues to flesh out the product by improving user experience and post-sale services.
  - Post-Sale: Modify booking, change flights after purchase.

3.2.4   The Power of the MVP

An **MVP** is the simplest version of a product that can be released to early adopters to validate the concept and gather feedback. This approach helps startups avoid the costly mistake of building features that users may not want.

3.2.4.1   MVP Example: Pebble Watch

The **Pebble Watch** is a classic example of a successful **MVP**. **Pebble** leveraged the **Kickstarter** crowdfunding platform to validate the demand for a smart watch that worked with both iOS and Android. The company did not build out a fully featured watch initially. Instead, they created a simple watch with just the core features – basic notifications and customizable watch faces – and relied on user feedback to guide future updates and improvements.

Through **Kickstarter**, **Pebble** raised over **$10 million**, proving the demand for the product before investing in full development. This **MVP** strategy minimized risks, reduced costs, and allowed the Pebble team to iterate based on feedback.

3.2.4.2   Insights on Building an MVP

1. **Don't Burn Money on a Product No One Wants!**
   An **MVP** helps ensure that you're investing resources in something that customers actually want. Test the market before pouring money into features or functionalities that may not be needed.
2. **Validate Your Assumptions:**
   - Write articles and seek feedback from your target audience.
   - Hold seminars or webinars to gauge interest.
   - Leverage social media platforms to test concepts and gather opinions.
3. **Remember the "Minimum" in MVP**
   The **MVP** should only contain the essential features that solve the core problem. Avoid feature creep and ensure that the product is lean and efficient.
4. **Perseverance and Continuous Learning Are Crucial**
   Use the feedback loop from your **MVP** to learn and improve continuously. Successful products are not built overnight; they require iteration and adaptation.
5. **Criteria for an MVP:**
   - **Minimum Features:** Only essential features that offer core functionality should be shipped.

- **Monetization**: Some early adopters should be willing to pay for the product, indicating that there is real demand.
- **Feedback Loop**: Early adopters should provide feedback that can guide further iterations.

3.2.5 MVP for a Product Case Scenario

Now let's take a look at how the Product Case Scenario can also make use of the MVP approach to build its car-sharing mobile application.

What **QuikDrive** needs is to create a basic product within a short period of time, push it onto the market, gather the first feedback, and assess its competitiveness. Figure 3.4 shows the steps in building an **MVP**.

1 The **first** step to building the **MVP** is to perform a market analysis that will shed some light on the market demand for **QuikDrive**'s platform for car owners and car renters.
2 The **second** step is for **QuikDrive** to conduct a market segmentation of target customers, based on needs and budget. For example, let's say **QuikDrive** wants to test the market segment of users on a budget, who only want the cheapest, no-frills car rentals. Then **QuikDrive** can simplify the potentially tedious process of choosing a rental car by offering only one type or model of car. In other words, the MVP in that case would not include options of car types, instead focusing on one car.

   By doing so in the early stages, it would give itself the room to grow and allow the company to focus its resources on getting the product right for that one car type. This kind of differentiation could also help **QuikDrive** to stand out from the competition and build a brand following for the company.
3 In the **third** step, the product team should design and map out the user process flow, focusing on mapping how users will interact with the car-sharing mobile app. Starting from opening the mobile app all the way to the final process of renting a car. This is similar to the customer journey mapping exercise you saw in a previous video.
4 Once the design process is done, the team will move on to the **fourth** step, which is to prioritize the product features so as to build the **MVP** version as quickly as possible. This also helps determine which features belong in the **MVP** version, and which can come later, in future versions or iterations.
5 The **fifth** step is to build and launch the **MVP**. **QuikDrive**'s MVP would include the basic features, such as sign-up and login, managing bookings, and mobile payment.

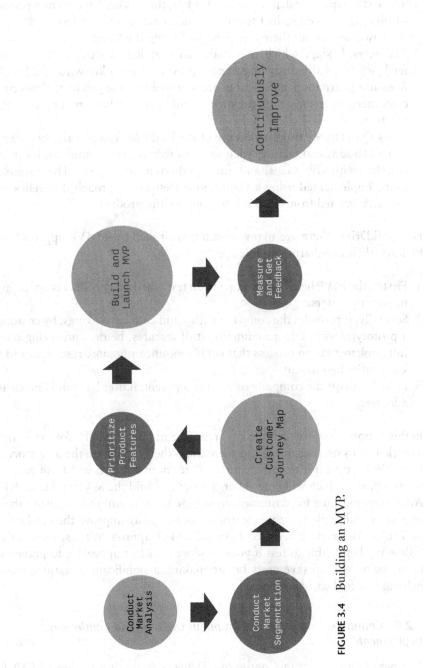

FIGURE 3.4   Building an MVP.

6 The **sixth** step, after deploying the **MVP** to the market for a certain period of time, is for the product team to conduct surveys to get feedback from the customers about their experiences of using the **MVP**.

7 The **seventh** step, which is actually an ongoing process, is to use the feedback to continuously improve the product. This is known as the **Build-Measure-Learn** loop: a cyclical process of building the product, measuring customers' reactions and responses, and learning how to improve the product.

As **QuikDrive's** team makes use of the **Build-Measure-Learn** loop, they can add additional features such as a rewards system, reminders, location searches with GPS maps, and integrated payment systems. These should all be implemented using a Continuous Delivery approach that relies on the data learned from feedback to improve the product.

For **QuikDrive**, there are many advantages of using the **MVP** approach to building their car-sharing mobile app.

1 Firstly, the **MVP** helps the product team test whether a product is appealing to potential users.
2 Secondly, it provides the company with significant cost savings, by creating a prototype with only a minimum set of features, before embarking on a full implementation process that entails significantly more resources and a substantial investment.
3 Lastly, it helps the company to acquire a potential user base and find early adopters.

In this segment, you've seen the key steps to building an **MVP**. You start with a market analysis, then market segmentation, then you design the user process flow. Next, you prioritize the features, determining which will form part of the **MVP**, and which will come later. Then, you build the **MVP** and launch it. After allowing time for customers to engage with it, you then measure their responses and apply what you learn, to continuously improve the product.

You've also seen the benefits of using the **MVP** approach. These include the following: being able to test if your product is in fact appealing to potential users; being able to save costs before making a significant investment; and helping you find early adopters.

3.2.6 Continuous Integration, Continuous Delivery, and Continuous Deployment

The next key concept in Continuous Delivery is the integration of **CI/CD** pipelines, which ensure that software updates are seamlessly integrated, tested, and delivered to production with minimal disruption.

- **Continuous Integration (CI)**: Developers frequently merge their code into the main branch, ensuring that the product is always in a working state. Automated testing is performed to identify issues early.
- **Continuous Delivery (CD)**: Once code is integrated, it is automatically prepared for release. This means that the software can be deployed to production at any time, even if it is not immediately released.
- **Continuous Deployment**: In this stage, every change that passes automated tests is automatically deployed to production. This means updates are delivered to users rapidly and frequently, ensuring that new features and fixes are always live.

3.2.6.1 The Challenges of Traditional Software Delivery

In traditional software delivery, the process of building and releasing software was often fraught with inefficiencies, delays, and challenges. One of the most significant issues was the integration phase, which typically occurred at the end of a project after developers had completed their work. Integration was a painful process, often taking weeks or even months as code from various developers had to be merged, tested, and debugged. This approach resulted in unpredictable timelines and last-minute rushes to meet deadlines. Figure 3.5 illustrates the traditional software delivery method.

Another major challenge in traditional method was the numerous **handoffs between different teams**. Developers would complete their work and pass it on to testers, who would then validate the code before handing it over to the release team. Once the release team finalized the build, it was passed on to operations and support teams for deployment and ongoing maintenance. This sequence of handoffs created silos between teams, with each group focusing only on their specific tasks and having limited visibility into the entire development lifecycle. These silos often led to miscommunication,

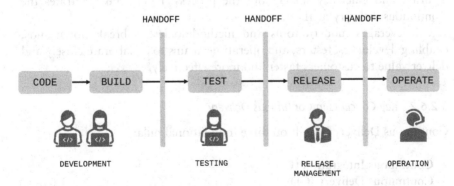

FIGURE 3.5 Traditional Software Delivery Method.

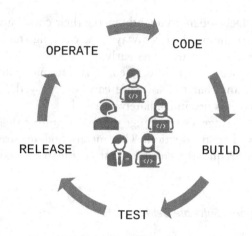

OPERATE

CODE

RELEASE

BUILD

TEST

FIGURE 3.6 Continuous Delivery Method.

delays, and inconsistent results, as teams encountered problems that could have been resolved earlier if there was better collaboration.

For instance, developers might code new features without fully considering how they would be tested or deployed, leaving testers and operations teams to struggle with unforeseen issues later in the process. Similarly, release and operations teams might face difficulties in deploying code that wasn't optimized for the production environment. This "over-the-wall" approach led to missed deadlines, untested code being released, and production issues that required extensive rework.

In today's digital age, businesses can no longer afford these inefficiencies. To remain competitive, organizations are adopting **Continuous Delivery (CD)** practices, which focus on automation, collaboration, and the frequent delivery of high-quality software. The goal is to reduce the time between writing code and delivering it to production while ensuring reliability, security, and efficiency throughout the process. Figure 3.6 illustrates the Continuous Delivery method.

CD leverages modern tools and methodologies to break down silos, enabling developers, testers, and operations teams to collaborate closely and deliver value to customers faster and more effectively.

3.2.6.2 Key Concepts in Continuous Delivery

Continuous Delivery is built on three foundational pillars:

1 **Continuous Integration (CI)**
2 **Continuous Delivery (CD)**
3 **Continuous Deployment (CD)**

Together, these practices ensure that software is constantly being integrated, tested, and ready for release in a streamlined and automated manner.

1. Continuous Integration (CI)

CI is a development practice in which developers frequently integrate code into a shared repository, ideally several times a day. Each integration is automatically verified through an automated build and tests, helping detect and address integration issues as early as possible.

Key Components of CI:
- **Version Control System (VCS):** A central repository like **Git**, where developers store and manage the codebase. This is where changes from multiple developers are integrated.
- **Automated Build:** Scripts compile the code and create executables automatically. This ensures that code from different developers can be merged without manual intervention.
- **Automated Testing:** Tests are automatically triggered after the build process to ensure the new code integrates properly and doesn't introduce new bugs.
- **Feedback Mechanism:** Developers receive immediate feedback on whether the code was successfully integrated or whether there were errors, allowing for quick resolution of issues.

Example: CI in Action

Imagine Steve, who works from home, and Annie, who works in the office, are both developing features for a mobile app. With CI, Steve and Annie frequently commit their code to the same repository. Automated tests ensure their code is successfully integrated, and if any issues arise, they receive instant feedback. This system prevents the painful process of "integration hell" at the end of a project and ensures that any issues are caught early.

To facilitate this, Steve and Annie use a **CI Server** (such as Jenkins or CircleCI) that automatically builds their code, runs unit tests, and checks whether the integrated code works as expected. If all tests pass, they receive a **green build** – a signal that their integration was successful. If not, they are alerted immediately to resolve the issue. This process ensures that integration is a continuous, non-disruptive activity rather than a last-minute event.

2. Continuous Delivery (CD)

Continuous Delivery takes the principles of CI a step further. In addition to integrating code frequently, CD ensures that the code is always ready to be deployed. This means that the software is tested in environments that closely resemble the production environment, ensuring that the code can be deployed with confidence at any time.

Key Concepts of Continuous Delivery:

- **Deployment Pipeline**: This refers to a series of automated stages that code passes through, from development to production. It usually involves multiple environments like development, testing, staging, and production.
- **Automated Testing**: Besides unit tests, automated testing at this stage involves more extensive testing like integration tests, performance tests, and security tests. These tests ensure that the code behaves as expected in production-like environments.

Example: Deployment Pipeline in Action

Steve and Annie's team set up a **deployment pipeline** where, after the code passes the initial CI tests, it is automatically deployed to a **development environment** for further testing. Next, the code is deployed to a **staging environment**, where it is tested against real-world scenarios that simulate production. Once all tests pass, the software is ready for deployment to production at any time.

For example, **Facebook** uses Continuous Delivery to ensure that small changes to its platform are tested in stages and can be quickly deployed across its massive user base. Each code change undergoes rigorous testing across development, staging, and production-like environments to minimize downtime or errors during deployment.

3. Continuous Deployment (CD)

Continuous Deployment automates the entire process of delivering code changes to production environments. Once the code passes all necessary tests in the deployment pipeline, it is automatically deployed to the live production environment without requiring manual approval.

Key Components of Continuous Deployment:

- **Automated Deployment**: Every code change that passes automated tests is immediately deployed to the production environment.
- **Monitoring and Rollback**: Once deployed, the production environment is continuously monitored to detect any issues. If a problem is detected, the system automatically rolls back to a previous stable version to minimize disruption.

Example: Continuous Deployment in Action

Companies like **Netflix** and **Amazon** have embraced Continuous Deployment, deploying small, frequent updates to their platforms multiple times a day. This allows them to introduce new features and fixes faster, with immediate feedback on how those changes perform in the real world. For instance, **Netflix** uses a deployment pipeline that continuously tests new code in a production-like environment and then deploys it to users as soon as it passes all tests.

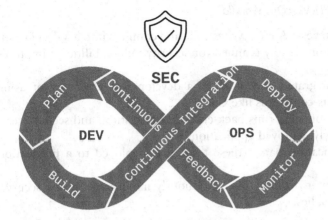

FIGURE 3.7 DevSecOps Integration and CI/CD Delivery Process.

3.2.6.3 DevSecOps and Security Integration

With the rise of **DevOps,** there's an increasing emphasis on integrating security into the development and delivery process. **DevSecOps** introduces automated security checks within the CI/CD pipeline to ensure that software is not only functional but also secure. Figure 3.7 illustrates the **DevSecOps** Integration and CI/CD delivery process.

Security Tools in DevSecOps:

- **SAST (Static Application Security Testing)**: Analyses code at rest to find security vulnerabilities without executing the application.
- **SCA (Software Composition Analysis)**: Scans the codebase for any known vulnerabilities in third-party libraries or open-source components.
- **DAST (Dynamic Application Security Testing)**: Scans the running application for security vulnerabilities in real-time environments.

3.2.6.4 Shift Left Approach

In **DevSecOps,** the **Shift Left** approach is a practice that emphasizes identifying and resolving issues earlier in the development cycle. This involves integrating security testing and checks into the early stages of development rather than waiting until the product is near deployment.

Example: Many organizations now use tools like **SonarQube** and **Fortify** to automate code scanning for security vulnerabilities, helping developers fix security issues early in the process.

3.2.6.5 A Typical DevSecOps Workflow

1 A developer (Steve or Annie) writes code and commits it to a VCS like **Git**.
2 The code is automatically scanned for security vulnerabilities using tools like **SAST**.
3 The code is integrated and tested in a **development environment** using infrastructure-as-code tools like **Chef**.
4 A test automation suite runs back-end, UI, integration, and security tests against the newly deployed application.
5 Once the application passes these tests, it is deployed to a **production environment**.
6 The production environment is continuously monitored for any security threats or anomalies.

3.2.6.6 Collaboration in DevOps: Bridging Development and Operations

A key aspect of Continuous Delivery and **DevOps** is increased collaboration between development and operations teams. In traditional environments, development teams were responsible for writing code, while operations teams managed deployment and infrastructure. However, **DevOps** removes this barrier, fostering a collaborative environment.

Key Aspects of Development Team Collaboration:
• Automate processes as much as possible to reduce manual intervention.
• Write secure code and perform regular vulnerability assessments.
• Create a clear release bill of materials (**BOM**) and link it to issue trackers with source control systems.
• Provide escalation paths for deployment glitches or security breaches.

Key Aspects of Operations Team Collaboration:
• Work with development teams to understand root causes of issues and solutions.
• Migrate configuration data from production back to staging and development environments for testing.
• Monitor production systems for security threats and optimize infrastructure configurations for scalability.

Example: DevOps Collaboration at Spotify
Spotify uses **DevOps** practices to manage its rapidly growing platform. The development and operations teams work together to ensure that updates to the platform can be delivered quickly, with minimal risk of downtime or

disruptions. By fostering collaboration and automating key processes, **Spotify** ensures that its platform is always up to date and secure.

3.2.6.7   Continuous Delivery Conclusion

In today's digital landscape, **Continuous Delivery (CD)** and the integration of DevOps principles are essential for businesses to remain competitive. By adopting **Continuous Integration (CI)**, **Continuous Delivery (CD)**, and **Continuous Deployment (CD)** practices, organizations can automate their software delivery process, reduce risks, and ensure faster time to market. Furthermore, the integration of security through **DevSecOps** ensures that the product is not only functional but also secure at every stage of development. This shift to automation and collaboration is transforming the way digital products are delivered, creating a more efficient, reliable, and secure development lifecycle.

3.2.6.8   Summary: Building and Delivering Products with Continuous Delivery

In the world of digital products, **Continuous Delivery** enables teams to ship features quickly, respond to feedback in real time, and ensure high product quality through automation. By starting with an **MVP** and leveraging the **Build-Measure-Learn** cycle, teams can validate their ideas and avoid costly mistakes. Combining this with **CI/CD pipelines** allows for smoother and faster releases, ensuring that the product can evolve continuously with the market and user needs.

3.3   Product Stack

A **Product (Tech) Stack** refers to the collection of apps, technologies, and resources that product managers and development teams use to build and bring digital products to market. The term "stack" is borrowed from the development community, where it's used to describe the combination of tools, frameworks, and technologies required to create and run a product or service. These technologies work together to create a seamless experience for both developers and end users.

A **Tech Stack** typically includes a mix of front-end and back-end technologies, databases, programming languages, and cloud or server technologies. For digital products, these stacks are crucial in ensuring that the product performs efficiently, scales with demand, and delivers value to users.

Just like building a house requires the right materials and tools, developing a digital product relies on selecting the right Tech Stack. Imagine trying to construct a home without sturdy bricks or proper blueprints – it might stand for a while, but it won't hold up over time. The same is true for software. Without a well-thought-out Tech Stack, the development process can quickly fall apart. A strong Tech Stack lays the foundation, supports the structure, and ensures everything works together seamlessly, just like a well-built house that's designed to last.

3.3.1 Tech Stack Components

A typical Tech Stack can be broken down into the following main components as shown in Figure 3.8:

1 **Front-end Tech Stack**
2 **Back-end Tech Stack**
3 **Full Stack Set**
4 **Deployment Infrastructure**

1. Front-end Tech Stack
The **front-end** is what the user interacts with – also known as the client side. A strong front-end Tech Stack ensures the product has a visually appealing, responsive, and intuitive user interface (UI). The core technologies that make up a front-end Tech Stack include the following:

- **HTML (Hypertext Markup Language)**: Structures the content on a web page.
- **CSS (Cascading Style Sheets)**: Styles and formats the content, defining the layout, colours, fonts, etc.

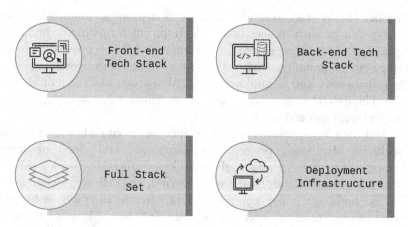

FIGURE 3.8 Tech Stacks Components.

- **JavaScript**: Powers dynamic content on web pages and enables interactive user experiences.
- **Front-end Frameworks and Libraries**: These include popular tools such as the following:
  - **React.js**: A JavaScript library for building UIs, especially for single-page applications.
  - **Vue.js**: A progressive JavaScript framework used for building UIs.
  - **Angular.js**: A JavaScript framework often used for building complex web applications.
  - **Bootstrap**: A CSS framework that helps to build responsive and mobile-first web pages.

2. Back-end Tech Stack

The **back-end** is the server side of the product that powers the front-end. It manages the logic, database interactions, user authentication, and server configuration. A typical back-end Tech Stack includes the following:

- **Server-side Programming Languages**: These are used to handle server-side logic, with popular choices being:
  - **Node.js**: A JavaScript runtime used for building fast and scalable network applications.
  - **Python**: A versatile language often used for data-heavy applications or application programming interfaces (APIs).
  - **Java**: A powerful object-oriented language used in enterprise-level applications.
  - **Ruby**: A dynamic language used in web development, particularly with the Ruby on Rails framework.
- **Back-end Frameworks**: These frameworks help structure server-side code and often handle database connections, user authentication, and routing.
  - **Express.js**: A minimal and flexible Node.js framework used to build web applications.
  - **Django**: A Python framework known for its simplicity and "batteries-included" philosophy.
  - **Spring Boot**: A Java framework that simplifies building production-grade applications.
- **Databases**: These store and manage application data. Some popular database technologies include the following:
  - **MongoDB**: An NoSQL database that stores data in JSON-like documents, used for scalability.
  - **MySQL**: A relational database known for its reliability and widely used for web apps.

- **PostgreSQL**: An open-source relational database with advanced features for complex queries.
- **APIs:**
  - Interfaces that allow different software systems to communicate and share data.
  - **Examples**: RESTful APIs, GraphQL
- **Web Servers:**
  - Software that processes incoming requests from clients (browsers) and serves them content.
  - **Examples**: Apache, NGINX, IIS (Internet Information Services)
- **Application Servers:**
  - Platforms for running server-side applications.
  - **Examples**: Node.js, Tomcat, Jetty
- **Containerization and Virtualization:**
  - Tools for creating isolated environments to run applications, making deployment easier and more scalable.
  - **Examples**: Docker, Kubernetes

3. Full Stack Set
Full Stack refers to a set of technologies that cover both front-end and back-end development. Some popular Full Stack sets include the following:

- **LAMP Stack:**
  - **Linux (OS), Apache (Server), MySQL (Database), PHP (Language).**
  - It is one of the earliest stacks for dynamic web applications, often used for PHP-based projects. While it has limitations in scalability, it's popular for simple web applications.
  - **Use Case**: A small blog website or content management system (CMS).
- **MEAN Stack:**
  - **MongoDB (Database), Express.js (Back-end Framework), Angular.js (Front-end Framework), Node.js (Runtime).**
  - This stack is popular for creating dynamic websites and applications using JavaScript on both the front-end and back-end.
  - **Use Case**: E-commerce websites or SaaS applications.
- **MERN Stack:**
  - **MongoDB (Database), Express.js (Back-end Framework), React/ Redux (Front-end Library), Node.js (Runtime).**
  - MERN is used to build single-page applications that require fast and dynamic user interactions.
  - **Use Case**: Social media platforms or dashboard applications.

4. Deployment Infrastructure
Deployment infrastructure refers to the environment and tools used to host, deploy, and manage software applications. The software can be deployed

either **on-premises** or in the **cloud,** depending on the organization's requirements. Below is an updated list of components and options for deploying software.

- **Cloud Providers**
  Cloud platforms offer scalable and flexible infrastructure for hosting and managing applications. They provide on-demand services for computing, storage, and networking. Cloud deployment reduces the need for maintaining physical hardware and allows for automatic scaling based on demand.
  - **Public Cloud:** These are cloud environments offered by third-party providers and shared by multiple users.
  - **Private Cloud:** A cloud environment dedicated to a single organization, providing more control and privacy.
  - **Hybrid Cloud:** Combines public and private clouds to allow for flexibility in where workloads are hosted.

Examples:
  - **Amazon Web Services (AWS)**
  - **Google Cloud Platform (GCP)**
  - **Microsoft Azure**

- **On-Premises Platforms**
  On-premises platforms involve deploying and managing software in a private data centre within an organization's physical infrastructure. This option offers more control over hardware, security, and compliance but requires significant resources for maintenance and scaling.

Examples:
  - **VMware vSphere**
  - **Red Hat OpenShift**
  - **Microsoft Hyper-V**

- **Content Delivery Networks (CDN)**
  CDNs are used to improve performance by caching and distributing content (static and dynamic) across global servers. This reduces latency and improves the user experience by serving data from the closest geographic location.

Examples:
  - **Amazon CloudFront**
  - **Cloudflare**
  - **Akamai**

- **Containerization and Orchestration**
  Containerization allows applications to be packaged along with their dependencies, ensuring they can run consistently across different environments. **Orchestration** tools manage and automate the deployment of containers across multiple environments and ensure scalability, load balancing, and fault tolerance.

Examples:
- **Docker** (Containerization)
- **Kubernetes, Docker Swarm** (Orchestration)

E **Serverless Architectures**
Serverless architectures allow developers to deploy code in the form of functions without worrying about the underlying server infrastructure. The cloud provider automatically handles scaling, patching, and server maintenance.

Examples:
- **AWS Lambda**
- **Google Cloud Functions**
- **Azure Functions**
F **Load Balancers**
Load balancers distribute traffic across multiple servers to ensure high availability and reliability of the application. They prevent server overload and ensure optimal performance even during high traffic periods.

Examples:
- **AWS Elastic Load Balancer (ELB)**
- **NGINX Load Balancer**
- **HAProxy**

- **CI/CD (Continuous Integration/Continuous Deployment) Pipelines**
  CI/CD pipelines automate the processes of integrating, testing, and deploying code. They reduce manual intervention and ensure that new code can be rapidly deployed to production environments with minimal risk.

Examples:
- **Jenkins**
- **CircleCI**
- **GitLab CI**
- **Travis CI**

- **Infrastructure as Code (IaC)**
  IaC tools automate the provisioning and management of infrastructure using code. This allows for consistent, repeatable deployments and simplifies scaling and maintenance.

Examples:
  - **Terraform**
  - **AWS CloudFormation**
  - **Pulumi**

- **Monitoring and Logging Tools**
  Monitoring tools track application performance and resource utilization, while logging tools collect and analyse log data to help identify and troubleshoot issues in real time.

Examples:
  - **Prometheus** (Monitoring)
  - **Datadog** (Monitoring)
  - **ELK Stack (Elasticsearch, Logstash, Kibana)** (Logging)
  - **Splunk** (Logging and Monitoring)

- **Database Management and Scaling Tools**
  Database management tools handle scaling, backups, and disaster recovery in production environments. These tools allow databases to scale alongside the application and ensure data integrity and availability.

Examples:
  - **Amazon RDS**
  - **Google Cloud SQL**
  - **Azure SQL Database**
  - **MongoDB Atlas**

- **Security and Compliance Tools**
  Security tools help ensure that applications are secure and compliant with industry standards. These tools help monitor vulnerabilities, manage identity and access control, and protect data.

Examples:
  - **AWS Shield**
  - **Palo Alto Networks Prisma**
  - **HashiCorp Vault**
  - **Snyk**

3.3.1.1 Cloud vs. On-Premises Deployment Options

- **On-Premises**: Best for organizations that require full control over their infrastructure and need to meet strict regulatory requirements. It provides more customization options but requires significant resources for management and maintenance.
- **Cloud**: Provides flexibility, scalability, and cost-efficiency, as well as automation for deployment, scaling, and monitoring. It also offers a range of services, from Infrastructure-as-a-Service (IaaS) to Software-as-a-Service (SaaS), depending on the organization's needs.

Hybrid cloud solutions can offer the best of both worlds by combining on-premises infrastructure with cloud resources, allowing for flexibility and better management of workloads.

3.3.1.2 Summary: Deployment Infrastructure

Organizations have many options when it comes to **deployment infrastructure**, whether through **on-premises solutions** or cloud providers like **AWS**, **GCP**, and **Azure**. These deployment environments, coupled with tools for containerization, orchestration, automation, and monitoring, ensure that products can be developed, tested, deployed, and scaled efficiently in response to changing demands. By leveraging the right deployment infrastructure, teams can accelerate time to market, improve reliability, and enhance the overall user experience.

3.3.2 Programming Languages and Frameworks in a Product Stack

The programming languages and frameworks used in a Tech Stack largely determine how the product will perform, scale, and integrate with other services. Here are some commonly used programming languages and their associated frameworks:

- **JavaScript**:
  Frameworks: **React.js, Angular.js, Vue.js, Node.js**
  Use Case: Front-end and back-end development for interactive web apps, SaaS platforms, and real-time applications.
- **Python**:
  Frameworks: **Django, Flask**
  Use Case: Back-end development, API development, data-heavy applications, machine learning models.
- **Java**:
  Frameworks: **Spring Boot**

Use Case: Enterprise-level applications, back-end services for large-scale systems.
- **Ruby:**
  Framework: **Ruby on Rails**
  Use Case: Web application development, especially for startups and MVPs.

3.3.3 Examples of Tech Stacks

3.3.3.1 Example 1: Netflix (Tech Stack shown in Figure 3.9)

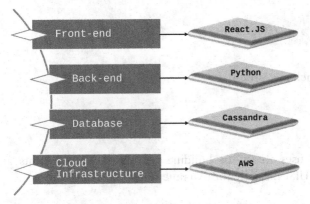

FIGURE 3.9   Tech Stack for Netflix.

1 **Front-end Layer**
   React.js: Netflix uses React as its primary front-end framework for building interactive and high-performance UIs.
2 **Back-end Layer**
   Python: Used for data science, automation, and analytics tasks, helping **Netflix** optimize content recommendations and performance.
3 **Database Layer**
   Cassandra: A highly scalable, distributed NoSQL database used by **Netflix** for storing and managing massive amounts of user data, including watch history, preferences, and recommendations.
4 **Cloud Infrastructure Layer**
   AWS: Netflix runs its entire platform on **AWS**, which provides the cloud infrastructure to deliver streaming services worldwide.

3.3.3.2 Example 2: Airbnb (Tech Stack shown in Figure 3.10)

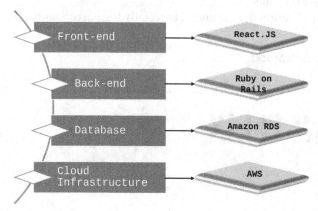

FIGURE 3.10 Tech Stack for Airbnb.

1 **Front-end Layer**
   React.js: Airbnb uses React for building reusable UI components and managing the UI, especially for dynamic single-page applications.
2 **Back-end Layer**
   Ruby on Rails: Airbnb's primary back-end framework, **Ruby on Rails,** is used for building robust web applications and managing the business logic of the platform. It helps **Airbnb** quickly develop and iterate on features.
3 **Database Layer**
   Amazon RDS: Airbnb leverages **Amazon RDS** (Relational Database Service) for scalable, managed **MySQL** database services.
4 **Cloud Infrastructure Layer**
   AWS: Airbnb runs its platform on **AWS,** using its cloud infrastructure to support scaling and handling global traffic.

3.3.4 Benefits of Using Tech Stacks

1 **Scalability**: A well-designed Tech Stack ensures that the product can handle growing user demand and larger datasets without performance degradation.
2 **Efficiency**: Tech Stacks allow developers to work efficiently by providing pre-built libraries, frameworks, and tools that simplify tasks like database management, API integration, and front-end design.

3 **Maintainability**: Modern Tech Stacks come with built-in tools that help manage and maintain the codebase over time. This reduces the likelihood of bugs and ensures that the product is easy to update.
4 **Flexibility**: A robust Tech Stack can be adapted to suit the evolving needs of the business. As products grow, additional components like databases or cloud services can be added or swapped out as needed.
5 **Collaboration**: Tech Stacks often include tools that facilitate collaboration across development teams. For example, using Git for version control ensures that multiple developers can work on the same project without conflicts.
6 **Security**: Many Tech Stacks offer built-in security features, such as encryption and secure authentication, to help protect the product and its users.
7 **Learning Curve**: Selecting the right Tech Stack can reduce the learning curve for development teams. Familiarity with common languages and frameworks enables teams to be more productive from the start, avoiding delays caused by having to learn new, unfamiliar technologies.
8 **Time to Market**: By using a well-established Tech Stack, development teams can accelerate the product development process and reduce the time to market. Pre-built libraries, APIs, and frameworks allow teams to focus on building core product features, rather than reinventing basic functionalities, leading to faster delivery of new features and updates.

3.3.5 *Product Stack Conclusion*

A **Product Stack** is a vital component in developing digital products, ensuring that the right tools, languages, and frameworks are in place for building, deploying, and scaling applications. By selecting the right Tech Stack, organizations can optimize the performance, scalability, and maintainability of their products while keeping up with evolving user needs. Whether for a startup, an e-commerce website, or a SaaS company, the right Tech Stack can make all the difference in delivering value efficiently and securely.

3.4 Conclusion

Continuous Delivery and the **Product Stack** are vital components of successful digital product development. By automating the release process, **Continuous Delivery** allows teams to deploy new features and improvements rapidly, maintaining a competitive edge. Meanwhile, a well-structured **Product Stack** ensures that teams have the tools they need to collaborate efficiently and scale their products as needed. Together, these approaches provide the foundation for delivering high-quality, user-centred products in today's fast-paced digital landscape.

4

CRAFTING THE MARKETING STRATEGY AND CAMPAIGN

4.1 Introduction

In today's digital landscape, crafting a comprehensive marketing strategy is essential for successfully launching and growing a product. This chapter explores how product managers can develop effective Go-to-Market (**GTM**) plans that align with the product's unique value proposition and business objectives. It begins with defining clear marketing goals, whether it's expanding into new markets, driving revenue growth, or increasing product adoption.

Next, we delve into the marketing mix – the 7 P's (product, price, place, promotion, people, process, and physical evidence) – which helps ensure that every aspect of the product's market entry is thoughtfully planned. We'll also explore the **PESO** model (PESO media) to effectively allocate marketing resources and leverage different media channels to engage customers.

Omnichannel strategies are critical in today's customer-centric world, and this chapter highlights how to create seamless experiences across multiple touchpoints, ensuring that your message is consistent and engaging. Additionally, we will discuss the importance of collaborating with key stakeholders, such as **Sales**, **Marketing Communications** (**MarCom**), and **Support** teams, to drive unified marketing efforts that ultimately deliver customer satisfaction.

4.2 Marketing Strategy

A **GTM strategy** is a comprehensive action plan that outlines how a company will launch, market, and sell a product to reach customers and achieve

DOI: 10.1201/9781003614180-4

competitive advantage. It covers everything from identifying target customers and positioning the product to developing distribution channels and creating a marketing campaign. For a **product manager**, the **GTM** strategy serves as a roadmap that ensures the product is well-positioned to capture the target audience's attention and meet market needs.

The purpose of a **GTM** strategy is to ensure that the product resonates with the intended audience and achieves the business objectives. A well-designed **GTM** strategy aligns all the stakeholders, from marketing and sales to customer support, enabling the product manager to introduce the product effectively, acquire customers, and create a positive market impact. This orchestration is crucial, as it allows a seamless transition from product development to product launch, ensuring customers have a clear understanding of the value the product offers.

4.2.1 Go-to-Market Strategy Plan

The **GTM Plan** is a critical roadmap for successfully launching a product into the market, and it consists of **seven key steps**. These steps provide a comprehensive framework for product managers to navigate the entire launch process, from identifying the market to introducing the product, as shown in Figure 4.1.

1 **Identify Target Market:**

- This step defines the specific segment of customers for whom the product is designed. Understanding their needs, behaviours, and preferences helps to tailor the product and messaging to attract the right audience.
- The intent of this step is to determine the specific customer segments that will benefit most from the product. By clearly defining the target market, the product manager can align product features, messaging, and distribution efforts with the needs and preferences of that audience.
- A Product Manager needs to understand how to conduct market research to identify and analyse market segments, assess market opportunities, and determine the right audience for the product.

2 **Set Objectives and Goals:**

- This step establishes clear objectives using **OKRs** (Objectives and Key Results) and setting **SMART** Goals (Specific, Measurable, Achievable, Relevant, Time-Bound) to guide the launch strategy.
- This step involves establishing measurable goals for the product launch, such as revenue targets, customer acquisition, or market share growth. Setting clear **OKRs** helps keep the entire team focused and aligned.

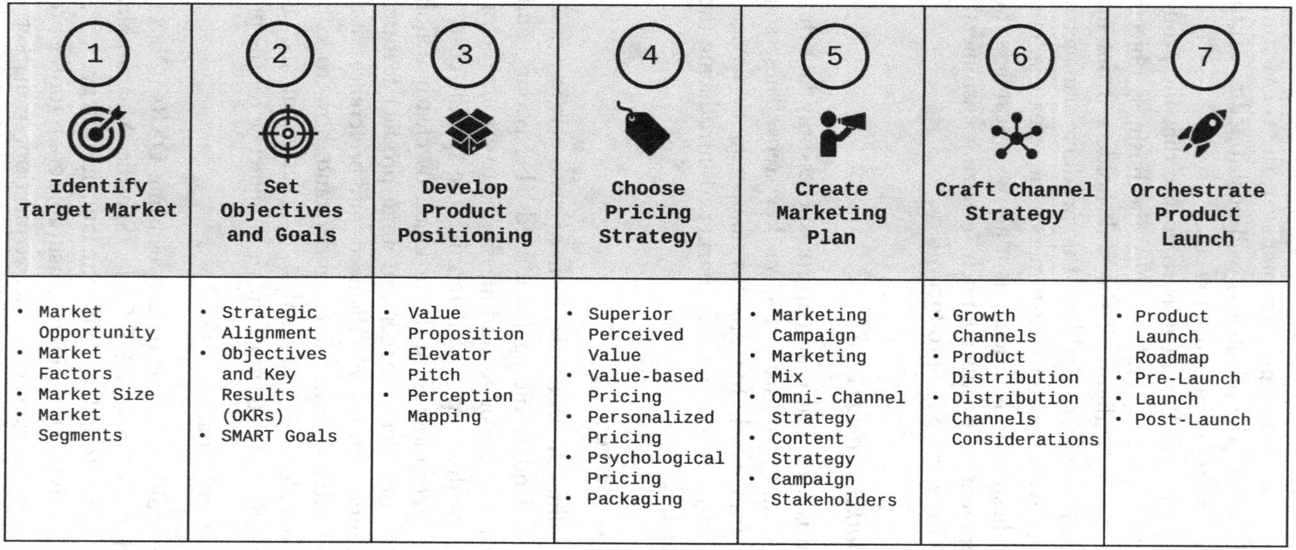

1 Identify Target Market	2 Set Objectives and Goals	3 Develop Product Positioning	4 Choose Pricing Strategy	5 Create Marketing Plan	6 Craft Channel Strategy	7 Orchestrate Product Launch
• Market Opportunity • Market Factors • Market Size • Market Segments	• Strategic Alignment • Objectives and Key Results (OKRs) • SMART Goals	• Value Proposition • Elevator Pitch • Perception Mapping	• Superior Perceived Value • Value-based Pricing • Personalized Pricing • Psychological Pricing • Packaging	• Marketing Campaign • Marketing Mix • Omni-Channel Strategy • Content Strategy • Campaign Stakeholders	• Growth Channels • Product Distribution Channels • Distribution Considerations	• Product Launch Roadmap • Pre-Launch • Launch • Post-Launch

FIGURE 4.1 Go-to-Market Strategy Plan.

- A Product Manager must be able to define **SMART** Goals and use OKRs to ensure that the launch is strategic and outcome-driven, ultimately tying back to the overall business objectives.

3 **Develop Product Positioning**:
- This step crafts a positioning strategy that highlights the unique value of the product to differentiate it from competitors, using tools like the **Value Proposition Canvas** and **Customer Perception Mapping**.
- This step focuses on crafting the product positioning to communicate how the product meets customer needs better than competitors. It involves defining the product's value proposition, brand messaging, and differentiation strategies.
- A Product Manager needs to utilize tools like the **Value Proposition Canvas** and **Customer Perception Mapping** to clearly articulate the unique selling points of the product and ensure consistent messaging across all channels.

4 **Choose Pricing Strategy**:
- This step selects an appropriate pricing model, which may include value-based, personalized, or psychological pricing, to align with customer expectations and maximize market adoption.
- Selecting the right pricing strategy is essential for positioning the product in the market. This step involves evaluating pricing models, such as value-based pricing, personalized pricing, or psychological pricing, to maximize the product's perceived value.

5 **Create Marketing Plan**:
- This step drives a specific goal through various channels and touchpoints using marketing campaigns.
- This step involves developing a comprehensive marketing plan that outlines the tactics and campaigns to drive product awareness and engagement. It details how the product will be promoted through various marketing channels, including online and offline campaigns.
- A Product Manager must work with the MarCom team to develop a targeted marketing plan that aligns with the product's positioning, drives engagement, and generates demand.

6 **Craft Channel Strategy**:
- This step develops the right level of distribution, support, and control to ensure that the product reaches customers efficiently.
- Developing a channel strategy determines how the product will be distributed to customers. This step involves deciding whether to use direct, indirect, or hybrid channels, and managing the relationships with channel partners to ensure a seamless distribution process.
- A Product Manager must collaborate with Sales and Distribution teams to identify the most effective sales channels, negotiate partnerships, and ensure that customers have easy access to the product.

7 **Orchestrate Product Launch:**
- This step create a comprehensive launch plan that introduces the product to the market with impact.
- This final step involves executing a well-planned product launch, which includes pre-launch preparations, launch activities, and post-launch follow-up. It is about introducing the product to the market, building excitement, and ensuring the product's availability.
- A Product Manager needs to coordinate the entire launch process, manage timelines, align stakeholders, and track performance metrics to ensure that the product launch is successful and meets the established objectives.

4.2.2 A Strong Marketing Strategy

Marketing Strategy is about creating a strong **GTM** plan for defining the approach and methods that will be used to attract customers and create a strong market presence for the product. It requires a clear understanding of customer needs, competitive positioning, and value messaging to formulate a strategy that resonates with the target audience.

Apple is well known for its meticulous marketing strategies when launching new products, especially the **iPhone**. The marketing strategy focuses on creating a sense of exclusivity and excitement around new features and technological advancements. **Apple** doesn't just sell the **iPhone** as a device; they sell it as an experience and a lifestyle choice, emphasizing sleek design, high performance, and innovative features. This approach is part of **Apple's GTM** strategy, where the value messaging – focused on innovation and quality – appeals directly to their target customers, creating strong demand even before the product is launched.

4.2.2.1 Key Aspects of a Strong Marketing Strategy

1 **Value Messaging:** The first step in a marketing strategy is to define how the product delivers value to the customer. Value messaging is the articulation of what sets the product apart and why customers should choose it over competitors.

Example: Spotify positions itself as a music streaming service that gives users access to millions of songs anytime, anywhere. Its value messaging focuses on providing personalized music recommendations, offline access, and a vast music library, which attracts users seeking convenience and customization in music streaming.

Example: Netflix emphasizes its original content, vast selection of movies and shows, and convenience as a streaming service without advertisements. The value messaging is focused on personalized entertainment, content diversity, and uninterrupted viewing, which appeals to customers seeking a flexible, on-demand viewing experience.

2 **Understanding Customer Needs**: A marketing strategy should always be customer-centric. Product managers must leverage user personas and insights gathered during market research to define the key benefits that the product offers to its customers.

Example: YouTrip, a Singapore-based multi-currency wallet, uses a marketing strategy focused on the needs of travellers looking for a hassle-free and cost-effective way to manage different currencies. By eliminating foreign exchange fees, YouTrip addresses a key pain point for travellers, effectively targeting this audience segment.

Example: Netflix understands that customers want convenience, choice, and personalized content. By using algorithms to recommend content based on viewing history and preferences, Netflix caters directly to the unique tastes of each customer, creating a highly personalized viewing experience that encourages retention.

3 **Customer Acquisition Tactics**: Defining tactics to acquire customers is critical. Tactics can include content marketing, social media, paid advertisements, influencer campaigns, and email marketing. The choice of tactic depends on the target audience and the best way to reach them.

Example: Grab, Southeast Asia's leading ride-hailing platform, utilized a mix of social media campaigns, promotional codes, and partnerships with local merchants to acquire users and rapidly expand its market share in the region. By focusing on localized value propositions like cashless payments and ride rewards, **Grab** effectively attracted a large user base.

Example: Netflix employs a mix of content marketing, social media campaigns, and influencer collaborations to acquire new customers. It uses high-quality trailers, teasers, and interactive content on platforms like **YouTube**, **Instagram**, and **Twitter** to attract viewers. The company also leverages word-of-mouth marketing by encouraging users to share their favourite shows and movies, making use of social proof to bring in new subscribers.

4 **Competitive Positioning**: Understanding the competitive landscape and positioning the product against competitors is vital for the marketing strategy. It is crucial to communicate what makes the product different and why it is a better choice.

Example: When **Netflix** launched in new markets, it positioned itself against traditional cable TV services by emphasizing flexibility and a vast content library that could be accessed at any time, without advertisements. This differentiation helped **Netflix** acquire customers looking for a better, more personalized entertainment experience. **Netflix** positions itself not just against traditional cable services, but also against emerging streaming competitors like **Disney+, Hulu,** and **Amazon Prime Video.** By focusing on a mix of high-quality licenced content, a large library of original series and films, and exclusive deals, **Netflix** consistently reinforces its position as a leader in the streaming industry, offering unparalleled choice and convenience.

4.2.3 Summary of Marketing Strategy

In this section, we explored the essential components of developing a successful marketing strategy and executing effective marketing campaigns. Crafting a marketing strategy starts with understanding the market landscape, setting clear marketing goals, and defining the target audience. We discussed the importance of formulating a GTM plan, which includes identifying the target market, setting objectives, positioning the product, and selecting an appropriate pricing strategy.

In the upcoming sections, we will further detail how these strategies translate into actionable campaigns, effective distribution channels, and impactful product launches, ensuring that the product reaches its audience with the right message, at the right time, and through the right channels.

4.3 Marketing Campaign

Marketing Campaign focuses on driving a specific goal through various channels and touchpoints using well-designed marketing campaigns. A **Marketing Campaign** is a strategic and organized effort to:

1 **Raise Awareness**: Ensure that potential customers know about the product, its features, and its value.
2 **Generate Demand**: Encourage customers to consider and ultimately purchase the product.
3 **Create Differentiation**: Set the product apart from competitors by highlighting its unique selling points.

To achieve these objectives, marketing campaigns use a combination of strategies and channels, depending on the target audience and overall marketing goals.

4.3.1 The Marketing Mix Framework

To design and implement an effective marketing campaign, businesses often use the **Marketing Mix** framework, which consists of various elements to shape their approach to market their products or services.

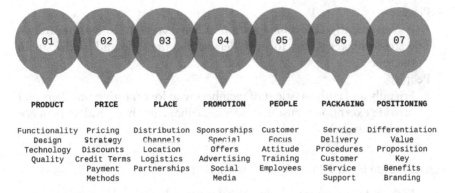

PRODUCT	PRICE	PLACE	PROMOTION	PEOPLE	PACKAGING	POSITIONING
Functionality	Pricing	Distribution	Sponsorships	Customer	Service	Differentiation
Design	Strategy	Channels	Special	Focus	Delivery	Value
Technology	Discounts	Location	Offers	Attitude	Procedures	Proposition
Quality	Credit Terms	Logistics	Advertising	Training	Customer	Key
	Payment	Partnerships	Social	Employees	Service	Benefits
	Methods		Media		Support	Branding

FIGURE 4.2   Seven P's of Marketing Mix.

Originally, the marketing mix was defined as the 4 Ps: Product, Price, Promotion, and Place. For service businesses, People was included as a fifth P. Then later on, two additional categories, Packaging and Positioning, were added. The **Marketing Mix** can take different forms, including the **5 Ps** (Product, Price, Place, Promotion, People) or the **9 Ps** (adding Packaging, Positioning, Process, and Physical Evidence) of marketing. Each "P" plays a crucial role in ensuring that the campaign reaches and engages its target audience effectively. An example of a marketing mix is shown in Figure 4.2 which contains the 7 P's.

Examples of the Marketing Mix in Action:

4.3.1.1   5 Ps – Segway Tour Shop

Steve is considering starting a mini Segway tour shop catering to travellers and tourists in **Sentosa**. To position his business effectively, Steve can consult the **5 Ps** of marketing in the following manner:

1 **Product:**
   • By-the-hour Segway rentals designed for people visiting Sentosa for a short duration. The product includes a limited liability form to be signed by participants and a monetary deposit to cover potential damages.
2 **Price:**
   • Affordable mini Segway tour packages tailored to meet the budget constraints of travellers and tourists. Additionally, a 10% discount is provided on packages for customers referred by a travel agency.
3 **Promotion:**
   • A **Facebook** page, **Instagram** page, and **Twitter** handle are used to promote the business, along with paid promotions on travel agency websites to reach potential customers.

4 **Place:**
  - A conveniently accessible location in Sentosa, close to existing transit systems, makes it easy for travellers to find the shop and participate in the tours.

5 **People:**
  - Friendly and enthusiastic staff members who love meeting travellers and provide exceptional customer service, enhancing the overall experience for customers.

4.3.1.2 Example 2: 7 Ps – High-End Restaurant

For a **high-end restaurant** that aims to offer an exclusive and luxurious dining experience, the **7 Ps** of marketing can be considered as follows:

1 **Product:**
  - Gourmet cuisine with a focus on locally sourced ingredients, ensuring that customers enjoy fresh, high-quality dishes.

2 **Price:**
  - Premium pricing is used to reflect the quality and exclusivity of the dining experience, aligning with the expectations of customers seeking luxury.

3 **Place:**
  - The restaurant is located in a fashionable district, featuring an elegant interior design that provides a sophisticated ambiance.

4 **Promotion:**
  - Marketing efforts include collaborations with food bloggers, social media campaigns, and loyalty programmes that reward repeat customers.

5 **People:**
  - Highly trained chefs and courteous, professional waitstaff provide an exceptional level of service that ensures a memorable dining experience.

6 **Process:**
  - The restaurant provides a seamless reservation and dining experience – from booking a table to receiving impeccable food service – enhancing customer satisfaction.

7 **Physical Evidence:**
  - The luxurious ambiance, well-designed menus, and positive online reviews all serve as physical evidence of the restaurant's quality, reinforcing the brand's value.

4.3.2 Marketing Mix in Car-Sharing Platform Case Scenario

Let's use the **QuikDrive** Car-Sharing Platform to see how it creates a marketing mix to find the right blend of Product, Price, Place, Promotion,

People, Packaging, and Positioning to gain and maintain an advantage over their competitors.

Let's examine these **7 P's** in more detail. First, we'll look at steering questions for each of the **7 P's**. Then, we'll look at how **QuikDrive's** product marketing is shaped as a result. Figure 4.3 shows the detailed breakdown of **QuikDrive's** Marketing Mix.

1 When considering the first P, *Product*, ask: How can your product meet your customer's needs? And, is your product right for the customer?

    QuikDrive provides a platform in the form of a website and mobile app, that brings car owners and renters together, manages rental bookings, and collects payment. It takes between 30% of the total income, which covers car insurance and operating expenses. In return, it provides roadside assistance, customer service, and vehicle inspection tests.

2 When it comes to *Price*, reflect on: What is the value of your product? What is your pricing strategy?

    QuikDrive aims to provide an attractive option for car owners and renters by excluding a membership subscription fee. They will also automate sign-ups of new members, including driver licence and credit card verification.

3 When considering the *Place*, ask: How will the products reach those customers? What are the delivery channels?

    QuikDrive is offering a pay-per-use service to renters which operates in shopping malls, residential estates, office buildings, hotels, airports, in addition to bus and rail stations in Singapore. It uses the one-way car-sharing model, which enables renters to begin and end their trip at different locations through free-floating zones, or station-based models with designated parking locations.

    QuikDrive also has a close partnership with a leading bus and rail operator in Singapore, to complement Singapore's public transportation. Furthermore, **QuikDrive** partners with well-known hotels and airlines to offer rental packages for travellers visiting Singapore.

4 When it comes to *Promotion*, decide: Does your product come with special offers and special promotions? Does it come with free additional services?

    QuikDrive leverages online and mobile advertising to increase awareness of their services. They also sponsor special events such as the Singapore Formula 1 Race to promote their services and spread brand awareness.

5 When considering *People*, determine: Do you have the right people responsible for the success of your product, from development, marketing, sales, and support?

    QuikDrive hopes to create a seamless and delightful experience for every customer, be it the car owner or renter using the platform. Their goal is to improve the car-sharing experience of customers by employing both

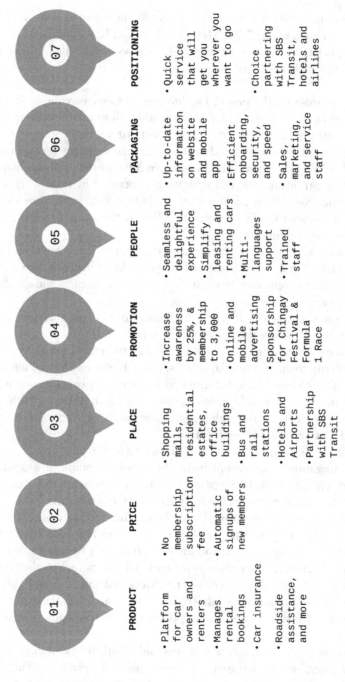

PRODUCT	PRICE	PLACE	PROMOTION	PEOPLE	PACKAGING	POSITIONING
• Platform for car owners and renters • Manages rental bookings • Car insurance • Roadside assistance, and more	• No membership subscription fee • Automatic signups of new members	• Shopping malls, residential estates, office buildings • Bus and rail stations • Hotels and Airports • Partnership with SBS Transit	• Increase awareness by 25%, & membership to 3,000 • Online and mobile advertising • Sponsorship for Chingay Festival & Formula 1 Race	• Seamless and delightful experience • Simplify leasing and renting cars • Multi-languages support • Trained staff	• Up-to-date information on website and mobile app • Efficient onboarding, security, and speed • Sales, marketing, and service staff	• Quick service that will get you wherever you want to go • Choice partnering with SBS Transit, hotels and airlines

FIGURE 4.3 QuikDrive's Marketing Mix.

web and mobile technology to simplify the process, and improve the experience of leasing and renting cars.

This cannot be accomplished without the right people across departments. For example, **QuikDrive's** Support Centre agents speak the four main languages in Singapore: English, Mandarin, Malay, and Tamil. These agents are trained to be courteous, friendly, and respectful and are able to communicate effectively with customers and give recommendations that will suit their needs.

6 When it comes to *Packaging*: Does your product appeal to your customers from initial contact to purchase, from installation to usage, service and support?

QuikDrive's car-share platform, available via website and mobile app, will provide up-to-date information on rates, promotions, user guides, and vehicle locations. Registration on the platform is designed for efficient onboarding, security, and speed.

For maximum ease of use, the **QuikDrive** sales, marketing, and service staff are equipped with the knowledge and skills to provide delightful end-to-end experiences for the customer.

7 And finally, when considering the *Positioning*, ask: How can you differentiate your product from competitors? How do you position your product in the minds and hearts of your customer?

QuikDrive provides a quick, convenient service that will get you wherever you want to go, aligning to the target market's need for fast convenience. QuikDrive's positioning strategy will be to differentiate itself from competitors by its unique value proposition of choice partnering with local transit, hotels, and airlines.

You've seen how the 7 P's provide you with steering questions to answer about your product, resulting in a marketing mix with which to bring a product to market. These questions include the following:

1 **Product**: How can your product meet your customer's needs?
2 **Price**: What is the value of your product?
3 **Place**: How will the products reach those customers?
4 **Promotion**: Does your product come with special offers and special promotions?
5 **People**: Do you have the right people responsible for the success of your product, considering individuals in development, marketing, sales, and support?
6 **Packaging**: Does your product appeal to your customers from initial contact to purchase, from installation to usage, and from service to support?
7 **Positioning**: How can you differentiate your product from competitors?

With these marketing mix questions in mind, think about how you can apply them to create your own marketing mix for your new product.

4.3.3 *Defining Marketing Goals*

Setting clear and actionable marketing goals is fundamental to a successful product launch. Marketing goals should be well-defined to guide the team and stakeholders towards a unified objective and measure the success of marketing initiatives. Below are examples of common marketing goals:

1 **Market Expansion:** This goal focuses on growing the product's market presence.
   - **Example:** Increase market share by launching products or services in two new geographic regions within the next year. A product manager will need to identify the right regions, research local customer needs, and plan entry strategies that resonate with those audiences.
2 **Revenue Growth:** This goal focuses on driving financial outcomes by acquiring more customers or increasing spend from existing customers.
   - **Example:** Achieve a 15% increase in annual revenue by acquiring and retaining high-value enterprise-level customers. This goal would require targeted campaigns, personalized outreach, and a focus on building relationships that encourage loyalty and upselling.
3 **Lead Generation:** Lead generation aims to attract potential customers who are interested in the product or service.
   - **Example:** Generate 1,000 high-quality leads per quarter to support the sales team's efforts and fuel the sales pipeline. This can be done through a mix of inbound content marketing, targeted advertising, and webinars.
4 **Product Adoption:** This goal is aimed at getting more users to start using a recently launched product or feature.
   - **Example:** Increase the adoption rate of a recently launched software product by 25% among existing customers within six months. This could be achieved through in-app notifications, onboarding support, tutorials, and webinars.
5 **Brand Awareness:** Improving brand visibility is crucial for long-term growth.
   - **Example:** Improve brand visibility and recognition by increasing website traffic by 30% and social media engagement by 20% over the next year. This can be driven by **SEO** optimization, influencer partnerships, and engaging content that sparks social sharing.

4.3.4 *Omnichannel Strategy for Engaging Customers*

An **omnichannel strategy** is essential for creating a seamless and integrated experience across all customer touchpoints, ensuring that customers receive consistent messaging and services as they engage with a brand across different channels – whether online or offline. The idea is to create an interconnected experience, where a customer can start their journey on one channel (such as a website) and continue on another (such as a physical store) without disruption.

Example of Leveraging an Omnichannel Strategy:

1 Sephora:
   - **Rich In-App Messaging**: The **Sephora** app uses in-app messages to keep users informed about upcoming promotions, exclusive products, and events.
   - **Personalized Push Notifications**: The app sends personalized push notifications based on user preferences and past purchases, encouraging them to engage further.
   - **In-Store Experience**: In-store technology allows **Sephora** employees to access customer profiles, including their preferences and favourite products, enabling personalized recommendations and a cohesive shopping experience.
   - **Integrated Approach**: Whether browsing online, booking an in-person consultation, or making in-store purchases, **Sephora** uses an omnichannel approach to ensure customers have a unified and enjoyable experience.
2 Nike:
   - **Nike App and Store Integration**: **Nike's** omnichannel strategy includes seamless integration between its app, website, and physical stores. Customers can use the **Nike App** to locate nearby stores, check inventory, and even reserve items to try on in-store.
   - **Personalized Content**: The app also offers personalized training programmes, exclusive content, and product recommendations, which keeps customers engaged both online and in-store.
   - **Loyalty Programme**: The **NikePlus** loyalty programme spans online and offline, allowing customers to earn rewards regardless of how they shop, creating a more integrated customer experience.

4.3.5 Marketing Campaign Stakeholders

A successful marketing campaign is a collaborative effort that requires the involvement of multiple stakeholders who contribute different expertise to achieve the campaign's goals:

1 MarCom:
   - Responsible for crafting the messaging, visuals, and content for the campaign.
   - Ensures all campaign materials align with the brand's value proposition and are consistent across all channels.
2 Sales:
   - Uses the campaign to close deals and convert leads into customers.

- The sales team needs a deep understanding of the campaign's messaging and goals to effectively engage with prospects.
3 **Support:**
  - Provides post-purchase assistance to customers and addresses any questions or concerns related to the campaign.
  - Ensures customers receive a positive experience, even after the initial transaction.

The **product manager** acts as the glue that brings these stakeholders together, ensuring that all teams are aligned with the marketing campaign's objectives and that collaboration is efficient. The product manager:

- Works with **MarCom** to develop messaging that reflects the product's value proposition and is consistent with the overall marketing strategy.
- Engages with the **Sales** team to ensure they are well-equipped with the right materials and information to convert leads into customers.
- Collaborates with **Support** to prepare them to handle customer inquiries and provide a seamless experience during and after the campaign.

4.3.6   Content Marketing Campaign

A **content marketing campaign** is a strategic initiative that focuses on creating, distributing, and promoting valuable content to attract, engage, and retain a target audience. The main purpose of a content marketing campaign is to establish authority in the industry, build trust with potential customers, and generate leads that can be nurtured into sales.

4.3.6.1   PESO Model for Content Marketing Campaigns

The **PESO model** – **PESO** media – is an effective framework for maximizing content reach and ensuring a comprehensive content marketing strategy. Figure 4.4 shows the diagram depicting the **PESO** model.

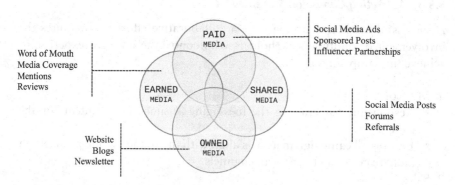

FIGURE 4.4   PESO Model.

1 **Paid Media:**
   - Paid media involves paying to promote content, such as through social media ads, sponsored posts, or influencer partnerships.
   - **Example: LinkedIn Ads** are often used to promote B2B content, like whitepapers or webinars, to target a specific professional audience.
2 **Earned Media:**
   - Earned media includes any free publicity gained from word-of-mouth, media coverage, mentions, or reviews.
   - **Example: Apple** frequently receives earned media coverage whenever it launches a new product, as tech blogs and mainstream media write about it without the company having to pay for the exposure.
3 **Shared Media:**
   - Shared media refers to content distributed through social media, such as posts that followers like, share, or comment on, as well as forums and referrals.
   - **Example: Starbucks** encourages its customers to share their coffee experiences on social media with branded hashtags, creating a ripple effect that amplifies the brand's reach.
4 **Owned Media:**
   - Owned media includes the channels that a brand fully controls, such as its website, blog, or newsletter.
   - **Example: HubSpot** uses its blog to share insights about digital marketing, positioning itself as a thought leader and attracting potential customers interested in learning more about inbound marketing.

By strategically combining **PESO** media, the **PESO** model helps brands build a balanced content marketing campaign that reaches the right audience, generates engagement, and ultimately drives conversions.

4.3.7 *Marketing Campaign in Car-Sharing Platform Case Scenario*

Let's walk through a Marketing Campaign based on the **QuikDrive** Car-Sharing Platform case scenario to have a look at the role of the product manager in developing a marketing campaign by preparing the MarCom, sales, and product support teams.

1 **Clean Drive Time! Campaign**
   QuikDrive plans to launch their "**It's Clean Drive Time!**" campaign – the company's first integrated marketing campaign in Singapore. To own a car in Singapore, people must register their vehicles and purchase a Certificate of Entitlement, or COE. COE prices have been escalating, and at the same time the work-from-home trend means that car owners aren't using their cars as much.

QuikDrive has recognized an opportunity to leverage those underused cars, and at the same time: effectively help car owners cover their COE costs. This presents an opportune moment for QuikDrive to entrench their eco-friendly car-sharing service in the minds of both car renters, and owners, with the launch of a new platform.

With QuikDrive, as is often the case, the product manager's key role during the marketing campaign is to prepare the various teams and to ensure alignment across product stakeholders such as Marketing, Sales, and Support. We'll use QuikDrive's new marketing campaign to illustrate what the product manager needs to do to prepare the different stakeholders for a marketing campaign and ensure a cohesive marketing campaign.

2 Business Objectives of Marketing Campaign

QuikDrive plans to achieve the following three target objectives with its new campaign:

 A. Increase brand awareness and promote its image of sustainability.
 B. Increase profits by 25% within the next year.
 C. Increase its user base by 3,000.

3 MarCom's Team

To address the first objective of increasing brand awareness and promoting its image of sustainability, QuikDrive's product manager works with the company's MarCom team on the company's new marketing campaign: "It's Clean Drive Time!"

To help develop the campaign, the MarCom's team is driven by the following key questions:

 A. How do we create brand and market awareness for the product?
 B. How can we leverage promotional events planning and execution?
 C. How do we manage the demand funnel for sales to follow up on?

Let's explore how these questions drive the team to develop the campaign. QuikDrive's "It's Clean Drive Time!" campaign will be co-developed with Singapore-based creative agency, Tree Canvas – also known for its sustainability advocacy. The main theme of the campaign is that QuikDrive helps car renters during "Clean Drive Time!" by providing the best available eco-friendly cars for weekend shopping sprees, date nights, or day trips to drive up to the coastal beaches. The campaign is designed to show how the platform offers the "quickest way to get the best eco-friendly car for whatever you want or need to do" – a tagline created by QuikDrive's product manager for QuikDrive's press release.

The campaign effort will also include audience-targeted television, radio, social, and digital advertising, as well as a partnership with a Singaporean actress, known for her strong support of environmental protection.

QuikDrive also hopes to reignite its **"Enterprise Car-Share Programme"** through this new campaign. This programme targets corporate accounts who want to demonstrate their corporate sustainability. This programme helps companies reduce the cost of owning their own fleet of cars and offers employees access to cars when they need to get things done.

Another way in which **QuikDrive's** product manager can help the **MarCom's** team is by providing product data sheets, pricing and proposal templates, and answers to frequently asked questions, which also helps the sales team.

4 Sales Team

To address **QuikDrive's** second objective for the marketing campaign: "to increase profits by 25 percent within the next year," **QuikDrive's** product manager works with the sales team. To this end, the sales team starts by asking these three questions. These questions help drive the campaign for the sales team. They are as follows:

A. How will the product help the customer and their clients?
B. What sales tools can be created to make the product easier to sell?
C. What special offers and promotions can we use to increase sales?

Let's explore how these questions drive the second objective of the campaign. The product manager will need to invest in sales to provide a payback for having a motivated and supportive sales team driving the product's success. The following are some key activities that can do just that.

A. First, they can help create a profitable business for **QuikDrive** by helping sales in managing the financials and leveraging financial assessment metrics, such as **NPV, ROI,** and break-even analysis.
B. Second, by enhancing marketing campaign effectiveness through customer qualification. For instance, by defining the value proposition, identifying the car renters, as well as identifying an appropriate celebrity influencer to support the campaign.
C. Third, by assisting sales in building corporate accounts for car-fleet rental. They can do this by creating value messages, as well as tactics and strategies for the sales and programme onboarding process.
D. Fourth, set up the sales support as well as any tools required. Tools such as a product data sheet, a competitive comparison table, and additional incentives for the sales team.

E And fifth, they can leverage channel programmes if the revenue model supports channel partnerships.

5. Product Support

Product Support is the third key element that supports the marketing campaign, as it ensures that customers obtain the most value from use of the product after the sale. To address the third objective of the marketing campaign and increase its user base of 3,000, the **QuikDrive** product manager needs to work closely with the product support team.

To drive this part of the process, the support team asks the following questions:

A. What training and resources are needed to assist customers and resolve issues via the company's social media account?
B. How can we help create content for the marketing campaign using customer support knowledge about customers' problems, needs, and pain points in the customer journey?
C. Which promotions will be deployed, and when, so that product support is well-equipped to answer any customer queries?

Let's dive into the answers.

With the launch of the new campaign, **QuikDrive** can expect a heightened customer awareness as well as higher expectations about support levels. In addition, it can expect a reduced ability to perceive product differentiation through superior technology. As such, the campaign needs to be backed by extensive service staff to deal with customer queries about promotions, pricing, insurance coverage, the onboarding process, invoicing needs, and the emergency help required for vehicle breakdowns.

The product support team can also help the sales team to follow up on sales leads from the new campaign. For example, corporate sign-ups or business queries for the **Enterprise Car-Share Programme**. Typically, these types of queries and leads are likely to come through the Support Line – a function of the product support team.

4.3.7.1 Summary: QuikDrive's Campaign

You've seen how product managers play a key role in ensuring alignment across teams, such as MarCom, sales, and support by providing the common thread needed for a cohesive marketing campaign.

The role involves leveraging the campaign to help the marketing team drive up both brand and product awareness. It involves helping the sales team craft the right pitch and increase sales. And it involves helping the support team create a delightful customer service and support experience.

Now that you've seen how **QuikDrive** can launch its new marketing campaign with the support from the three key stakeholders – marketing, sales and support – you can do the same for a product of your choice. What key objectives would you set such, knowing how they can be well-supported by these three teams?

4.3.8   Summary: Marketing Campaign

The marketing mix, particularly the 7 **P's**, was introduced as a framework for designing a comprehensive marketing strategy. Additionally, we examined how marketing campaigns drive specific business goals through targeted channels and touchpoints. The **PESO** model (PESO media) was highlighted as an effective way to structure campaigns across various media channels.

We also explored omnichannel strategies to ensure seamless engagement with customers, creating a cohesive experience across multiple platforms. The role of key stakeholders such as Sales, MarCom, and Support in executing marketing campaigns was emphasized, showcasing how product managers can orchestrate efforts for maximum impact.

4.4   Conclusion

This chapter underscores the pivotal role that a well-structured marketing strategy and campaign play in driving the success of a product. It highlights how product managers can create value through a deep understanding of their target market, clear marketing goals, and effective product positioning. By applying the marketing mix of the 7 **P's**, product managers can develop comprehensive strategies that address all aspects of customer engagement, from pricing to promotions.

The chapter also emphasizes the importance of leveraging a **GTM** strategy and an omnichannel approach to reach customers across multiple touchpoints seamlessly. Engaging various stakeholders, such as Sales, MarCom, and Support, is essential to executing a cohesive marketing campaign that drives business growth and product adoption.

In conclusion, a successful marketing strategy must be rooted in customer insights, clear goals, and the ability to adapt to changing market dynamics. By aligning all elements of a marketing campaign, product managers can ensure that their product not only reaches the right audience but also delivers sustained value, leading to long-term success in the market.

5
MANAGING SALES CHANNELS AND LAUNCHING PRODUCTS

5.1 Introduction

The success of any product in the marketplace relies not only on its design and functionality but also on how effectively it is distributed and made accessible to customers. Sales channels serve as the essential conduits between a product and its customers, and choosing the right channels can determine the trajectory of business growth. In this chapter, we explore the importance of crafting a robust channel strategy tailored to meet business objectives and market demands. We'll cover various types of sales channels, including direct and indirect approaches, and discuss how growth channels can accelerate product scaling efforts.

Product distribution is a critical factor in ensuring a product's availability to target audiences, and understanding the nuances of managing distribution channels is key to maintaining customer satisfaction and operational efficiency. Product managers must also consider several factors, such as channel reach, costs, and customer service, to optimize distribution. Finally, this chapter will guide you through the stages of a successful product launch, emphasizing the integration of channel strategies and distribution efforts to ensure a smooth and impactful introduction to the market.

5.2 Sales Channels Management

Sales Channels Management is an essential aspect of bringing a product to market, as it directly influences how the product reaches customers and generates revenue. The goal is to develop the right channel strategy to ensure that the product is available to the target market through the most efficient

DOI: 10.1201/9781003614180-5

and effective distribution methods. This section will cover key topics such as *Business Growth*, *Channel Strategy*, *Growth Channels*, *Scaling the Product*, *Product Distribution*, and *Distribution Channel Considerations*.

5.2.1 Business Growth

Effective sales channel management can significantly help a business grow by expanding its reach and optimizing distribution. Figure 5.1 shows three ways in which sales channels can contribute to business growth.

1 Reach Customers Who Don't Buy Directly from the Producer:
   Indirect sales channels allow businesses to reach customers who may not purchase products directly from the producer or manufacturer. By leveraging intermediaries such as distributors, wholesalers, or resellers, companies can tap into customer bases they may not have reached otherwise.
   Example: Apple reaches customers who may not purchase directly from **Apple** stores by partnering with large retailers like **Walmart, Target,** and **Best Buy.** These indirect channels give **Apple** access to customers who prefer to buy from familiar retail chains, thus boosting sales.

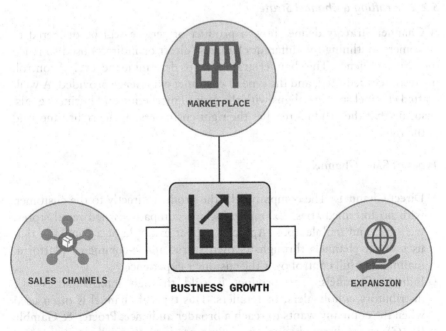

FIGURE 5.1 Ways to Grow Your Business.

2 Sell Your Product Through Marketplaces to Customers Looking for Choices and Deals:

Selling through *online marketplaces* like **Amazon, eBay,** or **Alibaba** allows businesses to reach a large pool of potential customers seeking convenience and competitive pricing. Marketplaces also attract customers looking to compare multiple options and find the best deals.

Example: Samsung lists its products on **Amazon,** allowing customers to easily browse, compare, and purchase **Samsung** products alongside other brands. This strategy not only increases product visibility but also allows **Samsung** to capture customers seeking a variety of choices and deals.

3 Expand in New Geographic Regions:
Leveraging *distribution partners, international retailers,* or *localized* e-commerce *platforms* can help businesses enter new geographic regions. Global expansion allows companies to grow their market share and increase revenue.

Example: **Nike** partnered with local retail stores in India to expand its presence in the market. By using a combination of direct online sales and local retail partnerships, **Nike** ensured its brand presence in multiple regions, catering to different customer preferences and increasing sales volume.

5.2.2 Crafting a Channel Strategy

A **Channel Strategy** defines how a product or service will be delivered to customers, outlining the different channels (direct or indirect) used to reach the target audience. The channel strategy helps determine the level of control, the resources required, and the type of customer experience provided. A well-crafted channel strategy aligns with the overall marketing and business goals, ensuring that the product reaches the right customers, at the right time, and in the right way.

Types of Sales Channel:

• **Direct Channels**: The company sells the product directly to the customer, with no intermediaries. Examples include company-owned retail stores, websites, and mobile apps. **Apple** is a great example of a company that uses direct channels through its own stores and e-commerce platform, maintaining full control over the customer experience.
• **Indirect Channels**: The product is sold through intermediaries like distributors, wholesalers, or retailers. This type of channel is often used when the company wants to reach a broader audience. **Procter & Gamble (P&G)** uses indirect channels by selling products through retail partners like supermarkets and pharmacies.

Hybrid Channels combine elements of both direct and indirect approaches, allowing the company to provide a multi-faceted experience for customers. For instance, **Nike** sells its products both through its website (direct) and through retailers like **Foot Locker** (indirect).

5.2.2.1 Example: Channel Strategy – Tesla

Tesla primarily uses a direct sales model, bypassing traditional dealerships and selling cars through company-owned showrooms and its website. By doing so, **Tesla** maintains complete control over the customer experience, from initial contact to after-sales support. This channel strategy allows **Tesla** to educate potential customers about electric vehicles, provide a personalized experience, and directly address customer concerns – all while maintaining brand consistency.

5.2.3 Growth Channels

Growth Channels are the platforms and mediums used to acquire new customers, engage existing customers, and drive sales. Identifying the right growth channels for a product is crucial for achieving scalability and market expansion. Growth channels can be either physical or digital, depending on the target audience and product type.

Types of Growth Channels:

- **Digital Channels:** Digital platforms such as e-commerce websites, online marketplaces, social media, search engines, and affiliate marketing are often used to reach a large audience quickly and cost-effectively. For example, **Amazon** and **Shopify** provide access to global markets through their digital channels, helping brands acquire new customers.
- **Physical Channels:** These include direct sales, retail stores, trade shows, and events. **IKEA** uses physical stores as a major growth channel, providing customers with an in-store experience where they can see, touch, and test products before purchasing.

5.2.3.1 Example: Growth Channel Strategy – Airbnb

Airbnb initially focused on **digital growth channels** to acquire users. Through content marketing, **SEO**, and word-of-mouth referrals, **Airbnb** attracted travellers seeking affordable and unique accommodations. Additionally, **Airbnb** used **growth hacking** techniques like engaging with communities on **Craigslist** to boost early user acquisition and scale rapidly.

5.2.3.2 Key Characteristics of a Growth Channel

To identify the most effective growth channels for your product, it's important to understand the characteristics of an ideal growth channel:

1 **Targeted Reach**:

- The ability of the channel to connect with a specific segment of the market is crucial for targeting the right audience effectively.
- **Example: LinkedIn Ads** allow **B2B** companies to target specific professionals based on industry, role, and location. This targeted reach ensures that the message is being delivered to the most relevant audience for a particular product or service.

2 **Scalability**:

- Growth channels should have the potential to grow and handle increasing volumes of customers, ensuring the product can reach a larger market without compromising quality.
- **Example: Meta (Facebook) Ads** are highly scalable, allowing businesses to start small with a limited budget and gradually increase ad spending as they see positive returns. This scalability is ideal for businesses looking to expand their reach over time.

3 **Measurability**:

- Growth channels must allow businesses to track and measure performance, making it easier to calculate **return on investment (ROI)** and optimize campaigns.
- **Example: Google Ads** provides detailed analytics on impressions, clicks, and conversions, enabling marketers to understand how well their ads are performing and make necessary adjustments.

4 **Cost-Effectiveness**:

- Channels should provide a high return on investment relative to costs. Businesses must consider both customer acquisition costs and the lifetime value of customers acquired through each channel.
- **Example: Email marketing** is often one of the most cost-effective growth channels. For many businesses, email provides a high return for relatively low costs, especially for retaining existing customers and driving repeat purchases.

5 **Engagement**:

- Growth channels should be capable of engaging customers and fostering ongoing relationships.

- **Example: Instagram** is an effective engagement channel for brands like **Coca-Cola**, which uses interactive content and branded hashtags to keep customers engaged and foster brand loyalty.

Factors to Consider When Growing the Product Business:

- **Channel Expansion:** Expanding the product to new channels, such as additional online marketplaces, international distributors, or retail partnerships.
- **Localization:** When scaling to new geographic regions, localization is critical to ensure that the product resonates with local audiences. This includes adapting product features, language, pricing, and marketing to suit local preferences.
- **Automation and Technology:** Leveraging automation tools like Customer Relationship Management (CRM) systems and sales automation software to improve channel management efficiency and support sales growth.

5.2.3.3   Example: Scaling Strategy – Spotify

Spotify scaled its music streaming service by partnering with mobile carriers and device manufacturers in different countries. This distribution strategy enabled **Spotify** to reach new markets by bundling its service with mobile plans or pre-installing the app on smartphones. Through these partnerships, **Spotify** was able to scale its product globally and expand its subscriber base.

5.2.4   Product Distribution

Product Distribution is the process of making the product available to customers through various sales channels. It involves managing inventory, logistics, and delivery methods to ensure that the product reaches customers in a timely and efficient manner. Product distribution plays a significant role in customer satisfaction, especially when customers expect fast and reliable delivery.

Distribution Models:

- **Direct Distribution:** The product is delivered directly from the manufacturer to the customer. For instance, **Dell** uses a direct distribution model, allowing customers to order customized laptops directly from their website, which are then manufactured and shipped directly to the buyer.
- **Indirect Distribution:** Involves intermediaries such as wholesalers, retailers, and distributors. **Unilever** uses indirect distribution to make its products available in supermarkets, convenience stores, and other retail outlets around the world.

- **Dropshipping**: A model where the retailer does not keep the product in stock but transfers customer orders to a third-party supplier who ships the product directly to the customer. **Shopify** store owners often use dropshipping as a cost-effective distribution strategy, especially for starting small e-commerce businesses.

5.2.4.1 Example: Product Distribution – Coca-Cola

Coca-Cola uses a multi-tiered indirect distribution model. The company sells its syrup concentrate to bottlers, who then produce the finished product, distribute it to retailers, and make it available to consumers. This approach allows **Coca-Cola** to benefit from the expertise of regional bottlers, reach a wide audience, and ensure that its products are available in markets around the globe.

An effective **Sales Channel Strategy and Plan** includes defining the channels that will be used, the resources required, the level of control desired, and the specific tactics for managing relationships with partners.

5.2.4.2 Example of Sales Channel Strategy – Microsoft

Microsoft uses a combination of direct and indirect sales channels to market its products:

- **Direct Sales**: Microsoft sells its software, such as **Microsoft 365**, directly through its website. This direct channel allows **Microsoft** to maintain customer relationships and maximize control over pricing and promotions.
- **Indirect Sales**: Microsoft also partners with value-added resellers (**VARs**), distributors, and retailers to reach a broader audience. For instance, the **Surface** line of laptops and tablets is sold through retail partners like **Best Buy** and **Amazon**, allowing **Microsoft** to extend its reach beyond its own stores.

5.2.4.3 Example of Sales Channel Plan – Shopify

Shopify employs a hybrid channel strategy that involves direct online sales and partnerships:

1 **Online Channels**: **Shopify** directly reaches its customers (entrepreneurs and business owners) through its website, providing detailed information on its platform and offering a free trial.
2 **Partnership Programmes**: **Shopify** has created a partner programme that involves web developers, designers, and agencies, which help promote the

Shopify platform to their clients. These partners earn commissions and bring new customers to Shopify, acting as an extended sales channel.

Channel Plan Components:

- **Channel Selection:** Choosing between direct, indirect, or hybrid channels based on customer preferences and company goals.
- **Channel Relationships:** Managing relationships with partners, including distributors, resellers, and retailers, to ensure alignment with sales goals and proper support.
- **Performance Metrics:** Setting up metrics to track channel performance, such as sales volume, customer acquisition rate, and partner satisfaction.

5.2.4.4 Distribution Channel Considerations

When developing a distribution strategy, it is essential to consider various factors that impact the efficiency and effectiveness of the product's journey to the customer. Figure 5.2 shows key considerations when selecting a distribution channel:

1 **Customer Service:**

- A strong distribution channel should provide excellent customer service, as this directly impacts the customer's experience.
- **Example: Zappos** is known for its outstanding customer service. The company's distribution channels include processes to ensure quick deliveries and easy returns, providing customers with a hassle-free experience.

2 **Technical Support:**

- For technology products, offering technical support through distribution channels can be a valuable differentiator.
- **Example: Microsoft** partners with authorized resellers who provide technical support for their products. This ensures that customers receive reliable assistance, building trust and confidence in the brand.

3 **Reach:**

- The reach of a distribution channel determines how widely a product is available to potential customers.
- **Example: Unilever** leverages an extensive network of wholesalers and retailers to ensure its products are available globally, even in remote locations, thereby maximizing market penetration.

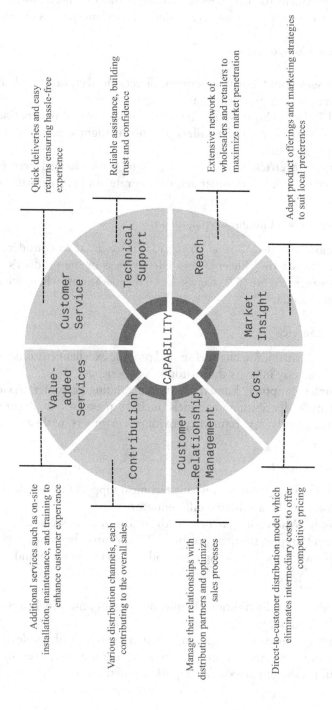

Quick deliveries and easy returns ensuring hassle-free experience

Reliable assistance, building trust and confidence

Extensive network of wholesalers and retailers to maximize market penetration

Adapt product offerings and marketing strategies to suit local preferences

Additional services such as on-site installation, maintenance, and training to enhance customer experience

Various distribution channels, each contributing to the overall sales

Manage their relationships with distribution partners and optimize sales processes

Direct-to-customer distribution model which eliminates intermediary costs to offer competitive pricing

Customer Service

Technical Support

Reach

Value-added Services

Market Insight

CAPABILITY

Contribution

Customer Relationship Management

Cost

FIGURE 5.2 Distribution Channel Considerations.

4 **Market Insight:**

- Distribution partners often have valuable insights into local market trends, customer preferences, and competitors.
- **Example:** Nestlé works with local distributors in different regions who provide market insights that help adapt product offerings and marketing strategies to suit local preferences.

5 **Cost:**

- The cost of using a distribution channel should be carefully evaluated to ensure it aligns with the desired profit margins.
- **Example:** Dell uses a direct-to-customer distribution model, which helps eliminate intermediary costs and allows the company to offer competitive pricing to customers.

6 **CRM (Customer Relationship Management):**

- Effective use of **CRM** tools helps businesses manage relationships with distribution partners, track sales performance, and ensure alignment with overall goals.
- **Example:** Salesforce is a widely used **CRM** tool that enables companies to manage their relationships with distribution partners and optimize sales processes.

7 **Contribution:**

- The contribution of each channel to overall sales should be assessed to determine its value and relevance.
- **Example:** Coca-Cola uses various distribution channels, including supermarkets, convenience stores, and vending machines. Each channel contributes to the overall sales, and the contribution is measured to optimize channel performance.

8 **Value-Added Services:**

- Offering value-added services through distribution channels can differentiate a product from competitors.
- **Example:** HP partners with resellers who provide additional services such as on-site installation, maintenance, and training. These value-added services enhance the customer experience and make HP's products more attractive compared to competitors.

5.2.5 Summary: Sales Channels Management

Sales Channels Management plays a vital role in ensuring that products reach the target audience effectively. By developing the right **Channel Strategy,**

leveraging **Growth Channels, Scaling the Product,** and creating an efficient **Product Distribution** network, product managers can maximize the market reach and impact of their product launches. Through real-world examples like **Tesla, Airbnb,** and **Coca-Cola,** we can see how effective sales channel management can be used to create a competitive advantage, improve customer experiences, and drive growth.

5.3 Market Launch

Market Launch is the final stage in the product journey where the product is introduced to the target market. This section will cover the **Market Launch Plan,** which is a systematic approach to launching a product that involves pre-launch preparation, launch activities, and post-launch follow-up. A product launch is the coordinated effort to bring a product to market, generate awareness, drive demand, and ensure a positive customer experience. It involves multiple teams working together to achieve a successful launch that aligns with business goals.

5.3.1 Product Brief

A **Product Brief** is a critical document in the pre-launch phase. It provides a high-level overview of the product, its value proposition, key features, and objectives for the launch. The product brief serves as a communication tool to align internal stakeholders – such as marketing, sales, and support teams – on the product's purpose and the strategy for launching it. The product brief typically includes the following:

- **Product Overview:** Description of the product, its features, and its value proposition.
- **Target Audience:** Details about the market segments being targeted.
- **Objectives:** Goals for the launch, such as revenue targets, customer acquisition, or market share.
- **Messaging:** Key messages and positioning statements to be used during the launch.
- **Launch Plan Overview:** Timeline and major activities for pre-launch, launch, and post-launch phases.

5.3.2 Types of Product Launches

Product launches can take different forms, depending on the objectives, target audience, and stage of the product lifecycle. Below are the main types of product launches:

1 **Soft Launch:**

- A **Soft Launch** is a limited release of a product to a smaller audience, often used to gather feedback, test features, and identify potential issues before a wider release. It allows companies to validate their assumptions and optimize the product.
- **Example:** Instagram was soft-launched to a small group of users to gather feedback before it was made available to the broader public. This helped refine the user experience before full-scale release.

2 **General Availability (GA) Launch:**

- A **GA Launch** is the official release of a product to the entire target market. It signifies that the product is now ready for public use and available to all intended customers.
- **Example:** Microsoft launched Windows 11 as a **GA** release, allowing all users to upgrade and access the new operating system.

3 **Three Tiers of Product Launches:**

- **Tier 1 – Strategic Product Launch:** A significant product introduction with high impact and a focus on strategic business goals. This type of launch often involves a large marketing budget and media coverage.

   Example: Apple's iPhone Launches are considered Tier 1, involving strategic planning, large-scale marketing campaigns, and global media attention.
- **Tier 2 – Product Launch Impacting Many Customers:** These launches focus on products that will significantly affect a large portion of existing customers or add substantial features to an existing product.

   Example: Google's Pixel Updates, which introduce major software enhancements that affect a wide range of users, are considered Tier 2 launches.
- **Tier 3 – Product Upgrade:** This involves incremental upgrades or enhancements to an existing product and is often communicated primarily to existing customers.

   Example: Spotify's Yearly UI Updates, which introduce minor changes to improve user experience, fall into Tier 3 launches.

Figure 5.3 depicts the three tiers of product launches.

5.3.3 Product Launch Roadmap

A Product Launch Roadmap is a visual tool used to plan, communicate, and track the progress of the product launch. It provides an overview of the

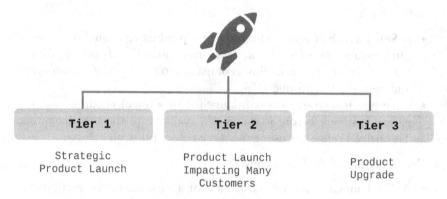

FIGURE 5.3   Three Tiers of Product Launches.

launch activities, timelines, and responsibilities to align all stakeholders on what needs to be done and when.

1 **Definition:** A Product Launch Roadmap is a high-level plan that outlines the steps involved in launching a product, including the key activities for each phase of the launch.
2 **Usage:** The roadmap is used by product managers to communicate the launch plan to internal stakeholders, coordinate efforts, and ensure that all teams are aligned.
3 **Contents:** A typical launch roadmap includes milestones, key activities, timelines, stakeholders, and dependencies.
4 **Stakeholders:** Product Managers, Marketing, Sales, Support, and Engineering teams.
5 **Purpose:** The roadmap ensures that all teams understand the launch timeline, their responsibilities, and how their contributions fit into the overall launch effort.

Figure 5.4 shows an example of a time-based Product Launch Roadmap.

5.3.4 *The Three Stages of a Product Launch*

This section describes a structured approach to successfully bringing a product to market. Each stage –**Pre-Launch, Launch, Post-Launch** – involves specific activities that ensure the product is introduced effectively, reaches the right audience, and continues to grow after the initial launch. Understanding these stages helps product managers coordinate efforts across teams, maximize impact, and drive long-term success for the product.

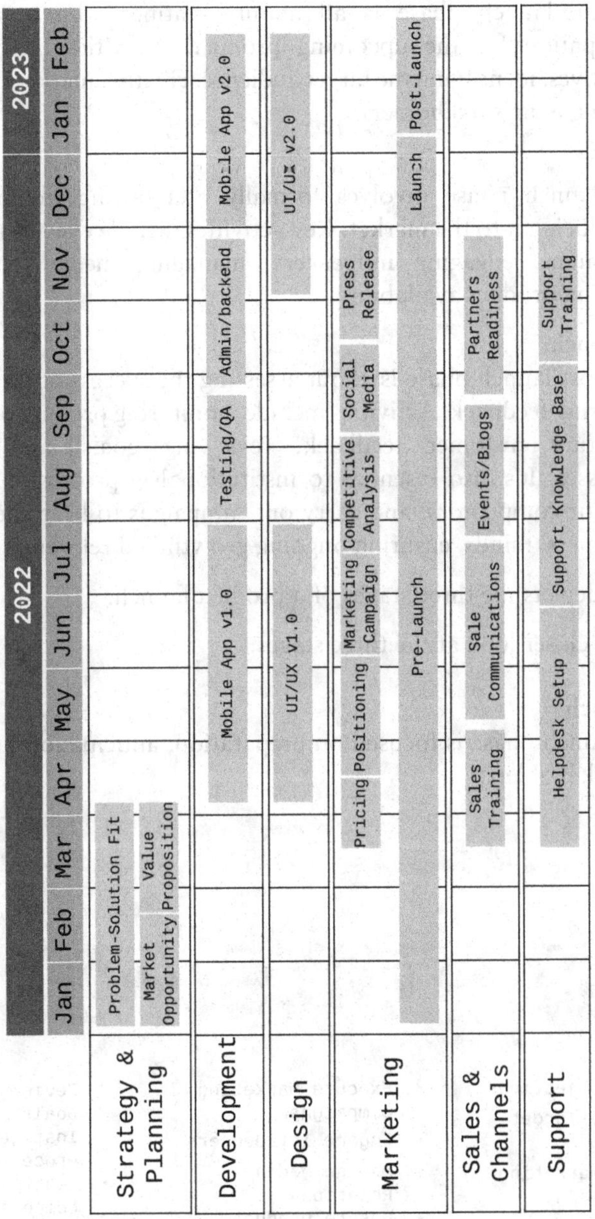

	2022												2023	
	Jan	Feb	Mar	Apr	May	Jun	Jul	Aug	Sep	Oct	Nov	Dec	Jan	Feb
Strategy & Planning	Problem-Solution Fit / Market Opportunity / Value Proposition													
Development					Mobile App v1.0			Testing/QA		Admin/backend		Mobile App v2.0		
Design					UI/UX v1.0						UI/UX v2.0			
Marketing					Pricing Positioning / Marketing Campaign / Competitive Analysis / Social Media / Press Release — Pre-Launch / Launch / Post-Launch									
Sales & Channels					Sales Training	Sale Communications		Events/Blogs		Partners Readiness				
Support					Helpdesk Setup	Support Knowledge Base				Support Training				

FIGURE 5.4   A Time-Base Product Launch Roadmap.

The following list the three stages of a product launch:

1 **Pre-Launch**:
   a The pre-launch phase is all about creating a buzz and building anticipation for the upcoming product. Activities include defining objectives, identifying the target audience, creating marketing collateral, and engaging stakeholders.

2 **Launch**:
   a The launch phase involves formally announcing the product and introducing it to the market. Key activities include executing marketing campaigns, engaging influencers, managing media relations, and ensuring product availability.

3 **Post-Launch**:
   a The post-launch phase is about assessing the success of the launch and gathering feedback. Activities include monitoring product performance, collecting customer feedback, reviewing goals, and optimizing processes. It's also essential to institutionalize processes, continue to monitor competitors, and carry out campaigns to keep the product in customers' minds, ensuring ongoing growth and relevance.

Figure 5.5 depicts the three stages of a product launch.

Let's take a closer look at the three stages:

1. Pre-Launch
The Pre-Launch phase is focused on preparation, anticipation building, and aligning stakeholders.

FIGURE 5.5 Three Stages of a Product Launch.

- **Checklist**:
  - Set clear launch objectives.
  - Develop the product brief.
  - Identify the target audience.
  - Create key messaging and marketing collateral.
  - Prepare the Product Launch Roadmap.
  - Engage with internal teams – Sales, Support, and MarCom.

- **Key Activities**:
  - **MarCom**: Develop promotional content, including blog posts, teaser videos, social media posts, and press releases.
  - **Sales**: Train the sales team on product features, benefits, and unique selling points to prepare them for customer inquiries.
  - **Support**: Train the support team to handle customer questions, provide troubleshooting, and create FAQs.

2. Launch

The Launch phase is the most critical stage, involving activities that introduce the product to the market and generate momentum.

Figure 5.6 depicts the five key activities for a successful product launch.

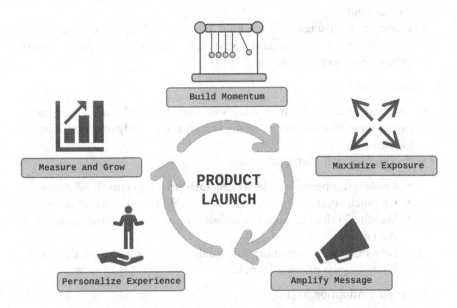

FIGURE 5.6   Key Activities for a Successful Product Launch.

The five key activities for a successful product launch include the following:

1 **Build Momentum**:

- Announce the product through media, influencers, and industry partners.
- Example: The **Alexander Wang × H&M** Hype Machine generated excitement by partnering with fashion influencers and showcasing exclusive previews of the collaboration.

2 **Maximize Exposure**:

- Execute online and offline campaigns to create widespread awareness.
- Example: **Apple** New Product Launch events are streamed live globally, attracting millions of viewers and maximizing exposure.

3 **Amplify Message**:

- Use public relations, partnerships, and influencer endorsements to amplify the product's message.
- Example: The **Nintendo Switch** Launch used partnerships with gaming influencers to create buzz and demonstrate the new console's unique features.

4 **Personalize Experience**:

- Customize communications based on audience segments to foster engagement.
- Example: **Samsung's Galaxy Fold** Launch included exclusive events and one-on-one consultations for early adopters, offering a more personalized experience.

5 **Measure and Grow**:

- Track key metrics such as sales, customer feedback, and engagement rates to measure the success of the launch and identify opportunities for growth.
- Product Launch Metrics:
  - **Leads**: Number of new leads generated through launch activities.
  - **Channels**: Performance metrics across different marketing channels.
  - **Website Traffic**: Changes in website traffic before, during, and after the launch.
  - **News Coverage**: Quantity and quality of news and media coverage related to the product launch.
- **Product Adoption Metrics**:
  - **Trials**: Number of users signing up for product trials.

- **Usage**: Metrics related to product usage, such as daily active users (DAU).
- **Retention**: Rate at which users continue using the product after initial adoption.

- **Product-market Metrics**:

  - **Revenue**: Revenue generated during and immediately after the product launch.
  - **Market Share**: Change in market share resulting from the product launch.
  - **Win Rate**: Percentage of sales opportunities won compared to lost during the launch period.

- **Example: Google Glass** failed partly due to insufficient market research and lack of a strong product-market fit. Monitoring and adapting based on feedback and metrics could have helped prevent its premature decline.

3. Post-Launch

The **Post-Launch** phase involves evaluating performance, making improvements, and ensuring that the product continues to meet customer needs.

Key Activities in the Post-Launch:

- **Review Launch Goals**:

  - Assess whether the launch goals were met. Analyse sales data, customer feedback, and engagement metrics.
  - Example: **Slack** reviewed user acquisition and activation metrics after launch to understand which channels were most effective in driving growth.

- **Institutionalize Process and Practices**:

  - Identify best practices and document lessons learned for future launches.
  - Example: **Dropbox** institutionalized its referral programme after its successful launch, using it as a blueprint for future customer acquisition efforts.

- **Monitor Competitors**:

  - Keep track of competitor activities, new releases, and market shifts.
  - Example: **Spotify** continuously monitors competitors like **Apple** Music and Tidal to stay ahead and adapt its product offerings.

- **Conduct Product Review Campaigns**:

  - Gather feedback through surveys, reviews, and customer interviews to improve the product.

- Example: **Airbnb** regularly conducts product review campaigns to collect guest feedback and improve its platform.

5.3.5 *Product Launch Plan in Car-Sharing Platform Case Scenario*

Let's walk through the **QuikDrive** Car-Sharing Platform to unpack the five key components of a Launch Plan as shown in Figure 5.7:

1 Problem Statement
2 Market Opportunity
3 Value Proposition
4 Pricing Strategy
5 Product Positioning

Background

QuikDrive is getting ready to launch their new car-sharing service in Singapore. They've created a launch plan to ensure a successful introduction of their new platform to the market.

Their launch plan aims to achieve three main objectives. Firstly, it aims to employ both web and mobile technology, which will simplify the process of leasing and renting cars, improving the experience for **QuikDrive's** members. Secondly, it aims to increase the adoption rate by removing membership subscription fees and automating the sign-ups of new members. Thirdly, it aims to leverage data analytics and machine learning for real-time and

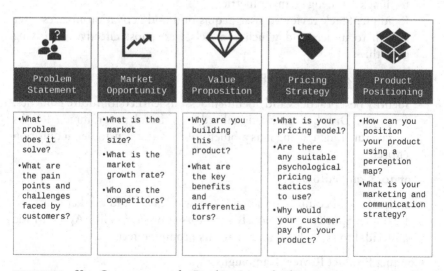

Problem Statement	Market Opportunity	Value Proposition	Pricing Strategy	Product Positioning
•What problem does it solve? •What are the pain points and challenges faced by customers?	•What is the market size? •What is the market growth rate? •Who are the competitors?	•Why are you building this product? •What are the key benefits and differentiators?	•What is your pricing model? •Are there any suitable psychological pricing tactics to use? •Why would your customer pay for your product?	•How can you position your product using a perception map? •What is your marketing and communication strategy?

FIGURE 5.7 Key Components of a Product Launch Plan.

flexible operations that improve the company's operational effectiveness and efficiency.

A product launch is best planned using a roadmap, which is a visual communication tool that illustrates how a new product will hit the market. This is called a **Product Launch Roadmap**.

It includes all the teams – from product strategy, to planning, development, marketing and sales, and support. It outlines all the tasks required to ensure that pre-launch, launch, and post-launch tactics are successfully executed.

This tool is highly valuable as it provides a shared source of truth for the broader team. One that outlines the vision, direction, priorities, and progress of a product over time – from initial concept to its launch into the market.

Let's take a look at the five key components that are important to include in a launch plan, by exploring **QuikDrive's** product launch plan now.

1. Problem Statement

The first key component of **QuikDrive's** launch plan is the **Problem Statement**. The problem statement helps the product manager and other team stakeholders understand the experience that **QuikDrive** aims to create, or the new market segment the company wishes to enter when building a new product or service.

QuikDrive's problem statement can be expressed in two ways because it is providing a service platform that solves problems faced by both car renters, and car owners. Here are two statements to describe the two problems.

Car drivers who don't own a car, due to the high cost of car ownership in Singapore, and seek a comfortable and convenient means to travel around at their own terms and at their pace, are dissatisfied with the existing available car rental options and are turning to car sharing as an alternative to owning a car.

Car owners who are faced with the problem of their car being heavily underutilized, which leads to parked cars causing wastage in both space and depreciating value, are seeking to turn their cars into income-generating assets.

2. Market Opportunity

The second key component of the launch plan is a description of the **Market Opportunity**. The product manager needs to perform a market analysis to determine the market opportunity, which then helps define who **QuikDrive's** target customers are, what they want, and how they make their decisions.

QuikDrive's market opportunity can be described as follows:

QuikDrive's market opportunity:
The target market is made up of two segments – the renters and the owners. For the renters, the main customer target segment consists of 18–35-year-olds, who will potentially be more open to the idea of renting cars for day-to-day use.

The target age group makes up about 35% of the population, which means there are about 500,000 licenced owners falling into that age category.

As for the owners, after conducting market research in the form of a survey, about 10% of private vehicle owners expressed interest in renting out their vehicles. This lower percentage is due to fears of potential damage to their vehicles, which might be caused by the renters. However, this statistic can likely improve with marketing of insurance-covered rides as well as thorough renter screening procedures.

3. Value Proposition

The third key component of **QuikDrive's** launch plan is the **Value Proposition.** The Value Proposition statement helps their target customers understand the value of the car-sharing service. It also helps the customers see exactly how the service benefits them, and why it offers them the best available option, when compared to the competition.

QuikDrive's value proposition is that it is a car-sharing platform that aims to bridge the gap between car ownership and the freedom to drive. **QuikDrive** empowers car owners by making it convenient for them to rent out their cars when unused, turning the car into a revenue-generating asset. **QuikDrive's** mobile digital key and virtual cash cards for top-up from the platform offers car renters convenient access to cars within their proximity and a hassle-free car rental experience.

4. Pricing Strategy

The fourth key component of **QuikDrive's** launch plan is their **Pricing Strategy.** Depending on its pricing strategy, **QuikDrive's** new service platform can either flourish or fail in the Singapore market. If the platform's price is pegged too high, customers will look for cheaper alternatives. And if the price is too low, **QuikDrive** may be able to capture the desired market share, but their profit margins will take a hit due to the higher cost of customer acquisition.

QuikDrive's pricing strategy is based on a "pay-per-use" model, where customers do not have to commit to long-term subscription plans but are still able to enjoy competitive and affordable rates.

QuikDrive aims to develop a well-established platform, such that car owners can trust **QuikDrive** to protect their cars while helping them to earn a passive income. And renters can trust **QuikDrive** to offer high-quality cars with attractive rental rates.

QuikDrive generates 12% of its revenues from its Enterprise Car-Share business and 88% from private car-share business.

5. Positioning Statement

The fifth key component of **QuikDrive's** product launch is its **Positioning Statement.** They need to craft the right positioning statement for the new platform. This will ensure they shape the distinct and clearly differentiated brand they want to entrench in the minds of their target customers.

QuikDrive's positioning statement can be boiled down to the following.

For city-dwelling car renters and owners, when you use **QuikDrive** car-sharing services, you get wheels when you need them, and cash when you don't.

5.3.5.1 Product Launch Roadmap

The **Product Launch Roadmap** is a valuable tool to plan a new product launch. This tool outlines key activities undertaken by all key stakeholders involved – from product strategy, planning, development, marketing and sales, and support – to ensure that pre-launch, launch and post-launch tactics are successfully executed.

Launching your product after many months of planning and building it is a critical milestone for the entire team. The question is whether you can do it successfully. If you don't do the product launch effectively, then not only will you not be able to create the desired level of awareness of your product, but you could potentially create a bad impression of it.

To ensure you carry out the product launch successfully, make sure to include the five key components discussed in this section. In addition, make sure you use a product launch roadmap to ensure that all bases are covered, across the various teams.

5.3.6 Summary of Market Launch

A **Market Launch** is a multi-faceted effort that requires careful planning, precise execution, and ongoing evaluation. From pre-launch preparation to the launch activities and post-launch follow-up, each stage of the launch plays a crucial role in the product's success. By developing a robust **Product Launch Plan**, leveraging different types of launches, and using a **Product Launch Roadmap** to keep teams aligned, product managers can maximize impact and ensure that their product resonates with the target audience. Effective market launches, like those of **Apple** and **Nintendo**, demonstrate the importance of coordination and strategy, while the failures of products like **Google Glass** highlight the value of adaptability and listening to customer feedback.

5.4 Conclusion

In this chapter, we explored the crucial aspects of managing sales channels and executing a successful product launch. Effective sales channel management is essential for driving business growth, as it helps organizations craft the right channel strategy to reach target markets efficiently. By understanding the various types of sales channels, leveraging growth channels, and scaling product distribution, businesses can ensure their products are accessible to customers while maintaining control over the customer experience.

In the second part of the chapter, we discussed the steps involved in preparing for and executing a market launch. The product brief serves as a foundation for outlining the key elements of the launch, while the different types of product launches allow companies to choose the best approach based on their objectives. A well-structured product launch roadmap, combined with attention to the three key stages – pre-launch, launch, and post-launch – ensures a smooth introduction of the product to the market, maximizing visibility, engagement, and sales.

Together, these insights equip product managers and their teams with the tools to strategically manage sales channels and launch products effectively, driving long-term success and growth.

6

ENGAGING CUSTOMER AND DESIGNING SEAMLESS EXPERIENCE

6.1 Introduction

In today's digital world, customer engagement is more critical than ever. As consumers become more tech-savvy, their expectations for seamless, personalized experiences grow. The ability to engage customers effectively – through tailored interactions across various touchpoints – can determine the success or failure of a product. This chapter focuses on how product managers can design and implement customer-centric strategies that meet these evolving needs.

Understanding customer behaviour, preferences, and expectations is essential to creating products that offer intuitive, personalized interactions. Through Omnichannel Engagement strategies, businesses can ensure that customers experience consistency whether they are engaging with a brand online, in-store, or through mobile apps. Additionally, adopting flexible architectures like Headless Commerce allows organizations to quickly adapt to changing customer needs and deliver personalized experiences at scale.

This chapter also introduces key concepts like the Flywheel Effect, which emphasizes the power of continuous engagement to drive long-term business growth. We'll explore how companies can leverage micro-moments – those brief instances when consumers are primed to make decisions – to create meaningful, real-time connections with their audience. By integrating these strategies into product design, product managers can help their organizations

DOI: 10.1201/9781003614180-6

build lasting customer relationships and deliver experiences that keep users engaged and loyal.

6.2 Effective Customer Service

Customer Service is the support provided to customers before, during, and after their purchase to ensure a great experience and to help them derive the most value from the product. Effective customer service can be a powerful differentiator, transforming customers into advocates and enhancing brand loyalty. It encompasses understanding customer needs, providing timely assistance, and solving their issues efficiently.

There are four key factors that enhance customer service:

1. **Personalized:**

   - Customer service starts with a human touch. Customers appreciate when interactions are personalized, showing that the company cares about them and their needs. Rather than viewing customer service as a cost, businesses should consider it an opportunity to build loyalty by exceeding customer expectations every time they interact.

2. **Competent:**

   - Great customer service means the team is knowledgeable about the company and its products. Customers want quick solutions, and for that, service professionals need to be competent in their responses. When support agents can easily solve customer problems and provide valuable insights, it builds trust and confidence in the brand.

3. **Convenient:**

   - Customers want to connect with support teams using channels they prefer, whether it's email, phone, live chat, or social media. Providing convenience is crucial for ensuring a positive customer experience. Make it easy for customers to reach out and access support whenever they need it.

4. **Proactive:**

   - Customers appreciate when companies anticipate their needs and reach out proactively. If there's a product issue, like a delay or downtime, communicating with customers in advance shows transparency and keeps them informed. Even if the news isn't good, being proactive in sharing information builds trust and keeps customers in the loop.

Figure 6.1 shows the four factors that enhance customer experience.

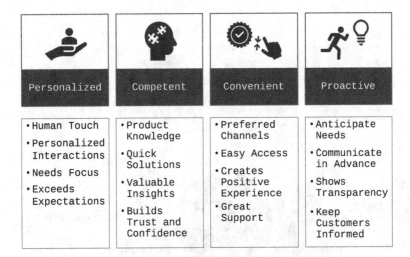

Personalized	Competent	Convenient	Proactive
• Human Touch • Personalized Interactions • Needs Focus • Exceeds Expectations	• Product Knowledge • Quick Solutions • Valuable Insights • Builds Trust and Confidence	• Preferred Channels • Easy Access • Creates Positive Experience • Great Support	• Anticipate Needs • Communicate in Advance • Shows Transparency • Keep Customers Informed

FIGURE 6.1   Key Factors That Enhance Customer Service.

6.2.1   Customer Touchpoint Wheel

The **Customer Touchpoint Wheel** illustrates the various stages of a customer's experience with a product, starting from pre-purchase to purchase and then post-purchase. These touchpoints provide opportunities to create a positive impression and foster loyalty.

Figure 6.2 shows the Customer Touchpoint Wheel.

1. **Pre-Purchase Experience:**

   - **Pre-purchase touchpoints** are largely influenced by marketing and brand activities. This includes advertising, social media, PR statements, websites, and direct promotions. The goal is to create an impactful initial impression of the brand to attract potential customers.
   - **Example:** A brand like **Nike** uses powerful marketing campaigns and collaborations with celebrities to create brand buzz, ensuring that customers have a positive pre-purchase perception.

2. **Purchase Experience:**

   - The **purchase experience** involves the customer interacting directly with the product in a retail setting or online. This stage includes aspects like product visibility, ease of navigation, and assistance provided during the buying decision.
   - **Example:** In a **Starbucks** store, the customer experience is enhanced by the cosy ambiance, well-arranged product display, and friendly service – all contributing to the customer's purchase experience.

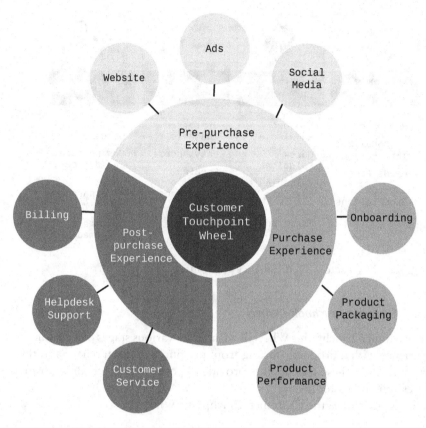

FIGURE 6.2 Customer Touchpoint Wheel.

3. **Post-Purchase Experience:**

- The **post-purchase experience** focuses on the customer's use of the product and whether it meets or exceeds their expectations. This stage helps determine whether the customer will continue to buy from the brand or not.
- **Example**: After buying an **Apple** product, customers receive ongoing support through AppleCare, ensuring that their experience with the product is seamless and helping drive repeat purchases.

Table 6.1 depicts a table that provides a comprehensive overview of customer touchpoints at various stages of the customer journey – **Before Purchase, During Purchase,** and **After Purchase.** By mapping out these touchpoints, businesses can better understand how customers interact with their brand and identify opportunities to enhance customer experiences. Each stage has

TABLE 6.1 Overview of Customer Touchpoints across the Customer Journey

Customer Journey Stage	Touchpoint Examples	Description
Before Purchase	Company blog	Educational articles that build credibility and generate product awareness.
	Customer reviews	Testimonials and ratings on platforms like Google, Yelp, and product websites to establish trust.
	Social media	Platforms like Facebook, Instagram, LinkedIn for engaging with customers, sharing content, and answering queries.
	Digital advertisements	Google Ads, Facebook Ads, and Instagram Ads used to target prospective customers and create brand awareness.
	Influencer marketing	Collaborations with influencers to endorse products and increase reach.
	Email newsletters	Promotional emails sent to prospects with special offers, product information, and updates.
	Webinars and events	Hosting online or offline events to educate and inform potential customers about the product's value.
	Friends and family	Word-of-mouth recommendations and referral programmes that encourage sharing.
During Purchase	Website checkout flow	The overall experience of purchasing online, including adding items to cart, entering payment details, and completing the checkout process.
	Conversations with support and sales teams	Live chat, email, or phone interactions to assist customers in making informed decisions.
	Email marketing	Follow-up emails that encourage users to complete abandoned carts or offer limited-time discounts.
	Direct mailers	Personalized postcards or brochures sent to potential buyers with information about products and special offers.
	Retargeting ads	Ads targeted at users who visited the site but didn't make a purchase, shown on social media or websites.
	In-store experience	If applicable, in-store displays, product arrangements, and interactions with sales staff.

(Continued)

TABLE 6.1 (Continued)

Customer Journey Stage	Touchpoint Examples	Description
	Mobile app purchase experience	Features like seamless navigation, easy checkout, and payment options available in the mobile app.
	Product demos and trials	Providing potential customers with product demos or free trials to help them experience the value of the product.
After Purchase	Customer onboarding	Tutorials, onboarding videos, and emails to help customers understand how to get started with the product.
	CSAT surveys	Customer satisfaction surveys to gather feedback on the buying experience and overall satisfaction.
	Customer service channels	Multichannel support including chat, phone, email, and social media to address customer issues.
	Knowledge base or community forum	Self-help articles, FAQs, and community forums where customers can find answers or advice from peers.
	Email newsletters	Regular updates on product news, tips, and exclusive offers to keep customers engaged.
	Loyalty programmes	Reward programmes for repeat purchases, including points, cashback, or exclusive discounts.
	Personalized offers	Targeted discounts or offers sent after purchase to encourage continued engagement and loyalty.
	Product updates and improvements	Notifications about new features or updates that add value to the product and enhance the customer experience.
	Social media community	Engaging with customers post-purchase via social media platforms to build a sense of community.
	User-generated content	Encouraging customers to share experiences and reviews through photos, videos, or testimonials for social proof.

unique interactions that can significantly impact a customer's perception, satisfaction, and loyalty.

The **Before Purchase** touchpoints focus on creating awareness, building trust, and generating interest through strategies like content marketing, influencer endorsements, and social media engagement. The **During Purchase** touchpoints emphasize providing a seamless buying experience through personalized assistance, retargeting ads, and a well-designed checkout process. Finally, the **After Purchase** touchpoints are geared towards reinforcing brand loyalty by offering onboarding support, personalized communication, loyalty programmes, and effective customer service. Understanding and optimizing each of these touchpoints helps businesses provide a consistent, engaging, and customer-centric experience, ultimately driving customer satisfaction and retention.

6.2.2   Customer Engagement

To build lasting relationships with customers, product managers must focus on creating strong **customer engagement**. Two key factors drive effective engagement:

1. **Emotional Connection:**

   - Customers are more likely to stick with a business they feel emotionally connected to. Providing more value than expected leaves the customer feeling delighted, resulting in loyalty.
   - **Example:** Coca-Cola focuses on creating an emotional bond with customers by promoting happiness, shared moments, and nostalgia. Campaigns like "Share a Coke" encouraged customers to engage with the brand by finding and sharing bottles with their names, building an emotional connection.

2. **Customer-Centricity:**

   - Shifting from product-centric to customer-centric operations means improving engagement by prioritizing customer needs and satisfaction.
   - **Example:** Amazon is known for its customer-centric approach, constantly innovating to improve the shopping experience. Features like one-click ordering and personalized recommendations make customers feel that their needs are being prioritized.

6.2.3   Omnichannel Engagement Strategy

An **Omnichannel Engagement Strategy** focuses on providing a seamless customer experience across multiple channels and touchpoints. It involves integrating all available communication channels – such as social media, email, phone, live chat, in-store, and online – to ensure consistency and connectivity throughout the entire customer journey. Omnichannel Engagement allows customers to move between channels effortlessly, without any loss of context or disruption in their experience. It allows customers to transition between different platforms – like in-store, online, or mobile – without interruptions.

Many companies communicate and interact with customers across different channels. However, the level of customer service provided across multiple channels is often inconsistent and important customer data and information can often remain siloed. As a result, customer demands and business responses are often misaligned.

When a company launches a product into the market, it needs a great product support team to help provide continuous value and ensure a consistent experience with the use of the product after the sale.

Customer expectations have risen in recent years. Customers today demand increased interaction with brands and products, across multiple channels on the platform of their choice. The change in expectations has made way for two unique, but easily confused, approaches for providing customer service: Multichannel and Omnichannel.

In this section, you'll learn more about both approaches and why one is better than the other. To better understand **Omnichannel Engagement**, it is useful to contrast it with a **Multichannel approach** as shown in Figure 6.3.

6.2.3.1 Multichannel Customer Service

Multichannel customer service refers to the use of multiple channels to promote a product and engage with consumers. An Omnichannel approach does the same, but in addition it aims to understand the customer and uses data to provide a single, seamless customer experience.

In other words, Multichannel approaches address customer engagement, while Omnichannel approaches address customer engagement AND enhance customer experience.

Multichannel customer engagement strategies use multiple channels to promote and sell products and engage with customers. Such channels may include websites, social media platforms, applications, physical stores, and more. Similarly, Omnichannel approaches include a range of channels for interacting with customers.

With Multichannel approaches, the different channels, or pieces, are not being connected to each other to form a unified customer experience. But with an Omnichannel approach, the customers' buying journey or experience is brought together across the various channels.

Key Characteristics of Multichannel Approach:

1. **Channel Silos**: Each channel operates independently, without sharing information with other channels.
2. **Inconsistent Experience**: Customers may experience different levels of service depending on the channel they use, resulting in inconsistencies. For example, a customer may have to repeat their query if they switch from live chat to a phone call.

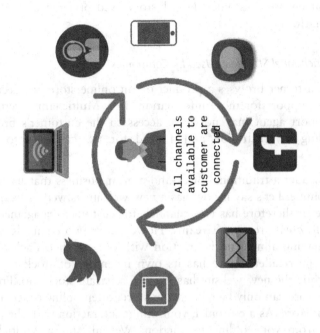

Omni-Channel Customer Service

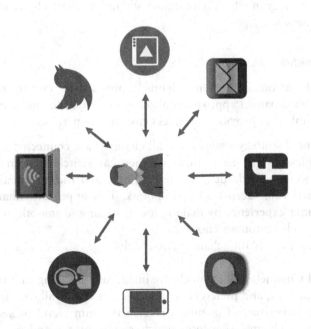

Multi-Channel Customer Service

FIGURE 6.3 Coordinated Engagement across Channels.

3. **Limited Integration**: The different channels do not have an integrated system that ensures customer data, history, and preferences are shared between platforms.

6.2.3.2   Multichannel Strategies Used by Companies

Example: A customer browses a product on an online store but decides to call customer support for more information. In a **Multichannel** setup, the customer support agent may not have access to the customer's browsing history, leading to **frustration** and a need for the customer to repeat information.

Example: Consider a traditional brick-and-mortar business that has moved its business online. Let's say it now has a new website as well as its original physical store. It therefore has two channels for customer engagement, and it uses both to create revenue streams. However, its two channels are still very siloed, having almost no interaction with one another. Each channel is separate. The retailer's store has its own inventory of stock to sell to customers, while the new website has its own separate stock too. Products purchased in-store can only be returned in-store; often online orders cannot be returned in-store. As a customer, your online interaction with the retailer is separated from your offline interaction. We call this a Multichannel Engagement strategy in which both online and offline channels are treated as separate businesses.

6.2.3.3   Omnichannel Customer Service

Now, let's take a look at an Omnichannel approach for customer service. Remember, Omnichannel approaches also have multiple channels, but those channels are linked to provide a seamless customer experience.

An **Omnichannel** strategy ensures that all channels are **connected** and work together seamlessly. This means that customers can switch between channels during their journey without any interruptions, and the information they provided is accessible across all touchpoints. This approach enhances the **overall customer experience** by making it consistent and smooth, regardless of which channels customers choose.

Key Characteristics of Omnichannel Approach:

1. **Connected Channels**: All channels are integrated, meaning that customer data, interactions, and preferences are accessible across all touchpoints.
2. **Consistent Experience**: Customers receive the same level of service no matter which channel they use, which results in a seamless customer experience.

3. **Personalized Interactions**: Since all customer information is available in real time, it allows for personalized interactions. For instance, if a customer adds items to their cart online and later visits a physical store, the sales associate can assist with the same items.

6.2.3.4 Omnichannel Strategies Used by Companies

Example: The Starbucks coffee company positions itself as more than just a coffee shop, or brand; it presents itself as an experience. Having an Omnichannel approach supports that.

One of the keys to Starbucks' experience lies in their mobile application and rewards programme. The Starbucks app allows for quick and easy payments. And the loyalty programme rewards users and offers value-added services, such as store locations and music recommendations. Let's examine Starbucks' Omnichannel approach to customer experience to demonstrate how a seamless experience is provided across multiple channels.

Starbucks' Omnichannel business initiative and its supporting technology is dubbed the "Digital Flywheel." It focuses on four distinct pillars: rewards, personalization, payment, and ordering. The app, together with a large loyalty programme, addresses the two basic customer needs of convenience and queue avoidance. Starbucks' "Digital Flywheel" helps bring the company to a new level of providing an Omnichannel experience to its customers.

While the rewards programme is primarily run through the rewards app on a customer's mobile device, customers can add money to their rewards account via multiple channels, including their mobile device, the company's website, and in stores.

Starbucks does an excellent job of providing a seamless experience to its customers. Every time a customer pays with a Starbucks card, using a physical card or the mobile app, that user accumulates rewards points.

The mobile app also allows the customers to find nearby stores, order drinks ahead of time, and view new menu items. And, with the Spotify integration, customers can view what songs are playing in that specific store and add them to their playlists.

Example: Home Depot has successfully implemented an **Omnichannel strategy** by integrating its website, mobile app, and in-store experience. Customers can browse products online, check stock availability, and reserve items for in-store pickup – all without losing any of the context. The sales team in-store can access the customer's preferences and help them complete the purchase, ensuring a **consistent and connected experience**.

Example: Circles.Life, a digital telco company, uses an **Omnichannel strategy** to enhance customer engagement. They offer support through multiple channels – such as chat, email, and phone – while also enabling customers to manage their accounts and purchase services through their mobile app. This integrated approach allows customers to switch between channels as needed, without any disruption, improving customer satisfaction and ensuring a seamless experience.

6.2.3.5 Summary of Omnichannel Engagement Strategy

Multichannel approaches to customer engagement use multiple ways to approach and engage customers. Some customers may prefer an in-store experience, while others prefer to communicate via email. Each channel may be an important touchpoint for your product, but the channels don't intersect to help foster a consistent message or a seamless customer experience.

Companies with Multichannel approaches to customer engagement create strategies for each distinct channel and focus on making each one engaging and easy to use for the majority of their customers, but they miss the opportunity to turn these disparate forms of engagement into one experience.

Omnichannel approaches, on the other hand, create a single and seamless customer experience. They provide customers with an integrated buying and usage experience. Customers can easily transition from shopping online on a desktop PC or mobile device, to the mobile phone, or to the store, and the experience will be seamless.

Omnichannel experiences are likely to build a sense of great customer service and foster a customer relationship with the company and product and hence have a positive impact on brand image and customer loyalty and retention.

Omnichannel approaches also unify sales, marketing, and support. This means customers can easily jump between channels, continuing their journey with a brand and product in a seamless manner.

To better engage your customers, you as a product manager need to think about creating consistent and personalized experiences for your customers and not only focus on getting each channel right. Ask yourself how to integrate or connect your channels so they form part of one great customer experience. Adopting an **Omnichannel Engagement strategy** means ensuring that customer data is readily accessible across all platforms, which in turn helps to provide a **cohesive customer experience**. Whether a customer reaches out via email, walks into a store, or uses a mobile app, they should feel as though they are dealing with a unified brand, receiving consistent information and support regardless of the touchpoint. Now think about how you can leverage an Omnichannel approach for your product of choice in relation to the customer touchpoints with your sales, marketing, and support channels.

6.2.4 Headless Commerce Architecture

Headless Commerce Architecture refers to a digital setup where the front-end (user interface) is separated from the back-end (commerce capabilities).

This approach enables businesses to add commerce features to more digital touchpoints, personalize the customer experience, and adopt new business models.

- **Adding Commerce Capabilities to More Digital Touchpoints:**
  - Businesses can integrate shopping features into websites, social media, and even smart devices, allowing customers to make purchases wherever they are.
  - **Example: Nike** allows customers to shop directly through their app, website, and social media platforms, ensuring an integrated experience across all digital touchpoints.

- **Enabling Personalized Shopping Experiences Across Touchpoints:**
  - Personalized recommendations and offers enhance the customer experience, making it more relevant and engaging.
  - **Example: Netflix** provides personalized content suggestions across all devices, creating a seamless and tailored experience for users.

- **Facilitating the Adoption of New Business Models:**
  - Businesses can introduce new subscription models, bundles, or curated shopping experiences by decoupling the front-end and back-end.
  - **Example: Shopify** merchants can use Headless Commerce to build custom front-end experiences while retaining the powerful commerce capabilities provided by the platform's back-end.

6.2.5 Flywheel Effect

The **Flywheel Effect** emphasizes that the best way to grow a business is through happy customers who advocate for the brand. Product managers should aim to make customers happy, who then recommend the product, creating a virtuous cycle of growth. Figure 6.4 shows the Flywheel Effect.

The three stages of the flywheel are as follows:

1. **Attract:**
   - Draw prospective customers with useful and engaging content. SEO, social media, and events all play a role in capturing the audience's attention.
   - **Example: Starbucks** attracts new customers by promoting loyalty programmes and personalized offers through social media and digital marketing channels.

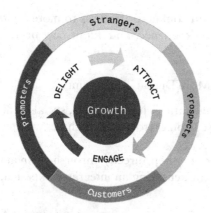

FIGURE 6.4 The Flywheel Effect.

2. Engage:

- Make it easy for customers to learn about and purchase your product at their own pace. Offer free trials, nurture campaigns, and self-serve purchasing options.
- **Example:** Starbucks' **Mobile Order & Pay** feature makes it convenient for customers to place orders in advance, reducing wait times and enhancing engagement.

3. Delight:

- Design your product to be easy to use and provide support resources to ensure customer satisfaction. Use customer feedback to improve the product and turn customers into advocates.
- **Example:** Starbucks uses personalized incentives through **spend-based rewards** to delight customers and encourage repeat purchases.

6.2.6 Summary of Effective Customer Service

Customer Service is the cornerstone of a successful product journey and a key differentiator for brands in today's competitive marketplace. A well-rounded customer service strategy that is personalized, competent, convenient, and proactive is essential for enhancing customer experiences and fostering brand loyalty. By focusing on **pre-purchase**, **purchase**, and **post-purchase** experiences, product managers can ensure that every interaction is an opportunity to strengthen relationships, address customer needs, and exceed expectations.

Customer Service also extends beyond solving issues; it involves building genuine connections with customers, providing seamless experiences, and ensuring ongoing engagement. The concept of **Omnichannel Engagement** and strategies such as the **Flywheel Effect** and **Headless Commerce Architecture** empower product managers to meet customers at every stage of their journey and create memorable experiences.

6.3 Conclusion

In this chapter, we explored the critical role of creating a seamless and engaging customer experience across multiple touchpoints. By understanding the **Customer Touchpoint Wheel** and optimizing every interaction, businesses can foster deeper relationships and emotional connections with their customers. This chapter demonstrated how modern **omnichannel engagement strategies** enable companies to unify customer interactions across platforms, ensuring that the experience remains consistent and fluid.

We also delved into the benefits of **Headless Commerce Architecture**, showcasing how businesses can stay agile and scalable in today's digital world by decoupling the front-end experience from back-end systems. Finally, the **Flywheel Effect** underscored the power of customer advocacy, turning delighted customers into brand advocates who drive future business growth.

A strong, strategic focus on customer engagement ensures that businesses not only meet but exceed customer expectations, turning every interaction into an opportunity to build loyalty and trust.

7

OPTIMIZING DIGITAL EXPERIENCE AND EMPOWERING EMPLOYEES

7.1 Introduction

In today's competitive landscape, creating exceptional digital experiences is at the core of customer satisfaction and long-term success. As digital products and services play an increasingly central role in people's lives, ensuring that these experiences are smooth, intuitive, and engaging is vital for organizations to stand out. Optimizing the digital experience goes beyond just providing a functional product – it involves continuously analysing user behaviour, personalizing interactions, and responding to evolving needs with agility.

However, delivering a superior digital experience cannot be achieved through technology alone. Empowering employees to take ownership of the customer journey is equally essential. When employees are equipped with the right tools, knowledge, and decision-making authority, they become key drivers of both customer satisfaction and product success. Empowered employees can deliver proactive support, enhance the user experience (UX), and contribute to product innovations.

This chapter explores how organizations can optimize the digital experience while fostering a culture of employee empowerment, showing that the synergy between technology and human engagement is the key to building lasting customer relationships and thriving in the digital era.

7.2 Optimizing Customer Service

7.2.1 Micro-Moments

Micro-Moments are intent-driven moments of decision-making and preference-shaping that occur throughout the consumer journey. In these

DOI: 10.1201/9781003614180-7

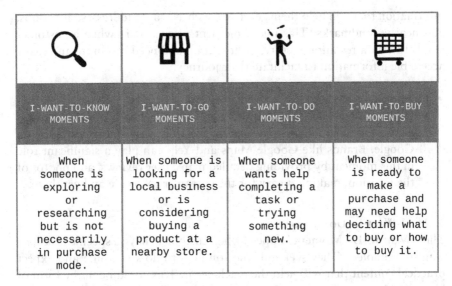

I-WANT-TO-KNOW MOMENTS	I-WANT-TO-GO MOMENTS	I-WANT-TO-DO MOMENTS	I-WANT-TO-BUY MOMENTS
When someone is exploring or researching but is not necessarily in purchase mode.	When someone is looking for a local business or is considering buying a product at a nearby store.	When someone wants help completing a task or trying something new.	When someone is ready to make a purchase and may need help deciding what to buy or how to buy it.

FIGURE 7.1 Four Micro-Moments.

moments, customers turn to their devices – often a smartphone – to act on a need: to learn something, do something, discover something, watch something, or buy something. By understanding these moments, product managers can better target and engage potential customers. Figure 7.1 depicts the four Micro-Moments defined by Google.

1. The I-Want-to-Know Moment
In the **I-Want-to-Know Moment**, customers are **seeking information** rather than making a purchase decision. They are doing research, learning about different products, or trying to gain insight into a specific topic. These customers aren't ready to buy yet – they want informative content like **blog posts, videos, articles,** and other materials that provide value and help them understand what they're interested in.

- **Example:**
  - A customer researching a new smartphone may search for "best features of Samsung Galaxy S25" to get detailed information on specs, comparisons, and reviews. Brands like **Samsung** or tech bloggers like **MKBHD** provide in-depth reviews and comparison videos, catering to this micro-moment by offering valuable and unbiased content.

2. The I-Want-to-Go Moment
During the **I-Want-to-Go Moment**, customers are interested in finding or travelling to a specific location. They are searching for **location-specific**

information that will help them get there, such as maps, addresses, directions, and nearby landmarks. This micro-moment often occurs when a customer wants to visit a restaurant, store, or attraction and needs accurate and easily accessible information to facilitate their journey.

- Example:
  - Imagine a traveller in Singapore who wants to find a popular hawker centre for lunch. They may search "best hawker centre near me" on **Google**. Brands like **Google Maps** and **Yelp** can play a significant role in this moment by providing detailed maps, user reviews, and photos of the location, making it easy for the customer to decide and get there.

3. The I-Want-to-Do Moment

The **I-Want-to-Do Moment** happens when customers have a specific **task** they want to complete. They seek guidance on how to do something and expect **practical content** that will help them achieve it. This could be in the form of **how-to videos, step-by-step guides, recipes,** or **DIY tutorials.** Customers in this moment are typically in problem-solving mode and want quick, helpful solutions.

- Example:
  - A person wanting to fix a leaky faucet may search for "how to fix a leaking faucet" on **YouTube**. Content from **Home Depot** provides easy-to-follow how-to videos that guide the customer step-by-step. By offering clear instructions, brands not only address the user's needs but also build credibility and trust.

4. The I-Want-to-Buy Moment

In the **I-Want-to-Buy Moment**, customers are ready to make a **purchase decision**. They want to know about the best deals, offers, coupons, and any details that will help them finalize their purchase. Brands need to be ready to provide options to **buy online quickly**, find in-store availability, or offer any other helpful information to convert their interest into a purchase.

- Example:
  - A customer is searching for "buy **Nike** running shoes on sale." **Nike** or online retail sites like **Amazon** and **ZALORA** can cater to this micro-moment by showing available deals, promotions, and easy purchase options. Providing customer reviews, free shipping, and a smooth checkout process enhances the experience and increases the chances of purchase.

7.2.1.1 The Importance of Micro-Moments in Product Strategy

Micro-moments are critical for product managers because they represent opportunities to engage customers in real time with exactly the information they need. By aligning content and experiences with each type of micro-moment, brands can improve **customer satisfaction**, build **brand loyalty**, and ultimately drive conversions.

Product managers need to understand these micro-moments and create targeted strategies that address the specific needs of users. For instance,

- **For I-Want-to-Go Moments:** Brands should ensure that their **location information** is accurate across all platforms, including **Google Maps**, their website, and social media. Utilizing local **SEO** strategies also helps to be visible in these moments.
- **For I-Want-to-Know Moments:** Companies can create **educational content** such as blog posts, FAQ pages, and video tutorials to provide the information that customers are looking for.
- **For I-Want-to-Do Moments:** Brands should produce **how-to content** – articles, guides, videos – that helps users accomplish their goals easily.
- **For I-Want-to-Buy Moments:** Companies need to optimize the buying experience by providing **purchase options, offers, and incentives** that encourage conversion, while also ensuring a smooth and hassle-free checkout process.

Table 7.1 shows strategies you can use to address micro-moments in your customer journey.

TABLE 7.1 Strategies to Address Micro-Moments in Customer Journey

Micro-Moment	Focus Area	Strategies
I-Want-to-Go Moment	Be found	Ensure accurate listings on **Google Maps**, provide up-to-date addresses, integrate maps on the website, leverage location-based **SEO**.
I-Want-to-Know Moment	Be informative	Create educational content like blog posts, articles, FAQs, videos, and reviews; build an easy-to-navigate knowledge base.
I-Want-to-Do Moment	Be helpful	Provide how-to guides, instructional videos, and tutorials; offer step-by-step blog posts or images that help customers accomplish tasks.
I-Want-to-Buy Moment	Be convincing	Showcase deals, coupons, and offers; provide detailed product information, customer reviews, and a seamless checkout experience.

By optimizing for these **micro-moments,** brands can ensure they are present when customers need them most, providing relevant, helpful, and timely content that drives action.

7.2.2 Customizing Digital Experience

To successfully create **customized digital experiences** for customers, a product manager must have a deep understanding of the customer journey. This journey includes every interaction a customer has with a brand – from first becoming aware of the product to becoming a loyal advocate. By leveraging models such as **McKinsey's Consumer Decision Journey** and **Customer Lifecycle Management (CLM)**, product managers can align their strategies to address customer needs at each stage and foster meaningful, long-lasting relationships.

Product managers need to understand that each stage of the customer journey presents unique opportunities to deliver value and personalize experiences. This requires analysing customer behaviour, identifying pain points, and using a data-driven approach to enhance engagement and satisfaction. The goal is to retain customers within the **Loyalty Loop** – ensuring that customers repeatedly choose the brand over others and even advocate for it to others.

This section will explore the different stages of **CLM** and link them to the **Consumer Decision Journey** model, providing product managers with a comprehensive framework to improve customer experiences, drive retention, and ultimately create brand advocates. It will also propose critical questions that product managers need to ask at each stage to ensure they are meeting customer expectations and retaining them within the loyalty loop.

7.2.2.1 The Consumer Decision Journey Model by McKinsey

The **Consumer Decision Journey** model by **McKinsey** as shown in Figure 7.2 describes the stages that customers pass through before, during, and after making a purchasing decision. It provides insights into how individuals interact with brands, and how businesses can build stronger relationships with customers by understanding their needs at every stage.

1. Trigger

The journey starts with a **trigger,** where a stimulus or an event causes a consumer to realize they have a problem or a need that requires a product or service to resolve. This trigger can be anything, such as an advertisement, a recommendation from a friend, or even recognizing a personal necessity.

- **Product Manager Focus:** Understand what triggers can lead potential customers to identify their needs and ensure that your brand is there when that happens.

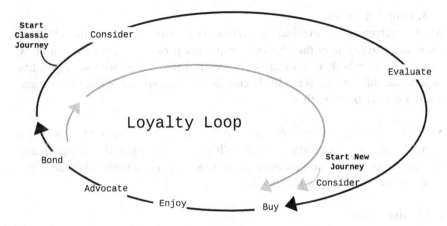

FIGURE 7.2 Consumer Decision Journey.

2. Initial Consideration Set
Once a need is identified, the consumer reflects on their **initial consideration set,** which consists of brands that they are immediately aware of, often due to previous brand marketing efforts or awareness campaigns. This initial set forms the shortlist of brands that the customer would consider to solve their problem.

- **Product Manager Focus**: Position your brand effectively so that it is a part of the customer's initial consideration set. Ensure that your brand message resonates and is memorable.

3. Evaluation
The **Evaluation** stage is where the consumer actively researches different brands and gathers information to decide which one best fits their needs. During this stage, customers read reviews, consult friends and family, and compare multiple sources to assess their options.

- **Product Manager Focus**: Provide comprehensive information about your product, including user reviews, detailed descriptions, and helpful content to make the evaluation process easier for customers.

4. Buying
After evaluating the options, the customer filters their choices and makes a final decision, initiating the **Buying** stage. The buying decision is influenced by factors such as product availability, pricing, convenience, and promotions.

- **Product Manager Focus**: Ensure a seamless purchasing experience by minimizing friction, simplifying checkout processes, and offering incentives that prompt consumers to finalize their purchase.

5. Ongoing Exposure

After purchasing the product or service, the customer enters the Ongoing Exposure stage, where they begin to enjoy the product, form their opinions, and evaluate whether it meets or exceeds their expectations. A positive experience during this stage leads customers to advocate for the brand and build a deeper bond with it.

- **Product Manager Focus**: Ensure that the product delivers on the promises made during earlier stages, and follow up with proactive support and engagement to enhance customer satisfaction, encourage advocacy, and strengthen the bond with the brand.

6. Loyalty Loop

Depending on the customer's satisfaction level, they may enter the **Loyalty Loop**, where they decide to continue purchasing from the brand, bypassing the evaluation stage in future decisions. A satisfied customer becomes a loyal advocate who not only makes repeat purchases but also promotes the brand to others.

- **Product Manager Focus**: Develop loyalty programs and foster strong relationships to keep customers within the loyalty loop, making them less likely to consider competitors.

7.2.2.2 *Infinity Loop and Loyalty Loop*

The **Infinity Loop** is a representation of a customer journey that never ends. Customers enter the loop when they become aware of a brand and continue in the loop with each interaction they have – be it purchasing, providing feedback, or sharing their experiences. The **Loyalty Loop** is a critical part of the **Infinity Loop**, representing loyal customers who choose to stay with the brand and repeatedly purchase from it, as shown in Figure 7.3.

The goal for product managers is to ensure that customers remain within the **Loyalty Loop** and do not get lost in the broader Infinity Loop where they might drift to competitors. Ensuring a seamless and delightful experience throughout the customer journey is key to achieving this.

7.2.2.3 *How Product Managers Utilize the Consumer Decision Journey Model*

Product managers can use McKinsey's Consumer Decision Journey to

1 **Identify Triggers**: Recognize and understand what drives customers to look for a solution.

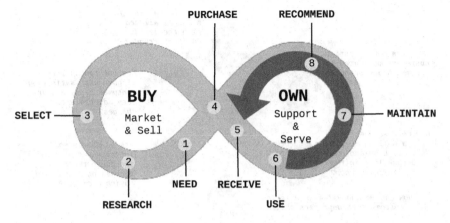

FIGURE 7.3   Infinity Loop and Loyalty Loop.

2 **Brand Awareness**: Ensure the brand is part of the **initial consideration set** by using targeted marketing and positioning strategies.
3 **Support Evaluation**: Provide detailed and transparent information that makes evaluating options easier for customers.
4 **Facilitate Buying**: Reduce friction during the purchasing process to make it easy for customers to choose the product.
5 **Post-Purchase Engagement**: Maintain engagement during the **ongoing exposure** phase to ensure satisfaction and reduce churn.
6 **Drive Loyalty**: Develop strategies to encourage repeat purchases and move customers into the **loyalty loop**.

7.2.2.4   Customer Lifecycle Management

CLM complements the Consumer Decision Journey by expanding it into six distinct stages: **Awareness, Acquisition, Conversion, Retention, Loyalty, and Advocacy**, as shown in Figure 7.4.

Each stage represents an opportunity to build a relationship with the customer, and product managers can align strategies to maximize value at each stage.

1. Awareness

The **Awareness** stage is when a potential customer first learns about your brand. Marketing campaigns, content, and promotions are aimed at building awareness and ensuring that your product becomes part of the customer's consideration set.

- **Key Questions for Product Managers:**

  - Are our marketing messages aligned with the latest consumer trends?

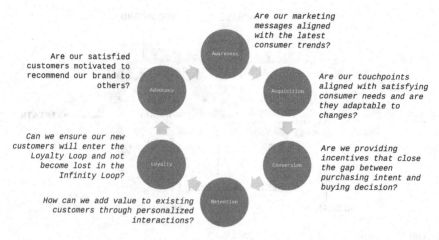

Are our marketing messages aligned with the latest consumer trends?

Are our satisfied customers motivated to recommend our brand to others?

Are our touchpoints aligned with satisfying consumer needs and are they adaptable to changes?

Can we ensure our new customers will enter the Loyalty Loop and not become lost in the Infinity Loop?

Are we providing incentives that close the gap between purchasing intent and buying decision?

How can we add value to existing customers through personalized interactions?

FIGURE 7.4 Customer Lifecycle Management.

- How well does our brand presence reflect the values and solutions that our target audience is seeking?

2. Acquisition

In the **Acquisition** stage, customers start engaging more with your brand. The goal is to draw customers to your product and convert their interest into meaningful engagement.

- **Key Questions for Product Managers**:
  - Are our touchpoints aligned with satisfying consumer needs, and are they adaptable to changes?
  - How can we leverage omnichannel strategies to ensure consistency across all touchpoints?

3. Conversion

The **Conversion** stage represents the moment when a lead becomes a customer by making their first purchase. It's about convincing the customer that the brand's value outweighs the competition.

- **Key Questions for Product Managers**:
  - Are we providing incentives that close the gap between purchasing intent and buying decision?
  - Are customers sharing their reasons for purchase? Are early impressions positive, neutral, or negative?

4. Retention

The **Retention** stage focuses on keeping existing customers engaged. A high level of retention is often an indicator of a successful product that meets customer expectations.

- **Key Questions for Product Managers:**

  - How can we add value to existing customers through personalized interactions?
  - Are we effectively addressing customer concerns to minimize churn?

5. Loyalty

In the **Loyalty** stage, customers repeatedly purchase from the brand, enter the **Loyalty Loop**, and become regular patrons. Brands must keep customers satisfied and engaged for them to remain loyal.

- **Key Questions for Product Managers:**

  - Can we ensure our new customers will enter the **Loyalty Loop** and not become lost in the **Infinity Loop**?
  - Are our customers invested enough to share suggestions for short-term extensions or longer-term innovations?

6. Advocacy

The final stage, **Advocacy**, is where loyal customers become active promoters of the brand. They share their positive experiences with others, thereby generating organic growth.

- **Key Questions for Product Managers:**

  - Are our satisfied customers motivated to recommend our brand to others?
  - How can we reward our advocates and leverage their voice for expanding brand awareness?

7.2.2.5 *Summary: Creating Customized Digital Experiences*

By understanding the **Consumer Decision Journey**, the **Infinity Loop**, and **CLM**, product managers can craft **customized digital experiences** that cater to each customer's unique journey.

- **Awareness to Advocacy:** Product managers need to focus on seamless transitions between stages, using data-driven insights to personalize each customer's experience. Each stage of the journey presents opportunities

to collect feedback, understand customer needs, and make continuous improvements.
- **Retention within the Loyalty Loop:** The ultimate goal for product managers is to retain customers within the **Loyalty Loop** by continuously delivering value. This involves creating personalized experiences, maintaining high-quality customer service, and actively listening to customer feedback.

By asking the right questions at each stage, product managers can anticipate customer needs, address pain points, and build **long-lasting relationships** that result in a growing base of loyal customers who actively advocate for the brand.

7.2.3   Customer Friction

Successful customer engagement relies on minimizing friction across various touchpoints in the customer journey. The following areas are common sources of friction that can impact engagement and prevent customers from moving through the stages of Awareness, Acquisition, Conversion, Retention, Loyalty, and Advocacy. Figure 7.5 depicts the five common sources of customer friction.

1. Brand Friction

Brand friction occurs when there is a lack of alignment between the brand's identity, values, and customer expectations. It may arise due to inconsistent messaging, unmet expectations, or a failure to establish trust with the target audience.

- **Inconsistency in Messaging:** When a brand conveys different messages across channels, customers may find it difficult to understand the brand's value proposition. For example, if a company claims to be eco-friendly but

Brand	Product	Price	Design	User Experience
Lack of alignment between the brand's identity, values, and customer expectations.	Offering does not meet customer expectations in terms of quality or reliability.	Customers perceive the price of a product or service as not providing adequate value.	Issues with Visual and functional aspects of product, which impact customer's experience	Negative ease of use and experience customers have when interacting with a product

FIGURE 7.5   Common Sources of Customer Friction.

is involved in unethical production practices, it leads to mistrust and a lack of engagement.

- **Lack of Trust and Credibility**: Customers need to feel that they can trust a brand to deliver on its promises. Negative reviews, poor customer service, and a lack of transparency can all contribute to brand friction and ultimately lead to disengagement.
- **Solution**: Product managers should ensure consistent branding and messaging across all channels and touchpoints, build transparency, and ensure all claims are substantiated by actions that build credibility.

Examples:

- **Netflix**: Netflix has faced brand friction in the past due to inconsistencies in its messaging related to subscription price increases. When **Netflix** attempted to separate its DVD rental service from its streaming platform and introduced a price hike, customers experienced confusion and backlash. This misstep showed the importance of consistent communication with customers regarding changes that affect them.
- **Apple**: **Apple** effectively addresses brand friction by maintaining consistent and well-aligned messaging throughout its product lifecycle. The brand's commitment to high-quality products, customer-centric design, and innovation is consistently communicated across its marketing campaigns, stores, and website, making it a well-trusted and admired brand globally.

2. Product/Service Friction
Friction related to the **product or service** arises when the offering does not meet customer expectations in terms of quality, reliability, or usefulness.

- **Product Quality Issues**: If the product fails to meet quality expectations, customers may feel dissatisfied and ultimately disengage from the brand. A product that frequently breaks down or falls short of the customer's needs will generate frustration and negative sentiment.
- **Poor Service Reliability**: Services that are unreliable or inconsistent also create friction, especially when customers depend on them. For example, unreliable delivery times or frequent outages in a digital service can lead to frustration.
- **Solution**: Product managers should focus on delivering consistent, high-quality products and services that meet customer expectations. Quality control, ongoing product improvements, and customer feedback loops should be built into the product development process.

Examples:

- **JetBlue:** JetBlue is known for minimizing product/service friction by providing quality services, such as ample legroom, free in-flight Wi-Fi, and free snacks, that align with customer expectations. By delivering on these service promises, **JetBlue** reduces customer frustration and creates a more enjoyable flying experience.
- **Samsung:** Samsung has faced product friction with incidents like the **Galaxy Note 7** battery explosions, which caused safety concerns and widespread recall. This incident highlighted the importance of rigorous product quality testing and delivering a reliable product to minimize product friction and retain customer trust.

3. Price Friction
Price friction occurs when customers perceive the price of a product or service as not providing adequate value compared to its cost. It can lead to hesitation or disengagement during the decision-making process.

- **Lack of Perceived Value:** If customers feel that the price is not justified by the value they will receive, they may look for cheaper alternatives. High prices that don't align with the perceived value can create a significant barrier to engagement.
- **Hidden Costs:** Unexpected fees or costs that are not clearly communicated also contribute to price friction. When customers encounter hidden charges at checkout, they may abandon their purchase altogether.
- **Solution:** Product managers can reduce price friction by offering clear and transparent pricing structures, ensuring alignment between pricing and value, and providing different pricing options or bundles that cater to diverse customer needs. Emphasizing the benefits and value that justify the price will help overcome concerns.

Examples:

- **IKEA:** IKEA has managed price friction effectively by offering affordable products that come with value. By emphasizing the "do-it-yourself" aspect, where customers assemble their own furniture, **IKEA** manages to keep prices competitive while maintaining product quality. This value-for-money proposition attracts customers despite the additional effort of assembly.
- **Singapore Airlines (SIA):** SIA operates in the premium segment of the airline industry, where pricing is higher compared to low-cost carriers. **SIA** manages price friction by emphasizing the value provided, including exceptional in-flight service, comfortable seats, and high-quality meals,

which justifies the higher ticket prices and creates a superior customer experience.

4. Design Friction

Design friction is caused by issues related to the visual and functional aspects of a product, which impact a customer's experience when interacting with it.

- **Complexity and Clutter**: When a product's design is overly complex, cluttered, or unintuitive, customers may struggle to use it effectively. A poorly designed interface, for example, can hinder users from easily finding what they need.
- **Poor Visual Appeal**: A lack of visual appeal in the design may make the product less engaging. A product that does not provide a pleasant aesthetic experience is less likely to resonate with customers and attract attention.
- **Solution**: Product managers can mitigate design friction by adopting a customer-centric design approach that prioritizes simplicity, clarity, and visual appeal. **A/B** testing can be used to identify design elements that resonate most with customers.

Examples:

- **Disney Theme Parks**: Disney's **My Disney Experience** and **Magic Bands** have been successful in reducing design friction by simplifying the theme park experience. Visitors can use **Magic Bands** to enter the park, reserve rides, and make payments – everything is accessible with a simple wristband. This cohesive design reduces friction, making the experience more enjoyable and seamless for customers.
- **TWG Tea**: TWG, a luxury tea brand, emphasizes an elegant and luxurious design both online and in-store. The physical stores are designed with a lavish, sophisticated aesthetic, which resonates with the brand's identity. However, for first-time buyers, navigating **TWG's** product range online can be confusing due to an overwhelming number of tea varieties. This design friction could be addressed by introducing a "Tea Finder" tool to guide new customers to the most suitable options.

5. User Experience (UX) Friction

UX friction relates to the overall ease of use and experience customers have when interacting with a product or service. Poor UX is a major source of disengagement.

- **Navigation Issues**: Difficulty navigating a website, app, or service can create a negative UX. If users cannot easily find what they are looking for, they are more likely to abandon the interaction.

- **Slow Performance and Responsiveness:** Poor responsiveness, long loading times, or lag in a digital interface can lead to significant frustration. In today's fast-paced digital environment, customers expect instant responses, and delays create disengagement.
- **Limited Flexibility:** A product or service that lacks flexibility can hinder the customer experience. For example, customers expect to be able to modify orders, easily cancel services, or reverse actions. The inability to do so can negatively impact engagement.
- **Solution:** Product managers should aim to create an intuitive and user-friendly experience by reducing the number of steps required to complete tasks, optimizing site speed, and providing clear pathways for users to accomplish their goals. Regular usability testing should be conducted to identify areas of improvement.

Examples:

- **Netflix:** Netflix reduces UX friction through a highly personalized recommendation engine, which suggests content based on a user's previous viewing habits. This makes it easy for users to find and engage with content without navigating a cluttered interface.
- **IKEA:** IKEA's online platform initially faced UX friction issues, particularly around product discovery and ease of navigation. However, IKEA has made strides in improving the UX by offering a feature where users can visualize how furniture will look in their homes using augmented reality. This helps customers make more informed decisions and enhances the overall UX.
- **SIA:** SIA has implemented a seamless UX across its website and mobile apps, allowing customers to easily book flights, select seats, and manage bookings. The app also provides flight updates and boarding information, making the journey as smooth as possible. The consistency in providing a high-quality UX is one reason why SIA remains a preferred airline for many travellers.

7.2.3.1 How Brands Addressed Friction Through Innovative Solutions

- **Disney Theme Parks: Disney's My Disney Experience** app and **Magic Bands** are great examples of reducing multiple types of friction:
  - **Brand Consistency:** The **Disney** brand is about magical experiences, and the app and **Magic Bands** extend that magic by making the park experience frictionless.
  - **Product Reliability:** Visitors can easily plan their park visits, book attractions, and make payments, reducing stress and ensuring reliability.

- **Design and UX:** The **Magic Band**'s design is intuitive, and the app provides a seamless way to experience all that the park has to offer.
- **Apple:** Apple's attention to UX and design consistency has allowed the company to create a frictionless journey for its users:
  - **Brand Consistency:** Apple's brand identity focuses on simplicity and ease of use, reflected in its products' design.
  - **Product Quality:** Each **Apple** product meets the highest standards of quality, reducing friction at the product level.
  - **UX:** From intuitive UI to seamless integration between devices, **Apple** ensures a delightful experience for its users.
- **Netflix:** Netflix's recommendation engine and easy-to-use interface are designed to eliminate **UX friction**:
  - **Brand Consistency:** Netflix's brand is centred around making entertainment easily accessible, which is delivered through its personalized recommendations.
  - **UX:** With an intuitive layout and a personalized homepage, **Netflix** makes it effortless for users to find something to watch without endless scrolling.

7.2.3.2 Summary: Customer Friction

Reducing customer friction across the brand, product/service, price, design, and UX is critical to improving customer engagement and retaining them within the **Loyalty Loop**. By learning from real-world examples like **Disney's Magic Bands, Netflix, JetBlue, IKEA, SIA, TWG, Samsung,** and **Apple,** product managers can better understand the pitfalls of customer friction and how to address them effectively. Minimizing **brand, product/service, price, design,** and **UX** friction leads to better engagement, higher retention, and ultimately, long-term customer loyalty. It is through the continuous elimination of friction that brands create memorable and seamless experiences that keep customers coming back and advocating for the brand.

7.2.4 Empowering Employees

The relationship between employee experience and customer experience is deeply interconnected, forming a **symbiotic relationship** that is vital for creating a winning customer experience. When companies empower and enable their employees, they foster an environment where empathy and genuine relationships with customers thrive – ensuring that customers keep coming back.

Empowered employees play a crucial role in shaping customer experiences by putting in the extra effort to recall customers' preferences, listen intently to complex requests, and respond with empathy. These small yet meaningful actions contribute significantly to enhancing customer satisfaction and building strong relationships.

Building a **positive company culture** and embodying company values are critical elements that influence the overall brand experience. Organizations that foster a culture of growth and development are more likely to have engaged and committed employees. Engaged employees, in turn, are motivated to deliver superior customer experiences consistently.

To achieve this, it is essential that employees are not only trained and rewarded for their contributions but also given a **conducive work environment** where they can grow, feel valued, and develop a sense of belonging within the organization. This empowerment leads to greater employee satisfaction, which is reflected in how they treat and engage with customers.

The following progression illustrates how **employee empowerment** drives exceptional customer experiences, as shown in Figure 7.6:

1 **Employee Empowerment and Training**: Employees are empowered by providing them with the necessary skills, resources, and authority to make decisions that benefit customers.

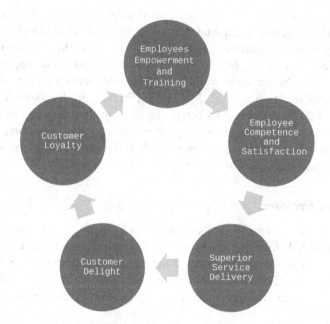

FIGURE 7.6 Empowering Employees.

2 **Employee Competence and Satisfaction**: When employees feel confident in their abilities and appreciated by their company, they are more satisfied and engaged in their roles.
3 **Superior Service Delivery**: Empowered and competent employees are more likely to deliver outstanding service, as they can address customer needs efficiently and with genuine care.
4 **Customer Delight**: When service exceeds customer expectations, it leads to customer delight, where customers feel valued and connected to the brand.
5 **Customer Loyalty**: Customer delight fosters loyalty, where satisfied customers become loyal advocates who repeatedly choose the brand and encourage others to do the same.

7.2.4.1 Summary: Employee Empowerment

In summary, **employee empowerment** is the foundation upon which exceptional customer experiences are built. Product managers and company leaders must ensure that employees are supported, trained, and empowered, as the quality of customer interactions directly depends on the experiences and satisfaction of the employees creating those interactions.

7.2.5 Case Study: United Breaks Guitars

Background:
The "**United Breaks Guitars**" incident is a powerful example of the impact that customer-generated content can have on a brand, especially in the age of social media. In 2008, Canadian musician Dave Carroll experienced a frustrating situation while flying with **United Airlines**. During a layover, Carroll and his band members witnessed **United's** baggage handlers carelessly handling their instruments, resulting in the damage of Carroll's valuable Taylor guitar, worth approximately $3,500. Despite multiple attempts to seek compensation from United Airlines over the course of a year, his requests were continuously denied and dismissed.

Frustrated by the lack of response, Carroll turned to an unconventional approach: he created a song called "**United Breaks Guitars**" and filmed a music video detailing his experience. The video, posted on **YouTube** on 6 July 2009, went viral almost immediately. Carroll's friends shared it on **Twitter** (now **X**) and other social media platforms, and it was picked up by bloggers and social news sites. Before long, mainstream media outlets caught on, amplifying the reach of the video. By the end of July, the video had been viewed 4.6 million times, and millions more saw it through external references and media coverage.

The impact on **United Airlines** was significant. Their brand reputation suffered, their customer service practices were questioned, and the video became a textbook example of what could go wrong when a company fails to handle customer complaints effectively. The video now has over 20 million views, and it has become a cautionary tale for businesses across industries about the importance of customer experience and the power of social media.

Lessons Learned:
The "United Breaks Guitars" incident provides valuable insights into the relationship between customer experience, social media, and brand reputation. Companies must be prepared for the potential backlash that can result from poor customer service, and they need to be agile in responding to customer complaints – especially when those complaints go public.

Here are some key lessons and discussion points from the case:

1 **Customer-Generated Communications Can Have a Huge Impact:**
The video demonstrated the incredible power of social media and customer-generated content. When Carroll felt unheard, he found a platform that allowed his message to reach millions of people. The humorous and catchy nature of the song made it relatable, and it struck a chord with others who had experienced similar frustrations with large corporations. **United Airlines** found itself facing a **PR** disaster, with damage control being extremely challenging given the viral spread of the video.

2 **Why Did Carroll's Video Garner So Much Attention?**
The video's success can be attributed to several factors:

- **Relatable Content:** Carroll's experience resonated with many viewers who had also faced poor customer service. The frustration of dealing with large, impersonal corporations is a feeling many can relate to.
- **Humour and Creativity:** Carroll used humour and creativity to convey his message, making the video entertaining rather than a standard complaint. This approach increased its shareability and audience appeal.
- **Timing and Social Media Amplification:** In 2009, social media platforms like **YouTube, Facebook,** and **Twitter** were growing rapidly, and content that was entertaining and relatable was often widely shared. Carroll's video was picked up by social media influencers and traditional news outlets, accelerating its reach.

3 **What Options Did United Have Once the Videos Had Been Launched?**
United had several options in responding to the video:

- **Ignore the Video: United** could have chosen to ignore the video, hoping it would eventually fade away. However, this approach would risk further damaging the brand and giving the impression that the company didn't care about its customers.

- **Issue an Apology and Compensate Carroll:** United could have publicly apologized to Carroll and offered compensation for the damage. This response would have been a step towards acknowledging their mistake and taking responsibility, potentially mitigating some of the damage.
- **Use the Opportunity for Improvement:** United could have used the incident as an opportunity to overhaul its customer service practices and demonstrate a commitment to change. They could have implemented new baggage-handling policies and communicated these improvements publicly to rebuild trust.

4 **How Well Did United Handle the Situation?**
United's initial response was inadequate. The airline did not take Carroll's complaint seriously, and by the time they did attempt to respond, the damage had already been done. United eventually offered compensation and issued a public statement, but it was perceived as too little, too late. The lack of a proactive approach and delayed response resulted in a significant blow to their reputation.

5 **Could United Have Anticipated This Situation?**
Yes, United could have anticipated the potential for a backlash. In an era when social media platforms were on the rise, customer complaints could easily gain widespread attention. A proactive approach – addressing the complaint when it was first raised, offering a sincere apology, and providing compensation – could have minimized the damage. Companies should always assume that dissatisfied customers have the ability to reach a wide audience and should handle complaints accordingly.

6 **Suggestions for Product Support Services to Provide Great Customer Service:**

- **Empathy and Prompt Response:** Customers want to feel heard and valued. Responding to complaints quickly and empathetically can prevent situations from escalating. United could have avoided the negative publicity by addressing Carroll's complaint in a timely and respectful manner.
- **Empower Employees:** Empowering frontline employees to resolve customer complaints can prevent issues from being escalated unnecessarily. Employees should have the authority to make decisions that benefit the customer, such as offering compensation for damaged items.
- **Training and Customer-Centric Culture:** Building a customer-centric culture where employees understand the importance of delivering great service is key. Employees should be trained to handle difficult situations effectively and to treat every customer interaction as an opportunity to build brand loyalty.

- **Monitoring Social Media:** Companies should actively monitor social media to identify and address negative sentiment before it goes viral. Engaging with customers online and addressing their concerns publicly can show that the company is listening and willing to improve.

7.2.5.1 Summary: United Breaks Guitars

The **United Breaks Guitars** case highlights the importance of proactive customer service and the potential consequences of ignoring customer complaints. In today's digital age, customers have the power to influence a brand's reputation through social media, and companies must be prepared to respond quickly and effectively to customer issues. By empowering employees, adopting a customer-first mindset, and being responsive to feedback, businesses can avoid the pitfalls that **United Airlines** experienced and instead create positive experiences that foster customer loyalty and advocacy.

7.2.6 Summary of Optimizing Customer Service

Optimizing customer service is about enhancing customer experiences through personalized digital journeys while empowering employees to deliver exceptional service. Additionally, creating an empowered, well-trained, and satisfied workforce is key to delivering these superior customer experiences.

The **United Breaks Guitars** case study serves as a reminder of how crucial it is to respond to customer complaints with empathy, transparency, and prompt action. Empowered employees play an essential role in delivering great service by acting as the front line in building and sustaining strong customer relationships. When employees feel valued and empowered, they are more likely to provide exceptional service, resulting in delighted customers who advocate for the brand.

Ultimately, building a seamless and empowering customer service strategy allows brands to minimize customer friction, foster deeper relationships, and keep customers within the **Loyalty Loop**. By addressing customer needs proactively and treating every interaction as an opportunity for engagement, brands can create a lasting impact that drives customer satisfaction, loyalty, and advocacy – ensuring sustained growth and long-term success.

7.3 Conclusion

In this chapter, we focused on how optimizing the **digital experience** and empowering employees are key to delivering superior customer service and driving business success. By identifying **micro-moments** in the customer journey and delivering personalized, relevant experiences at each stage, companies can enhance customer satisfaction and retention. Customizing digital interactions to meet the unique needs of users creates a frictionless experience that keeps customers engaged and loyal.

We also explored the importance of reducing **customer friction** by identifying pain points and streamlining processes to eliminate obstacles in the customer journey. In parallel, empowering employees plays a crucial role in ensuring that these optimized experiences are consistently delivered. By fostering a culture of empowerment, companies enable their teams to take ownership of customer interactions, resolve issues effectively, and proactively deliver value.

In conclusion, combining an optimized digital experience with a well-trained, empowered workforce creates a winning formula for long-term customer success and business growth.

8

SUPPORTING AND MAINTAINING PRODUCTS

8.1 Introduction

Providing excellent product support is vital to ensuring great customer experiences and the long-term success of a product. Chapter 8 explores two critical aspects of product support: **Technical Support** and **Product Maintenance**. The chapter highlights the importance of continuous support and improvements in creating a positive customer journey and ensuring optimal product performance. Readers will learn how well-structured technical support teams and proactive maintenance contribute to customer satisfaction, loyalty, and ultimately, the success of a product.

8.2 Technical Support

Imagine that you've built your new product and are preparing to launch it to the market. You know that you need a good support team, but what kind of support and how much of it will you need? More importantly, how could you ensure the support team is ready for your product to hit the market?

Technical Support is a crucial component of product support, addressing customers' technical issues and ensuring they can use the product effectively. To provide efficient technical support, it's important to understand the different levels of support and equip the support team to manage customer issues appropriately.

DOI: 10.1201/9781003614180-8

8.2.1   The Five Levels of Technical Support

Organizations use the **five levels of support** approach to provide structured and efficient product support, ensuring that customer issues are resolved in a timely manner while optimizing resource allocation. By categorizing support into different levels, companies can address simple, repetitive issues through pre-support and self-service, reducing the workload for support teams and empowering customers to find their own solutions. More complex issues are then escalated to the appropriate support level, ensuring that specialized expertise is applied where needed. This approach helps manage costs, improves response times, and ensures that customers receive the most effective support based on their specific needs, ultimately leading to a positive customer experience.

A typical support structure is represented by Figure 8.1.

1 **Proactive Assistance:**

- **Proactive Assistance** involves anticipating and addressing common customer issues before they even occur. It includes creating resources like FAQ sections, product guides, and community forums, allowing customers to find answers independently.
- **Example: Apple**'s support website offers a well-organized repository of help articles, tutorials, and troubleshooting resources, enabling users to resolve common issues independently before seeking formal support.

2 **Self-Help Resources:**

- **Self-Help Resources** includes providing customers with the resources they need to solve problems themselves. This can include knowledge

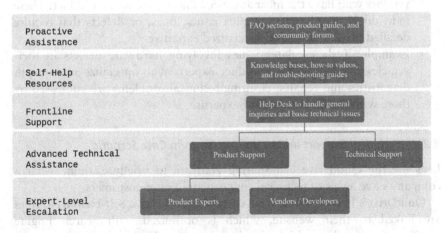

FIGURE 8.1   Five-Level Support Structure.

bases, how-to videos, and troubleshooting guides, interactive chatbots on a website, which empower customers and reduce the load on support teams.

- **Example:** Spotify's Help Centre allows users to search for answers to their questions, find account help, and troubleshoot issues without directly contacting support.

3 **Frontline Support (Help Desk):**

- The **Frontline Support**, often referred to as the **Help Desk**, handles general enquiries and basic technical issues. They provide solutions to common problems and escalate more complex issues to higher support levels if needed.
- **Example: Amazon's** Customer Service Team answers general enquiries about deliveries, returns, and product issues via chat, phone, or email.

4 **Advanced Technical Assistance (Product Support and Technical Support Staff):**

- **Advanced Technical Assistance** consists of product and technical support specialists who provide more in-depth assistance for issues that cannot be resolved by the help desk. They have a deeper understanding of the product and handle more complex problems, often involving troubleshooting and diagnostics.
- **Microsoft** offers a dedicated support team for their enterprise customers, handling advanced troubleshooting and technical diagnostics for issues like software compatibility or configuration.

5 **Expert-Level Escalation (Product Experts/Vendors/Developers):**

- **Expert-Level Escalation** involves product experts, developers, or vendors who have the most advanced knowledge of the product. These individuals may handle complex issues, bugs, or defects that require detailed investigation and specialized expertise.
- **Example: Tesla** escalates issues involving hardware defects in their vehicles to engineers or product experts who specialize in in-depth diagnostics and repairs, ensuring technical problems are addressed by those with the highest level of expertise.

8.2.2 *Technical Support in Car-Sharing Platform Case Scenario*

Let's use the **QuikDrive** Car-Sharing Platform to briefly examine what a company's five levels of technical support could offer customers.

QuikDrive's **Level 1 Proactive Assistance** and **Level 2 Self-Help Resources** are linked to their website, which is optimized with **Search Engine Optimization** to allow a higher ranking in a **Google** search when customers look for car-sharing services. The website's FAQ section lists answers to the top questions asked by **QuikDrive** customers. Additionally, the website provides key information and general user guidelines to pre-empt enquiries about pricing, the reservation process, and the rewards system by car-sharing and car-hiring customers.

QuikDrive's Level 3 Frontline Support comprises the **Help Desk** technicians. They are responsible for answering straightforward questions from customers. For example, how to install the **QuikDrive** mobile app, change passwords, make payment, determine a car's location, and so forth. During their interactions with customers, the **Help Desk** technicians are trained to ask a few basic questions that will determine if customers require assistance from the next line of support.

QuikDrive's Level 4 Advanced Technical Assistance typically handles more complex customer problems. These technicians are equipped with a more in-depth product knowledge to help solve technical glitches such as if the **QuikDrive** app crashes, unavailability of core services like reservations, server downtime, and problems with the digital key to unlock cars. Any issues that these technicians cannot resolve, will be taken up by the next line of support.

QuikDrive's Level 5 Expert-Level Escalation consists of product experts, such as designated superusers or individuals from **QuikDrive's** R&D department. If a customer's problem is escalated to this level, it may mean custom work is required to solve the issue, which could be costly to the company. Examples include severe security problems on the **QuikDrive** app such as leakages of customer account information, credit card details, or vehicle information.

8.2.3 *Methods of Providing Technical Support*

When customers make purchases, they often believe they're buying more than just a product. They have expectations about the level of "after-sales-support" associated with the product. This technical support could simply be the replacement of a faulty item, or a more complex set of arrangements that meet customer needs over the product's entire lifecycle.

Before a product is launched, the product manager must decide the type of technical support to be associated with the product. Different forms of support can be offered, based on the type of product and the customer usage.

The following lists several methods that technical support teams can use to assist customers:

- **Ticketing System**: Allows customers to create support requests and track their status, ensuring that issues are resolved in a systematic way.

- **Phone:** Provides immediate assistance for more urgent or complex issues where real-time communication is necessary.
- **Social Media:** Enables customers to seek help through social platforms, which are increasingly used as a customer service channel.
- **Email:** Allows customers to describe their issues in detail and receive personalized responses at their convenience.
- **Real-time Chat:** Offers immediate support via chatbots or live agents, providing an effective way to handle enquiries quickly.

8.2.4 Preparing the Product Support Team

Product managers need to take several important steps to prepare their product support teams:

- **Hire and Train Necessary Support Personnel:** Ensure that all team members have the right skills and product knowledge to handle customer enquiries effectively.
- **Create Frequently Asked Questions (FAQs):** Compile a list of common questions and issues, along with detailed answers, to help both the support team and customers resolve problems quickly.
- **Set Up Channels to Stay in Touch with Customers:** Use newsletters, email campaigns, and social media to stay connected with customers, provide updates, and gather feedback.
- **Prepare Troubleshooting Guides, Installation Guides, and Service Manuals:** Develop comprehensive documentation that support personnel and customers can use to troubleshoot and resolve issues.

8.2.5 Differentiating Customer Service and Technical Support

The product support team ensures that customers obtain the most value from the product they purchased. This team is usually divided into two distinct functions: **Customer Service** and **Technical Support**. **Customer Service** focuses on the overall customer experience, with the goals of keeping the customer satisfied, and keeping them as a customer over time.

Technical Support, on the other hand, has the goal of resolving technical issues as quickly, efficiently, and cost-effectively as possible.

While **Customer Service** and **Technical Support** are both essential to the overall support experience, they have different sets of goals:

- **Customer Service Goals:** Focuses on general customer enquiries, providing a positive experience, handling complaints, and ensuring overall satisfaction. The goal is to build and maintain strong relationships with customers.

- **Technical Support Goals:** Focuses specifically on resolving technical issues related to the product, helping customers with installation, usage, troubleshooting, and product defects. The goal is to ensure that customers can effectively use the product without technical barriers.

8.2.6   *Service and Support Feedback Loop*

A **Service and Support Feedback Loop** is used by product support teams to gather insights from customer interactions and use them to improve the product and support experience. The feedback loop involves four process steps:

1 **Gather Customer Feedback and Requests Information:**

- The first step is to collect feedback from customers, including pain points, feature requests, and areas for improvement. This information can be gathered through support tickets, surveys, and direct interactions.

2 **Share Feedback with Internal Team:**

- Once customer feedback is collected, it must be communicated with the product and development teams. This ensures that the internal teams understand the needs and issues faced by customers and can prioritize them accordingly.

3 **Create Action Plan Based on Feedback:**

- Develop an action plan to address the issues and opportunities highlighted by customer feedback. This may involve fixing bugs, adding new features, or improving existing ones to enhance the overall customer experience.

4 **Internal Team Reports on Outcomes:**

- Finally, the internal team must report on the outcomes of the action plan, including updates, improvements, and changes made based on customer feedback. Communicating these outcomes to customers shows that their feedback is valued and leads to continuous improvements.

8.2.7   *Ways to Improve Service and Support*

To deliver the best possible service and support, companies should consider the following approaches:

1 **Coordinated Case Management:** Ensure that customer enquiries are tracked and managed systematically, allowing for seamless handoffs between support levels if required.

2 **Omnichannel Options:** Provide multiple ways for customers to contact support (phone, email, social media, chat), allowing them to choose the most convenient channel.

3 **Self-Support Opportunities:** Offer self-service options like knowledge bases, FAQs, and how-to guides to empower customers to solve issues on their own.

4 **Loyalty Rewards:** Reward loyal customers with exclusive support benefits, such as faster response times or dedicated support personnel.

5 **24/7 Options:** Provide round-the-clock support for customers, especially for global products with users in different time zones.

6 **Personalization:** Personalize interactions by understanding customer history and preferences, ensuring that support is tailored to individual needs and that customers feel valued.

By building a comprehensive technical support strategy and ensuring continuous product maintenance, product managers can enhance customer satisfaction and drive the overall success of the product.

8.2.8 Summary: Technical Support

The **Technical Support** section explored the structure and strategies necessary for providing effective and efficient support for technical issues related to a product. We discussed the five levels of support – **Proactive Assistance, Self-Help Resources, Frontline Support, Advanced Technical Assistance, and Expert-Level Escalation** – each playing a vital role in addressing customer issues and ensuring a positive product experience. These levels help streamline the resolution process, allocate resources effectively, and enable specialized assistance when required.

We also covered various **methods of providing technical support,** such as ticketing systems, phone, social media, email, and real-time chat. These multiple channels ensure that customers can access support in a manner that is most convenient to them. Preparing a technical support team involves hiring and training the right personnel, creating detailed FAQs, maintaining customer contact channels, and developing troubleshooting guides – all of which empower the team to provide excellent support.

The section also differentiated **Customer Service** from **Technical Support,** highlighting their unique goals and responsibilities. Product Support, which consists of **Customer Service** and **Technical Support,** ensures that customers obtain the most value from the product they purchased. While customer service aims to maintain positive relationships, technical support focuses on resolving specific product-related issues. Specifically, the **Technical Support** which follows a product launch is essential in resolving technical issues quickly, efficiently, and cost-effectively across five levels through which problems are escalated.

Lastly, we introduced the **Service and Support Feedback Loop,** which involves gathering customer feedback, sharing it with the internal team, creating action plans, and reporting outcomes. This continuous loop is essential for improving the product and providing better customer experiences. To further enhance service and support, companies can adopt strategies such as coordinated case management, omnichannel options, self-support opportunities, loyalty rewards, 24/7 support, and personalization – all aimed at improving customer satisfaction and product performance.

As a product manager, you must consider the operational impact a new product launch will have on your organization. If you don't correctly forecast how the launch will affect your day-to-day operations, you could find yourself in a situation where you're unable to support your customers for days or even weeks. This may result in your most loyal customers vocalizing their disappointment and annoyance. Prevent this from derailing your product by ensuring that all five levels of technical support are in place before your product hits the market.

8.3 Product Maintenance

8.3.1 Introduction to Product Maintenance

Product Maintenance refers to the ongoing process of changing, modifying, and updating a product or service to keep it relevant to the evolving market, customer needs, and technology landscape. Product maintenance ensures that the product continues to provide value, adapts to technological advancements, and remains competitive. It includes both incremental updates and larger modifications that address product issues, add new features, and adapt to changes in customer requirements. Effective product maintenance is crucial for product longevity and customer satisfaction.

8.3.2 Key Reasons for Product Maintenance

Product maintenance is essential for ensuring that a product remains valuable and competitive throughout its lifecycle. There are four primary reasons for maintaining a product: **correcting faults, adapting to operating environment changes, future-proofing,** and **improving performance.** Figure 8.2 shows

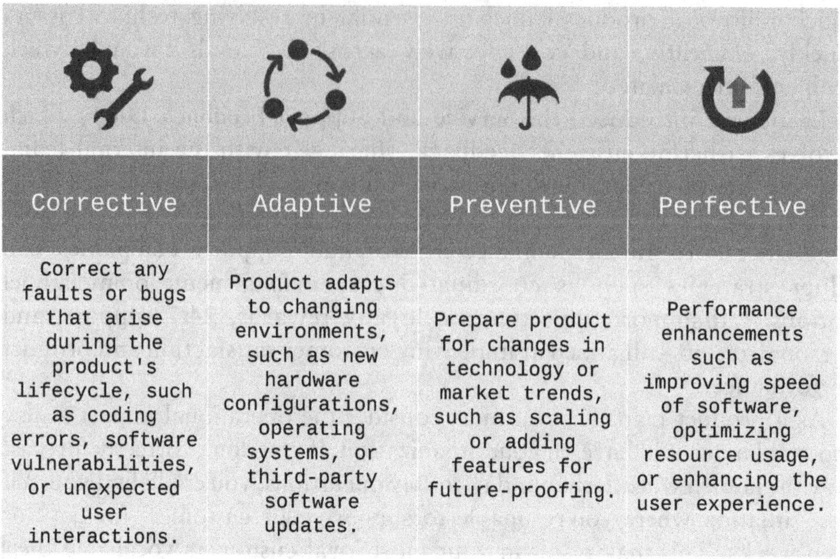

Corrective	Adaptive	Preventive	Perfective
Correct any faults or bugs that arise during the product's lifecycle, such as coding errors, software vulnerabilities, or unexpected user interactions.	Product adapts to changing environments, such as new hardware configurations, operating systems, or third-party software updates.	Prepare product for changes in technology or market trends, such as scaling or adding features for future-proofing.	Performance enhancements such as improving speed of software, optimizing resource usage, or enhancing the user experience.

FIGURE 8.2   Four Reasons for Product Maintenance.

the four reasons for product maintenance underscore the importance of continuous product maintenance in delivering long-term success.

1 **Correct Faults:**

- One of the primary reasons for product maintenance is to correct any faults or bugs that arise during the product's lifecycle. Faults can be a result of coding errors, software vulnerabilities, or unexpected user interactions that were not accounted for during development.
- **Example: Microsoft Windows** frequently releases updates to address security vulnerabilities, improve stability, and resolve bugs reported by users. These updates ensure that users have a smooth and secure experience, thereby maintaining customer satisfaction and trust.

2 **Adapt to Operating Environment Changes:**

- As technology evolves, products must adapt to changing environments. This includes adapting to new hardware configurations, operating systems, or third-party software updates. Maintenance ensures that a product is compatible with the latest technologies and remains functional across different platforms.
- **Example: Netflix** constantly updates its app to adapt to new smart TV models, operating system updates like iOS and Android, and to work seamlessly across different devices and platforms. This allows **Netflix** to

deliver a consistent streaming experience regardless of the device used by the customer.

3 **Future-Proofing:**

- Future-proofing refers to making updates that prepare the product for upcoming changes in technology or market trends. This may include adopting new technologies early, making the product scalable, or adding features that will become essential in the near future. Future-proofing helps ensure that the product stays relevant and minimizes major overhauls later on.
- **Example:** Tesla's over-the-air (OTA) software updates provide a way to future-proof its electric vehicles. By continuously adding new features, improving battery efficiency, and updating the autopilot system, Tesla ensures that its cars remain at the forefront of technological advancements without the need for hardware changes. This approach keeps customers satisfied and maintains the company's competitive edge.

4 **Improving Performance:**

- There is always room for performance improvements, no matter how good a product is. Performance enhancements may include improving the speed of the software, optimizing resource usage, or enhancing the user experience. Maintenance aimed at performance improvements ensures that the product remains fast, reliable, and engaging for users.
- **Example:** **Instagram** regularly updates its app to enhance performance by optimizing loading times, improving responsiveness, and minimizing crashes. These updates are essential to keeping users engaged and providing a seamless user experience.

8.3.3   Product Maintenance in Car-Sharing Platform Case Scenario

No matter how good a product is, you can always find ways to improve it. The same goes for mobile applications. There will always be a scope for improvement and upgrades. Let's use the **QuikDrive** Car-Sharing Platform to see how the four reasons for product maintenance are exemplified for its mobile application.

1 **Corrective Maintenance:** This is necessary when something goes wrong in a piece of software. This is often referred to as software errors, or bugs.

These can have a significant impact on the functionality of the software in general, and so must be addressed as soon as possible.

Imagine, for example, that **QuikDrive's** new mobile application had a software error or bug; perhaps something that caused the app to crash or prevented users from being able to make bookings, or even use their digital keys to unlock a car. Such errors could even include security problems to do with the leaking of sensitive personal information.

When such things go wrong, the appropriate type of maintenance is what we call "corrective" maintenance. Corrective maintenance can sometimes happen quickly, but sometimes requires further investigation to determine the root cause of the error or bug. Nevertheless, it's important to address such issues as quickly as possible.

2 **Adaptive Maintenance:** This is used to handle the changing requirements for your product. These can include changes to the operating system that supports your product, changes to authentication credentials, or hardware changes.

For example, **QuikDrive** users were logging on to the mobile app using a social media platform and had no prior problems doing so. But then suddenly all users were unable to log in from that social media site.

An investigation by the **QuikDrive** software developer uncovered that the social media site changed the way it authenticates users, with its application programming interface, or API. As a result, the **QuikDrive** app would need to be modified to accommodate this change. This is an example of the type of adaptive maintenance that product managers would do well to anticipate.

3 **Preventative Maintenance:** This requires looking into the future for likely problems, so that your product is better prepared to handle those problems through preventive measures.

Preventative maintenance can include handling latent problems that only arise after a certain amount of time. Or, so-called scaling issues, that arise as a product's customer base scales up, or grows, over time.

For example, **QuikDrive's** customer base has grown five-fold, from 1,000 to 5,000 members. Initially, after the successful marketing campaign and launch of the new mobile platform, the target was 3,000 members. While having 5,000 members presents exciting opportunities for **QuikDrive**, the product team is not sure if the application's server can handle the increased load.

What they know is that many users will be impacted if the server crashes during the rapid growth. **QuikDrive** can avoid a potential negative outcome by adding more servers as soon as they realize the customer base is growing more rapidly than originally anticipated.

In addition, the software team can make changes to the mobile software app to further increase its robustness and reliability, to accommodate the growing customer base.

4 **Perfective Maintenance**: After a new product is released to the public, product managers and teams expect issues and enhancement ideas to emerge from the product's usage in the real world.

For example, users may see the need for new features that further meet their needs and enhance their experience, and which the product team didn't anticipate themselves.

Let's assume, for instance, that **QuikDrive** users are able to sign in to their mobile app from their social media sites. When they do, they are either taken to their home page, or their profile page.

However, in a **QuikDrive** customer feedback survey, the team found that many users would prefer something different. The feedback indicated that the first thing customers want to see when they log in is their most recent activity, such as a booking. Making this change, based on this feedback, is what we call "perfective maintenance."

8.3.3.1 QuikDrive Case Scenario Summary

To deal with changing technologies and business environments, product maintenance is necessary for digital products like **QuikDrive's** mobile app.

You've seen how each type of product maintenance supports different problems and customers' needs. Corrective maintenance addresses issues such as errors, bugs, or faults. Adaptive maintenance addresses changes that impact your product. Preventative maintenance is about looking ahead and preventing foreseeable future issues. And perfective maintenance is all about refining and improving a product once it's been released to market.

Maintenance and support services go a long way in determining the success of an application. Focusing on the features of your digital product and ensuring it to be unique is the right way to think, but your job does not end there. You need to ensure you are prepared to provide adequate maintenance support to your customers. It involves constant monitoring, fixing, and updating the product features.

8.3.4 The Importance of Continuous Product Maintenance

Product maintenance is not a one-time activity but a continuous process that is crucial for retaining customers, meeting their expectations, and staying ahead in a competitive market. Whether it is fixing bugs, adapting to new technology, future-proofing the product, or improving its performance, product maintenance helps maintain a high-quality user experience that drives customer satisfaction.

For instance, consider a **mobile application** that allows users to order food online. Initially, the app may be functioning perfectly, but over time, changes in mobile operating systems, customer preferences, and market competition can demand modifications. The app will need updates to fix any issues that arise, adapt to new mobile OS versions, add new features like voice ordering or payment options, and improve speed and reliability to keep up with user expectations. Without continuous maintenance, such a product would quickly fall behind competitors and frustrate users, leading to customer churn.

In today's fast-paced tech environment, products must adapt quickly to changes in user behaviour and technology advancements. By prioritizing continuous maintenance, businesses can ensure that their products remain relevant, high-performing, and aligned with the evolving needs of their customers.

8.4 Conclusion

Effective product support and maintenance are the foundation of a product's long-term success. By providing well-structured technical support and ensuring continuous product maintenance, companies can significantly enhance customer satisfaction and loyalty. The five levels of support – from proactive assistance to expert-level escalation – allow organizations to manage customer issues effectively while optimizing resources. Meanwhile, the process of product maintenance helps address customer needs, adapt to evolving technology, and continuously improve the product's performance.

The combination of technical support and proactive product maintenance ensures that customers can rely on the product while benefiting from continuous enhancements. This results in a positive product experience and a strong relationship between the customer and the brand. By prioritizing these aspects of product management, businesses can create a customer-focused environment that drives long-term growth, customer retention, and product success.

9

LEVERAGING PRODUCT ANALYTICS FOR CUSTOMER INSIGHTS

9.1 Introduction

In today's digital landscape, product analytics plays a pivotal role in understanding customer behaviour, optimizing product performance, and driving business success. Within the **Digital Product Management (DPM)** framework, analytics serves as a core function that supports decision-making across all stages of the product lifecycle, from ideation and development to launch and ongoing support. This chapter introduces the power of product analytics in generating valuable insights about customer behaviour and preferences, which are essential for making informed, data-driven decisions.

By integrating product analytics into the **DPM** framework, product managers can align their strategic goals with real-world data, enabling them to improve customer experiences and meet business objectives more effectively. We explore key metrics such as the **AARRR** (Pirate Metrics) model and customer experience KPIs like **NPS** (Net Promoter Score), **CSAT** (Customer Satisfaction), and **CES** (Customer Effort Score). These metrics help product managers track and measure customer acquisition, engagement, satisfaction, and retention, providing a clear understanding of where products are excelling and where improvements are needed.

As product analytics is a key enabler of success throughout the product lifecycle, this chapter lays the groundwork for further exploration of how analytics drives customer retention and feature adoption, which will be covered in detail in subsequent chapters. Ultimately, this chapter highlights the importance of using data to inform decisions and guide the evolution of digital products.

DOI: 10.1201/9781003614180-9

9.2 Product Metrics and User Experience Insights

Product Analytics is the process of capturing and analysing data about how customers interact with a product or service to obtain valuable insights for product improvement. This approach allows companies to make data-driven decisions and validate product assumptions to better align with customer needs. Before launching a new product or feature, companies typically rely on qualitative data from potential customers, gathered through surveys and interviews, to validate their assumptions and design solutions. Once a product or feature is launched, the strategy shifts to analysing hard evidence, using real behavioural data to determine how users are interacting with the product. The insights gained from product analytics are crucial for understanding actual usage and identifying areas for enhancement, ensuring that the product continues to deliver value.

Through the analysis of real product data, product teams can gain insights into areas such as funnels, churn, friction, segmentation, interests, feature adoption, and more. This chapter will explore the many ways in which product analytics informs product strategy and provides the foundation for growth.

To build and maintain a successful product, understanding how users interact with it is essential. Product analytics provides a wealth of insights that help product managers make informed decisions to optimize user experience, increase engagement, and drive product growth. This section delves into the key metrics and insights that guide product development, ensuring that every aspect of the user journey is measured, analysed, and enhanced for maximum impact. Figure 9.1 shows the five main categories of product analytics.

Teams can effectively address challenges and capitalize on opportunities by measuring and tracking metrics based on the following five categories:

1 User Journey and Behaviour

- **User Journey Mapping:** By tracking user interactions across different stages, product analytics helps visualize the complete user journey. This allows product teams to identify opportunities for improvement at each touchpoint, ensuring a cohesive and engaging experience. For example, **Airbnb** uses journey mapping to understand where guests or hosts face challenges, allowing them to optimize the experience at every stage, from booking to checkout.
- **Funnels:** Understanding how users progress through different stages of the product and identifying where they drop off. This insight helps product managers optimize conversion paths, reducing drop-off rates.
- **User Behaviour Patterns:** Product analytics can identify recurring user behaviours, such as the times users are most active or which features they use most frequently. These insights help product teams tailor the

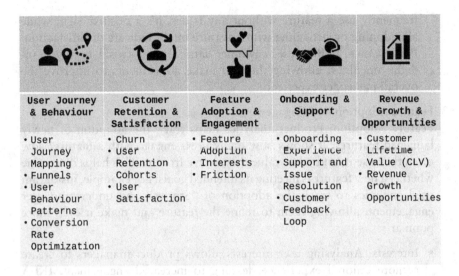

User Journey & Behaviour	Customer Retention & Satisfaction	Feature Adoption & Engagement	Onboarding & Support	Revenue Growth & Opportunities
• User Journey Mapping • Funnels • User Behaviour Patterns • Conversion Rate Optimization	• Churn • User Retention Cohorts • User Satisfaction	• Feature Adoption • Interests • Friction	• Onboarding Experience • Support and Issue Resolution • Customer Feedback Loop	• Customer Lifetime Value (CLV) • Revenue Growth Opportunities

FIGURE 9.1 Five Categories of Product Analytics.

experience and prioritize feature development. For instance, **LinkedIn's** notifications are timed based on user activity to maximize engagement.

- **Conversion Rate Optimization (CRO):** Analytics play a crucial role in tracking how users progress from one stage of the funnel to the next. Product managers can use this data to test and optimize different elements (e.g., CTAs, UI components) to increase the overall conversion rate. **IKEA** conducts A/B testing on its website design to determine which elements drive higher conversions, ultimately improving the online shopping experience.

2 Customer Retention and Satisfaction

- **Churn:** Analysing which users are leaving and why. Insights from churn data are crucial for refining the product to improve user retention. For example, **Netflix** analyses churn data to understand which user segments are most at risk and develop targeted retention strategies.
- **User Retention Cohorts:** By analysing user retention cohorts, product managers can determine which actions or behaviours are linked to higher retention rates. This data is useful for improving the onboarding process and ensuring users find value quickly. For example, **Slack** found that users who sent at least 2,000 messages had higher retention rates and used this insight to refine the onboarding process to encourage communication.
- **User Satisfaction:** Product analytics can indirectly measure satisfaction by analysing how users interact with key features or services. If users

frequently use a feature without any issues, it's a positive sign, while abandoning or struggling with a feature might indicate dissatisfaction. For instance, **JetBlue** uses customer data to track satisfaction with in-flight amenities, allowing them to make adjustments to improve the overall passenger experience.

3 **Feature Adoption and Engagement**

Feature Adoption: Product analytics helps track the adoption of newly launched features. It shows how many users engage with a feature, how often they use it, and what value they derive from it. This helps determine whether a new feature is meeting its intended goals. For example, **Instagram** used analytics to track the adoption of "Stories" and understand user engagement, allowing them to refine the feature and make it even more popular.

- **Interests**: Analysing user interests allows product managers to create a more tailored experience, leading to increased engagement. **IKEA** uses user interest data to recommend products that align with each customer's shopping behaviour, leading to higher engagement and conversions.
- **Friction**: Identifying barriers that make it difficult for users to achieve their goals. Reducing friction in the user experience helps enhance customer satisfaction. For instance, **JetBlue** identified friction points in its booking process and simplified them to make booking easier for travellers.

4 **Onboarding and Support**

- **Onboarding Experience**: Analytics helps monitor the effectiveness of the onboarding process, tracking whether users are successfully completing key onboarding steps. This helps product teams identify areas that may need adjustment to provide a better initial experience. For instance, **Dropbox** uses analytics to track onboarding steps, ensuring users understand how to upload and share files, which helps boost early engagement.
- **Support and Issue Resolution**: Product analytics can highlight areas where users are facing challenges, such as features with high error rates or support requests. This helps in reducing friction and improving customer support effectiveness by proactively addressing issues. For example, **Apple** uses analytics to identify common problems faced by iPhone users and releases software updates to address those issues promptly.
- **Customer Feedback Loop**: Product analytics provides insight into how users interact with feedback mechanisms, such as surveys or in-app

prompts. It can identify the best times to ask for feedback and what types of questions generate the most useful responses. For instance, **Netflix** asks users for ratings after watching content, which helps them refine their recommendation algorithms and improve user satisfaction.

5 Revenue Growth and Opportunities

- **Customer Lifetime Value (CLTV)**: Product analytics helps estimate the potential revenue a user might generate over their entire relationship with the product. Understanding **CLTV** allows product teams to focus on retaining high-value users and investing in strategies that enhance their experience. For instance, **Salesforce** uses **CLTV** to identify which enterprise clients bring the most value and tailor its services to nurture those relationships.
- **Revenue Growth Opportunities**: Analysing user behaviour allows product managers to identify upsell or cross-sell opportunities. This insight enables businesses to design personalized offers or additional services that align with user needs and behaviours. For example, **SIA (Singapore Airlines)** uses customer data to offer travel upgrades, personalized meal plans, and loyalty programme offers based on travel history.

9.3 Pirate Metrics: AARRR

Acquisition, Activation, Retention, Referral, Revenue (AARRR), also known as **Pirate Metrics**, is a framework for understanding customer behaviour throughout the product lifecycle. Startups use this model to track key milestones, from acquiring customers to generating revenue. Below, we will explore how product analytics helps product managers at each stage of the **AARRR** model, shown in Figure 9.2.

1 **Acquisition**: Product analytics helps track how users find the product and which channels drive the most effective acquisition. By analysing these acquisition funnels, product managers can optimize their marketing strategies and allocate resources to the best-performing channels.
   - **Question**: How do customers find out about our product?
   This helps product managers identify which marketing channels or campaigns are most effective in driving new users to the product.
   - **Metric**: Channel Conversion Rate
   Measure the percentage of users acquired from different marketing channels. This helps identify which channels are most effective in bringing new users to the product.

Acquisition	How do customers find out about our product?	Channel Conversation Rate
Activation	What actions do users take to indicate they have a great first experience?	Activation Rate
Retention	What are the reasons why users continue to engage with our product regularly?	Cohort Retention Rate
Referral	What motivates our customers to recommend our product to others?	Net Promoter Score (NPS)
Revenue	Which features or services are users most willing to pay for?	Average Revenue Per User (ARPU)

FIGURE 9.2 Pirates Metrics: AARRR.

2 **Activation**: Analytics helps track user engagement during the onboarding process, ensuring that customers successfully activate the product and find initial value. Tools like funnel analysis and **CRO** help identify and improve user touchpoints, increasing activation rates. **IKEA** conducts **A/B** testing on website elements to optimize user experience and boost conversions.

- **Question**: What initial actions do users take that indicate they are experiencing value in our product?
  Understanding this can help product managers identify key activation points, such as signing up, completing onboarding, or using a core feature, that lead to long-term engagement.
- **Metric**: Activation Rate
  Measure the percentage of users who reach a predefined activation event, such as completing onboarding or using a core feature for the first time. This metric highlights how well users are experiencing initial value in the product.

3 **Retention**: Retention is key to sustainable growth, and product analytics allows teams to understand and improve retention rates. **Cohort Retention Analysis** helps product managers identify behaviours linked to higher retention rates. Slack found that users who sent at least 2,000 messages were more likely to be retained, which influenced changes in their onboarding process to promote this behaviour. Additionally, analysing user retention cohorts enables product teams to identify effective onboarding elements, such as creating groups and encouraging active communication.

- **Question**: What are the reasons why users continue to engage with our product regularly?

Identifying patterns that drive retention allows product managers to optimize features, improve usability, and keep users coming back.

- **Metric**: Cohort Retention Rate
Measure the percentage of users that continue to use the product after a certain period (e.g., weekly or monthly). This helps identify what drives users to keep coming back over time.

4 **Referral**: Product analytics helps track referral patterns and understand why users share a product. By identifying influential features that prompt users to invite others, product managers can create referral incentives. For example, **Uber** uses referral analytics to encourage existing users to invite new riders through promotional offers.

- **Question**: What motivates our customers to recommend our product to others?
Understanding what drives users to refer can help product managers develop or enhance referral programmes that incentivize users to share the product with their network.

- **Metric**: Net Promoter Score (**NPS**)
Measure the likelihood of users recommending the product to others on a scale of 0–10. A higher **NPS** score indicates that users are more willing to refer others, highlighting the product's positive impact.

5 **Revenue**: Revenue analytics are used to monitor user behaviour and identify upsell or cross-sell opportunities. Revenue growth opportunities can be identified by analysing users' purchasing behaviours. **SIA** (**Singapore Airlines**), for example, uses customer data to offer personalized travel upgrades and meal plans, boosting customer loyalty and increasing revenue.

- Question: Which features or services are users most willing to pay for? Analysing this helps product managers understand what is driving revenue, where users see the most value, and identify opportunities for upselling or creating premium offerings.

- **Metric**: Average Revenue Per User (**ARPU**)
Measure the average revenue generated per active user over a specific period. This metric helps identify which features or services are contributing most to revenue generation.

These questions and metrics enable product managers to gain deeper insights into user behaviour at each stage of the customer journey, helping them make informed decisions to optimize user acquisition, activation, retention, referrals, and revenue growth, thereby ensuring the product meets user needs effectively and drives growth.

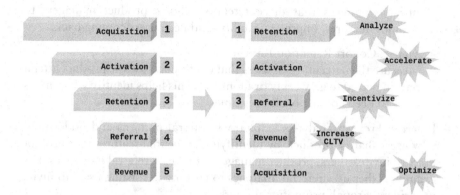

FIGURE 9.3   Paradigm Shift from AARRR to RARRA Metrics.

9.4   Shift in Pirates Metrics: AARRR to RARRA

As businesses evolve, there is often a paradigm shift away from focusing solely on acquisition to prioritizing retention. This shift, known as the **RARRA** model, reflects the need to continuously provide value to retain customers in a competitive market. This is shown in Figure 9.3.

The shift from **AARRR** (Acquisition, Activation, Retention, Referral, Revenue) to **RARRA** (Retention, Activation, Referral, Revenue, Acquisition) emphasizes the importance of focusing on retaining and nurturing existing users before seeking new ones. The **RARRA** framework prioritizes delivering continuous value to users to build loyalty and sustainable growth. Below are the five key areas of growth strategies corresponding to **RARRA**:

1 **Retention** – *What's the ideal customer journey?*

  • To drive retention, product managers need to understand and optimize the customer journey. Strategies like customer journey mapping, leveraging attractive features, and identifying behaviours that drive higher retention can help create a journey that keeps users coming back.

2 **Activation** – *How can we optimize touchpoints to activate more users?*

  • Activation involves optimizing touchpoints to get users to experience the product's value as early as possible. This can be done by reducing onboarding friction, guiding users through the buying journey with effective **CTAs**, and using visuals and walkthroughs to make the process intuitive.

3 **Referral** – *What features encourage users to invite others?*

  • A strong referral strategy encourages users to invite others by incentivizing recommendations. Product managers can use cash back or discounts for both the referrer and the new user, while leveraging email reminders and in-app messages to prompt users to share the product.

4 **Revenue** – *Which customer segments are most profitable?*

- Increasing revenue involves identifying the most profitable customer segments and driving up **CLTV**. This can be achieved through upselling and cross-selling, sending achievement emails, providing personalized

TABLE 9.1 Growth Strategy: From AARRR to RARRA

Metrics	Product Analytics	Growth Strategies
Retention	Retention Curve Cohort Analysis	What's the ideal customer journey? • Customer journey mapping • Leverage attractive features • What user behaviours drive higher retention?
Activation	Conversion Rate Optimization (CRO)	How can we optimize touchpoints to activate more users? • Reduce onboarding friction • Guide users through buying journey using effective CTAs • Use more visuals and walkthroughs
Referral	Social Sharing Analytics	What features encourage users to invite others? • Incentivize users to recommend to others • Offer cash back/discounts to both current users and those they refer • Use email reminders or use in-app messages
Revenue	RFM Analysis (Recency, Frequency, Monetary)	Which customer segments are most profitable? • Increase customer lifetime value (CLTV) through upselling and cross-selling • Send achievement and progress emails (e.g., savings made using your product) • Use behavioural data to send personalized offers (e.g., related products/services, product bundles, popular/trending products • Get user feedback on product experience
Acquisition	Funnel Analysis	Which channels bring in the most qualified users? • Use cohort analysis and RFM analysis to segmentize your users to identify acquisition channels are bringing in the most loyal customers

offers based on behavioural data, and gathering user feedback to improve product experiences.

5 **Acquisition** – *Which channels bring in the most qualified users?*

- Finally, to bring in new users effectively, product managers should focus on acquisition channels that attract loyal customers. This can be done using cohort and **RFM** analysis to segment users and identify the channels with the highest quality leads.

Table 9.1 lists the growth strategies based on the **RARRA** approach.

By shifting focus to Retention first, the **RARRA** approach ensures product teams nurture and provide value to existing users, creating a loyal base that helps fuel sustainable growth. This foundation of satisfied, engaged users helps build the momentum needed for effective acquisition and long-term success.

9.5 Customer Experience KPIs

There are three questions every product manager and their team should be asking: How likely is someone to recommend the product to a friend? How satisfied are customers with the product? And how much effort do customers need to go through to interact with the product, or resolve issues?

By using three different metrics, you – as a product manager – can answer these three critical questions. These **customer experience KPIs** are crucial in understanding and measuring customer satisfaction.

Figure 9.4 lists these three fundamental customer experience **KPIs**. These **KPIs** include **NPS** (Net Promoter Score), **CSAT** (Customer Satisfaction Score), and **CES** (Customer Effort Score):

1 **NPS** (Net Promoter Score): Product managers can use this metric to ask, "How likely are you to recommend this product to a friend or colleague?" A high **NPS** indicates strong customer advocacy, while a low **NPS** points to areas needing improvement. For instance, **Tesla** frequently scores highly on **NPS** due to its innovative features and customer loyalty. Figure 9.5 shows the Net Promoter Score formula.

Customers are asked to rate their answer to this question on a scale of 0–10, with 10 representing the highest likelihood of them recommending the product or service.

Based on the scores given by the surveyed customers, you'll place each customer in one of three categories. Firstly, those who give scores of 9 or 10, and are your most enthusiastic and loyal customers, are termed "**Promoters.**"

👍	Net Promotor Score (NPS)	Q1. How likely are you to recommend this product to a friend or colleague?
🙂	Customer Satisfaction Score (CSAT)	Q2. How satisfied are you with this product?
🏃	Customer Effort Score (CES)	Q3. How much effort did you personally have to put forth to resolve your issue?

FIGURE 9.4   Customer Experience KPIs.

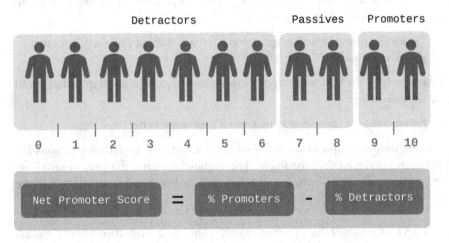

FIGURE 9.5   Net Promoter Score (NPS).

Secondly, there are those who score 7 or 8. These are the customers who are satisfied with the product, but not enthusiastic enough to promote it. We call these "**Passives.**"

Thirdly, those who score 0–6 are termed "**Detractors.**" These are unhappy customers who are unlikely to buy from you again. They may even discourage others from buying your product.

To calculate your **NPS**, you subtract the percentage of **Detractors** from the percentage of **Promoters.**

Let's use the **Car-Sharing Platform QuikDrive** as an example. Let's say that 50% of the respondents to the **NPS** survey question were **Promoters** and 10% were **Detractors.** So, we take 50% and we subtract 10%, which gives us an NPS of 40.

Now, you might be wondering what constitutes a good score. **NPS** scores can range from negative 100 (if all respondents are detractors and none are promoters) to positive 100 (where all are promoters and none are detractors). The closer to positive 100, the better. Here's a good rule of thumb:

a A score of 70 or more is outstanding
b 50–69 is strong
c 1–49 needs some improvement
d Anything below 0 is a red flag

In an **NPS** survey, it is always good practice to ask a follow-on question, based on the answer given by the customer. This can be easily done through an online survey.

For example, if the customer clicks on a high score of 9, the survey can then prompt the following question:

"Thanks for giving us such a high score! What was it about your experience that you liked so much?"

Conversely, if the customer gives a low score of 2, a follow-on question could be the following:

"What could we have done to make your experience better?"

Having follow-on questions helps you understand the underlying reasons for the scores given by the customers. These questions can offer insight into how customers view your brand, and what actions you need to take to improve the customer experience.

2 **CSAT** (Customer Satisfaction Score): This is a customer loyalty metric used by companies to gauge how satisfied a customer is with the product experience. Product managers can use surveys or in-app feedback to ask, "How satisfied are you with this product?". High **CSAT** scores reflect positive user experiences, as seen in **Netflix's** personalized content recommendations.

Here's an example of a CSAT question using the **Car-Sharing Platform QuikDrive**:

"How would you rate your overall satisfaction with QuikDrive?"

Respondents use 1-to-5 scale to answer the questions:

1 Customers who are very unsatisfied
2 Customers who are unsatisfied
3 Customers who are neutral
4 Customers who are satisfied
5 Customers who are very satisfied

In a **CSAT** survey, you can ask the customer to give a rating of 1–5, for various aspects of your product or service. For example, **QuikDrive** might want customers to rate all of the following aspects of the onboarding process. Its sign-up process, the process of reserving a car, the ease of navigating the website or platform, or the notification reminders for making bookings. In other words, you can use **CSAT** surveys to get customers to rate their satisfaction with the experience of using any one of your features.

Once you've received **CSAT** ratings, here's an easy way to calculate a **CSAT** customer satisfaction score.

a Start with the number of "Satisfied" respondents: those who scored 4 or 5, representing the "Satisfied" to "Very Satisfied" range.
b Next, divide that number by the number of total responses. Then multiply that by 100.
c So, if 100 customers respond to **QuikDrive's CSAT** survey. And if 80 of them rated their satisfaction as 4 or 5, out of 5. Then **QuikDrive** has an 80% CSAT score.
d **CES** (Customer Effort Score): **CES** helps determine how easy it is for users to resolve issues. Product managers can ask, "How much effort did you personally have to put forth to resolve your issue?". The goal is to reduce user effort, making it as seamless as possible for them to achieve their desired outcomes. The purpose of a **CES** survey is to help you find out if customers are having a difficult time performing certain actions when interacting with your product. That way you can take the necessary steps to streamline and improve the processes. The three best times to send a **CES** survey are after a purchase, after a subscription sign-up, and after a customer service interaction (or touchpoint). For example, **IKEA** aims to reduce **CES** by providing easy-to-understand assembly guides and customer support options.

In **QuikDrive's** case, a **CES** survey can focus on different aspects of interacting with **QuikDrive** service, such as making a car reservation, getting help from the **Help Desk,** or even leaving a review. To illustrate the types of questions to ask in a **CES** survey, we'll use **QuikDrive** as an example. To measure the effort their customers go through to use, or interact with, their product they could ask some of the following questions:

How easy was it to complete your car reservation using the QuikDrive app?
How easy did QuikDrive's Support Line make it for you to handle your issue?
How easy was it for you to write a review using the QuikDrive app?

Customers then rate their responses on a scale of 1–7, where 1 requires a high effort from customers, and 7 is easy or requires little effort. The total CES score is calculated by finding the average of all responses. This means taking the sum of responses and dividing it by the total number of survey respondents.

So, let's say you receive 50 survey responses. Then you add up the ratings for all 50 surveys, and let's say the total sum of customers' response ratings is 200. Then you'll divide the total of 200, by the 50 responses, which will give you a **CES** score of 4.

A score of 4 isn't great. Generally speaking, an average **CES** score of more than 5 is good. A score that is 5 and lower is not.

Regardless of your score, consider including an open-ended, follow-on question that asks for feedback to supplement the rating response. This way, as with the **CSAT** score, you'll get more context for the underlying reasons for subsequent improvement plans.

In this section, you learned three important metrics for measuring your customers' experience of using your product. Firstly, **Net Promoter Score,** which measures how likely a customer is to recommend a product to a friend. Secondly, **Customer Satisfaction,** which measures how satisfied a customer is with the product. And thirdly, **Customer Effort Score,** which measures how much effort customers need to go through to interact with your product, or resolve an issue with it.

As you can see, these three scores: **NPS, CSAT, CES,** are all useful measures of customer experience. But, what's important is what you do with the scores to drive and improve the customer experience!

Given these three metrics and the questions they help answer, consider how you might pre-empt customer experience issues when you develop a new product. And ask yourself how you can continually improve product features, based on subsequent survey data around these three metrics.

9.6 Sean Ellis' Survey

The **Sean Ellis' Survey** is an effective tool for measuring product-market fit. It asks users, "How would you feel if you could no longer use the product?" The three possible responses – "Very disappointed," "Somewhat disappointed," and "Not disappointed" – help determine the product's value to users. Furthermore, participants of the survey must correspond to one of these three mandatory conditions:

1 People who used the core product or the service.
2 People who have used the product or the service at least twice.
3 People who have used the product or the service in the last two weeks.

Figure 9.6 shows the crux of **Sean Ellis' Survey** based on the "magical 40%."

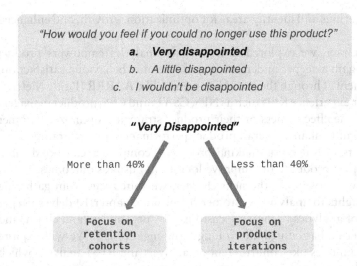

"How would you feel if you could no longer use this product?"

a. **Very disappointed**

b. *A little disappointed*

c. *I wouldn't be disappointed*

"Very Disappointed"

More than 40%   Less than 40%

Focus on
retention
cohorts

Focus on
product
iterations

FIGURE 9.6 Sean Ellis' Survey.

The goal is to have at least 40% of users answer "Very disappointed," which indicates strong user attachment to the product. This figure has emerged as a leading indicator of product/market fit, signifying a strong user attachment to the product and hinting at a readiness for scaling.

If more than 40% of users responded with "*Very disappointed*," product managers should focus on retention cohorts, as this indicates that the product resonates well with the users and is ready for growth. On the other hand, if less than 40% responded positively, product managers may need to consider iterating on product features, refining the value proposition, or even pivoting the product to better align with user needs and expectations. This could involve changing the target market, rethinking core features, or developing new use cases that better solve user pain points.

This structured approach allows product managers to gauge user sentiment, prioritize improvements, and determine whether their product is in a strong position for scaling or needs more refinement to meet user expectations effectively.

Companies like **Spotify** use surveys to gauge user sentiment and refine features to ensure they consistently deliver value.

9.7 Conclusion

This chapter has highlighted the essential role that data-driven insights through Product Analytics play in the continuous improvement of products and user experiences. By analysing key product metrics and user behaviours, product managers can gain a deep understanding of how customers interact with their offerings and identify areas for optimization, growth, and enhanced engagement.

In this chapter, we explored how product analytics empowers product managers to gain a deeper understanding of customer behaviour, satisfaction, and engagement. Through the use of key metrics like **AARRR** (Pirate Metrics) and customer experience KPIs such as **NPS**, **CSAT**, and **CES**, product managers can measure the effectiveness of their product strategies, optimize customer interactions, and enhance overall product performance. By integrating data-driven insights into decision-making processes, companies can build more customer-centric products and improve long-term business outcomes.

As we move forward to the next chapter, we shift focus from gathering customer insights to analysing customer retention. Chapter 10 delves deeper into the use of analytics to measure customer loyalty, understand churn, and identify patterns that contribute to long-term engagement. We will explore advanced techniques like cohort retention analysis and **RFM** analysis, which provide product managers with actionable insights to keep customers engaged and returning to their products.

10

ANALYSING CUSTOMER RETENTION AND JOURNEY

10.1 Introduction

Customer retention is one of the most critical factors in the long-term success of any product. In this chapter, we explore how product analytics can be applied to measure, understand, and improve customer retention. While acquiring new users is essential, keeping those users engaged and loyal to the product is equally, if not more, important for sustainable growth. By analysing customer behaviours, product usage patterns, and their journey from onboarding to long-term adoption, product managers can identify the drivers of loyalty and the causes of churn.

In this chapter, we introduce key tools and techniques such as **Cohort Retention Analysis**, **RFM analysis**, and **Customer Journey Analytics** to provide a comprehensive understanding of how to measure retention and identify patterns that affect user behaviour. We will also explore the **Customer Retention Curve** and delve into methods for optimizing customer engagement throughout their lifecycle. By leveraging these analytics, product managers can make informed decisions that improve customer satisfaction, enhance product value, and ultimately reduce churn.

This focus on retention is a natural progression from Chapter 9's exploration of customer insights, as it highlights the ongoing need to not only understand customer behaviour but also maintain a strong, lasting relationship with them.

DOI: 10.1201/9781003614180-10

10.2 Customer Retention Analytics

Customer Retention Analytics is the process of analysing user metrics and behaviour to understand the factors that drive customer retention and churn. It is often referred to as "survival analytics" because it focuses on understanding the survival rate of existing customers and leveraging that data to reduce churn. By gaining insights into why customers leave or stay, product managers can develop targeted strategies to keep them engaged.

10.2.1 Customer Retention Curve

One of the key tools for measuring customer retention is the **Retention Curve,** which shows the percentage of active users over time. The retention curve helps identify whether customers are sticking around or gradually moving away to find alternative solutions or products. A healthy product retention curve gradually flattens out over time, and a product can be said to have achieved product-market fit if the percentage of active users levels off at 50% or higher.

Many mobile apps lose the majority of users between Day 1 and Day 30. For example, research conducted by *Localytics* has shown that the average retention rate for mobile apps drops drastically to less than 5% within the first 90 days of use, highlighting the challenge of maintaining engagement in a competitive app market.

To flatten the retention curve and retain users effectively, product managers should optimize three key stages in the user journey: **Onboarding, Value Discovery (Aha! Moment),** and **Habit Formation.** Each of these stages plays a critical role in keeping users engaged and turning them into long-term customers. Figure 10.1 shows the three stages in the user journey and the recommended strategies to flatten the retention curve.

10.2.1.1 Optimizing the User Retention Flow Stages

1. Onboarding: First Impressions Matter
The onboarding experience is crucial because it represents the first interaction users have with the product. Optimizing this stage can significantly improve the likelihood of users continuing their journey. The goal of onboarding is to make it as easy as possible for new users to get started and find immediate value.

Steps Product Managers Can Take:

- **Tutorials and Interactive Walkthroughs:** Integrate interactive walkthroughs and product tutorials to help users get acquainted with the core features quickly. For example, *Slack* uses an engaging onboarding process that

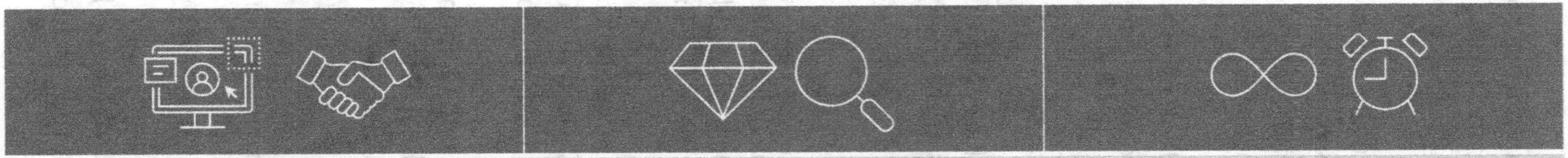

Onboarding: First Impressions Matter	Value Discovery: Demonstrating the Product's Worth	Habit Formation: Building a Routine with Users
Tutorials and Interactive Walkthroughs	Highlight Key Features	External Triggers
Slack introduces users to the workspace, highlighting how to send messages, set up channels, etc.	*Grammarly* prompts users to use the tool on different platforms, such as their browser or word processor.	*LinkedIn* sends notifications about connection requests, job opportunities, and content recommendations.
Remove Friction	Trigger Messaging Strategy	Motivation and Rewards
Duolingo allows users to start learning a language before creating an account.	*Calm*, a meditation app, sends reminders to users encouraging them to try guided meditations.	*Duolingo* uses streaks and rewards users with badges to motivate consistent practice.
Personalization	Show Success Metrics	Create FOMO (Fear of Missing Out)
Netflix asks users about their preferences during onboarding to recommend content.	*Fitbit* provides users with weekly activity reports, showing them how far they've come in reaching their health goals.	*Shopify* sends notifications about items left in users' shopping carts, reminding them that the items might sell out.

FIGURE 10.1 Strategies to Flatten Retention Curve.

introduces users to the workspace, highlighting how to send messages, set up channels, and more.

- **Remove Friction**: Streamline the sign-up process by minimizing required fields and making it easier for users to start exploring the product. For example, *Duolingo* allows users to start learning a language before even creating an account, reducing barriers to engagement.
- **Personalization**: Use information provided by users during signup to tailor the onboarding experience to their needs. *Netflix*, for example, asks users about their preferences during onboarding to recommend content that is more relevant, increasing the chances of initial engagement.

Impact: Winning at onboarding increases the likelihood of users staying engaged through the rest of the journey, providing a knock-on effect that helps flatten the retention curve.

2. Value Discovery: Demonstrating the Product's Worth
The next stage is helping users reach the **Aha! moment,** where they discover the product's true value. This is the point at which users realize why they need the product and how it can solve their problem.

Steps Product Managers Can Take:

- **Highlight Key Features**: Guide users to key features that deliver the most value. For example, *Grammarly* prompts users to use the tool on different platforms, such as their browser or word processor, so they experience its full capabilities.
- **Trigger Messaging Strategy**: Use segmented emails and push notifications to guide users towards activation events. For instance, *Calm*, a meditation app, sends reminders to users encouraging them to try guided meditations, emphasizing the app's value.
- **Show Success Metrics**: Showcase user success metrics to demonstrate progress. *Fitbit*, for example, provides users with weekly activity reports, showing them how far they've come in reaching their health goals, which reinforces the product's value.

Impact: Proving the product's worth ensures users remain engaged and see continuous value, thus motivating them to return.

3. Habit Formation: Building a Routine with Users
Once users understand the value of the product, the goal is to develop habits that keep them coming back. Habit formation helps embed the product into users' daily routines and fosters long-term loyalty.

Steps Product Managers Can Take:

- **External Triggers**: Use push notifications, email reminders, and calendar integrations as external triggers to encourage users to come back. For example, *LinkedIn* sends notifications about connection requests, job opportunities, and content recommendations to keep users engaged.
- **Motivation and Rewards**: Use motivation and gratification techniques, such as gamification and rewards, to encourage regular use. *Duolingo* uses streaks and rewards users with badges to motivate consistent practice.
- **Create FOMO (Fear of Missing Out)**: Create a sense of urgency to encourage repeat use. For example, *Shopify* sends notifications about items left in users' shopping carts, reminding them that the items might sell out.

Impact: By turning product usage into a habit, product managers can retain users over the long term and build a loyal customer base.

10.2.2   Cohort Retention Analysis

To further understand customer retention, one common approach is **Cohort Retention Analysis**, which involves tracking user engagement by grouping users based on shared characteristics or behaviours over specific periods. This analysis allows product managers to observe how different user segments perform over time and identify which factors contribute to higher retention rates and reduce churn.

Let's walk through an example to illustrate the steps involved in performing cohort retention analysis:

Imagine you are a product manager of a **Mobile Wellness Platform** that helps people lead healthier and more active lives by empowering them with data, inspiration, and guidance to reach their goals. The platform connects health and fitness tracker devices with software and services, including an online web portal, mobile app, data analytics, motivational and social tools, personalized insights, and virtual coaching through customized fitness plans and interactive workouts. Figure 10.2 shows a Cohort Retention Analysis for this platform.

1 **Formulate a Hypothesis**: Start by creating a hypothesis. In this case, one of your hypotheses might be that users who connect a health or fitness tracker device to the platform are more likely to stay engaged with the product compared to those who do not.
2 **Define an Acquisition Cohort**: Choose an acquisition cohort for analysis. For example, select users who signed up for the platform in January 2025. This allows you to track and compare users who joined during the same time frame.
3 **Break Down Behavioural Cohorts**: Break the acquisition cohort into two **behavioural cohorts** – those who have connected a health or fitness tracker

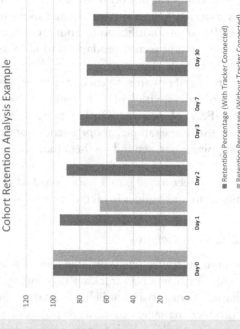

Cohort Retention Analysis Example

■ Retention Percentage (With Tracker Connected)
■ Retention Percentage (Without Tracker Connected)

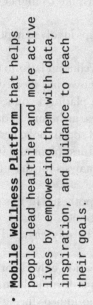

- **Mobile Wellness Platform** that helps people lead healthier and more active lives by empowering them with data, inspiration, and guidance to reach their goals.

- **Acquisition Cohort**: New customers who signed up for the platform in January 2025

- **2 Behavioural Cohorts**: Those who have connected a fitness tracker and those who have not.

- **Result**: Higher retention for users connected a fitness tracker

- **Actional Insights**: New user onboarding checklist or prompt existing users with in-app messages encouraging them to connect their fitness devices.

FIGURE 10.2 Cohort Retention Analysis Example.

device and those who haven't. This step helps isolate and examine the impact of specific behaviours on retention.

4 **Plot and Compare Cohort Data**: Plot the retention data for both behavioural cohorts over a specific period and compare the results. If there is a significant difference in retention rates between the two groups, this would validate your hypothesis. For example, users who connect their fitness tracker might show a higher retention rate over three months compared to those who did not.

5 **Act on Insights**: Based on the analysis, take actionable steps to improve retention. If connecting a health or fitness tracker indeed correlates with higher retention, you could make connecting the device an essential part of the onboarding process. You might add this task to the new user onboarding checklist or prompt existing users with in-app messages encouraging them to connect their fitness devices.

Example of Applying Insights:

- *Calm*, a wellness and meditation platform, found that users who completed their first meditation session immediately after signing up were more likely to continue using the product. As a result, they incorporated an onboarding process that actively encouraged new users to complete a session right away, which improved long-term retention rates.

By leveraging cohort retention analysis, product managers can validate assumptions, refine user onboarding processes, and encourage key behaviours that drive long-term engagement. This approach provides a data-driven method to create impactful improvements in user experience and retention, ultimately enhancing the product's value for its users.

10.3 RFM Analysis

10.3.1 Introduction to RFM Analysis

RFM Analysis is a customer segmentation technique that evaluates three key factors – **Recency, Frequency**, and **Monetary Value** – to understand the behaviour of different customers. By analysing these three components, product managers can create highly targeted marketing campaigns, improve customer retention, and boost customer lifetime value. Figure 10.3 shows the three questions to ask in an **RFM Analysis**.

1 **Recency**:

- *How recent was the last purchase?*

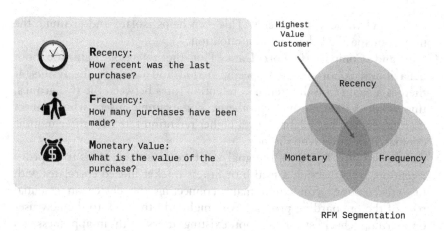

FIGURE 10.3 RFM Analysis.

- Customers who have made a recent purchase are more likely to engage with the product and respond to marketing campaigns. A recent purchase indicates active engagement and interest in the product or service.

Example: A customer who last used a *Netflix* subscription last week is more likely to renew their subscription compared to a customer who has not logged in for over six months.

2 **Frequency:**

- *How many purchases have been made?*
- Frequent customers indicate a strong attachment to the product and are more likely to respond to upsell or cross-sell opportunities. Frequent usage also indicates a higher likelihood of retention.

Example: Customers who frequently order through *Deliveroo* demonstrate strong loyalty and attachment to the convenience of food delivery.

3 **Monetary Value:**

- *What is the value of the purchase?*
- The value of purchases made by a customer helps to segment high-value and low-value customers. High-value customers are often a priority for retention efforts, as they contribute significantly to the revenue.

Example: A customer who consistently makes large purchases from *IKEA* has a higher monetary value compared to someone who occasionally buys smaller, inexpensive items.

10.3.2 Examples of Using RFM Analysis

1 Example – Amazon:

- *Recency*: The last purchase made by a customer on *Amazon* indicates their recent engagement. A customer who recently bought a product may respond better to related product suggestions.
- *Frequency*: Customers who make frequent purchases are likely enrolled in the *Amazon Prime* programme, indicating strong loyalty.
- *Monetary Value*: Customers who buy higher-priced electronics or appliances have a higher monetary value compared to those who purchase small household items.

2 Example – Lazada:

- *Recency*: If a customer recently shopped on *Lazada* during a sale, they are more likely to return for future promotions.
- *Frequency*: Customers who often shop during major sales like *Lazada 11.11* or *12.12* are highly engaged and contribute to *Lazada's* recurring revenue.
- *Monetary Value*: Customers who buy luxury goods on *Lazada* have a higher monetary value compared to those who buy smaller daily essentials.

3 Example –FairPrice Online:

- *Recency*: Customers who recently ordered groceries online from *FairPrice Online* indicate a recurring need and a preference for convenience.
- *Frequency*: Customers who order weekly groceries demonstrate a high frequency, signalling strong dependence on the platform.
- *Monetary Value*: A customer buying bulk household items or high-value products has a higher monetary value compared to a customer who only buys occasional snacks or drinks.

10.3.3 Customer Segmentation Using RFM Analysis

However, while RFM provides a static snapshot of past behaviour, **Customer Lifetime Value (CLTV)** helps extend this analysis to understand a customer's potential future value. **CLTV** can be classified into two types:

1 **Descriptive CLTV**: It measures the historical value that a customer has brought to the company, focusing on past transactions.
2 **Predictive CLTV**: It estimates the potential value a customer could generate in the future, based on observed patterns and behaviours.

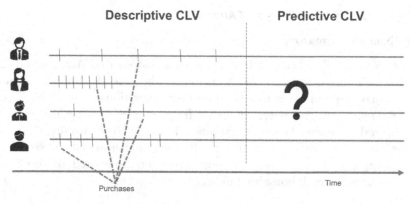

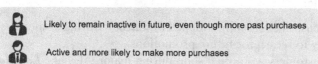

FIGURE 10.4 Customer Segmentation Using RFM Analysis.

To further enhance our understanding, we can segment customers into four types based on their purchasing behaviours and apply both **RFM** analysis and **CLTV** to tailor the marketing strategy accordingly.

Figure 10.4 illustrates how customer segmentation combined with **Descriptive CLTV** and **Predictive CLTV** can be used in **RFM** Analysis to determine which customer will likely to remain inactive in future, and which customer will still be active and more likely to make more purchases.

10.3.3.1 Customer Segmentation Using RFM Analysis

1 Multiple Purchases Done Consistently Over a Time Period

- **RFM Analysis**: These customers score high on Recency, Frequency, and Monetary Value. They frequently buy, engage actively, and bring high value to the business.
- **Descriptive CLTV**: Shows that these customers have contributed significantly over time.
- **Predictive CLTV**: Indicates that they are likely to continue being high-value customers.
- **Example**: A *Netflix* subscriber who consistently renews their subscription, watches multiple shows weekly, and engages with personalized recommendations.

- **Strategy**: Keep these customers engaged with VIP loyalty programmes, early access to new features, and exclusive offers.

2 **A Bunch of Past Purchases Done in a Distant Past but No Purchase over Recent Time Period**

- **RFM Analysis**: High Frequency and Monetary Value, but low Recency. They used to be good customers but haven't engaged recently.
- **Descriptive CLTV**: These customers have had a strong historical contribution.
- **Predictive CLTV**: Indicates a potential decline unless re-engaged.
- **Example**: A customer who used to order regularly from *IKEA* but hasn't made a purchase in over a year.
- **Strategy**: Win-back campaigns can be employed to re-engage them. Sending reactivation emails, personalized offers, and new product updates may encourage them to return.

3 **Few and Far between Purchases**

- **RFM Analysis**: Low Frequency and Monetary Value, and possibly medium Recency if they made a recent purchase.
- **Descriptive CLTV**: Shows low historical contribution due to limited engagement.
- **Predictive CLTV**: Indicates that the potential future value may be low unless engagement strategies are successful.
- **Example**: A customer who orders from *Lazada* occasionally, primarily during major sales like *11.11*.
- **Strategy**: Utilize limited-time promotions, discounts, and product recommendations to encourage more frequent purchases and move them up the value chain.

4 **Purchases That Trend Downwards in Frequency**

- **RFM Analysis**: Recency may be moderate, Frequency and Monetary Value are trending down.
- **Descriptive CLTV**: Indicates a declining trend in historical value.
- **Predictive CLTV**: Suggests that they may churn if trends continue, reducing future potential value.
- **Example**: A user on a *fitness and wellness platform* who was once highly engaged with virtual coaching sessions but has been interacting less frequently over the past few months.
- **Strategy**: Proactively re-engage with personalized content, motivational messages, and incentives to prevent churn and reignite their interest in the platform.

10.3.3.2 RFM Segmentation Strategy

The **RFM Segmentation Strategy** helps product managers divide customers into different segments based on their Recency, Frequency, and Monetary scores. A **3x3 matrix** allows us to categorize customers into nine distinct segments by combining the three RFM dimensions –**High, Medium,** and **Low** – to allocate an **RFM Factor** for each quadrant.

Table 10.1 represents the segmentation strategy.

TABLE 10.1 RFM Segmentation Strategy

Segment	RFM Factor	Customer description	Marketing strategy
Champions	High-High-High	Highly active customers who make frequent purchases of high value	Offer exclusive rewards, loyalty programmes, and VIP offers
Loyal Customers	Medium-High-High	Frequent buyers of high value but recent activity is moderate	Send personalized offers to reactivate recent purchases
Potential Loyalists	High-Medium-Medium	Recent purchasers who engage often but make mid-value purchases	Encourage repeat purchase with loyalty discounts
Occasional Shoppers	Medium-Medium-Low	Customers who purchase occasionally but have moderate engagement	Use targeted offers to increase frequency of purchase
At Risk Customers	Low-High-Medium	Customers used to be frequent but haven't purchased recently	Win-back campaigns, email reminders, re-engagement offers
Price Sensitive Customers	Medium-Low-Low	Occasional buyers who often look for deals	Offer discounts and limited-time promotions
Lapsed Customers	Low-Low-Medium	Customers who haven't made recent purchases but have some value	Win-back campaigns communicate product value
Lost Customers	Low-Low-Low	No recent purchases, no frequency, low value	Evaluate whether to target with special offers or drop

Explanation:

1 **Champions** are your most valuable customers, who frequently make high-value purchases. Focus on retaining them with VIP offers and exclusive rewards.
2 **Loyal Customers** are frequent purchasers with high value but moderate recent activity. Incentivize them to keep their purchases consistent with special reactivation offers.
3 **Potential Loyalists** are recent purchasers showing moderate engagement and purchasing value. Encourage them with discounts and promotions to convert them into loyal customers.
4 **Recent Buyers** have made a recent purchase but may need nurturing to increase their frequency. Use onboarding campaigns to familiarize them with the brand.
5 **Occasional Shoppers** buy every now and then. Target them with promotional offers to encourage more frequent purchases.
6 **At Risk Customers** are those who used to buy often but haven't made a purchase recently. A win-back campaign can encourage them to return.
7 **Price Sensitive** buyers tend to make occasional purchases when there are discounts. Run targeted campaigns during sales to motivate them to buy.
8 **Lapsed Customers** may still hold some potential value. A carefully planned win-back campaign could encourage them to return.
9 **Lost Customers** are unlikely to return and often require the most effort to re-engage. Consider whether a targeted approach is worth the investment.
10 **Descriptive CLTV** helps us understand which segments have historically contributed the most value to the business, allowing product managers to allocate resources to retain those customers effectively.
11 **Predictive CLTV** allows us to estimate the future value of customers in each segment, enabling proactive strategies for customer retention, upselling, and re-engagement.

By combining **RFM Analysis** with **Customer Lifetime Value** (CLTV) insights, product managers can effectively create a **customer-first approach,** focusing not only on high-value customers but also identifying segments that have the potential to become valuable over time. This combination of retrospective and prospective analysis helps businesses in creating more targeted and effective marketing strategies.

10.4 Customer Journey Analytics

Customer Journey Analytics (CJA) is the process of connecting data across different touchpoints to measure user behaviours throughout their journey, not just during the ideal paths.

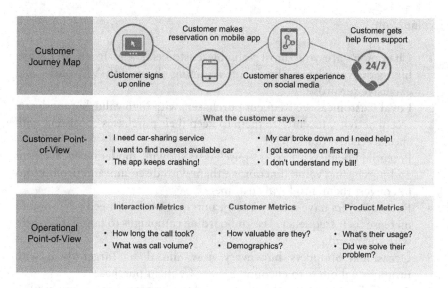

FIGURE 10.5 Customer Journey Analytics in Mapping Customer Experience.

Using **Car-Sharing Platforms like QuikDrive** as an example, the journey of car owners and car renters can be analysed to enhance user satisfaction.

Figure 10.5 depicts how **Customer Journey Analytics** is used to map customer experience.

1 **User Journey Map**: By tracking user interactions across different stages, product analytics helps visualize the complete user journey. For instance, **QuikDrive** uses journey mapping to understand where guests or hosts face challenges, allowing them to optimize the experience at every stage, from signing up online, making reservation, sharing experience on social media to getting help from support.

 By tracking user interactions across different stages, product analytics helps visualize the complete user journey. For instance, **QuikDrive** uses journey mapping to understand where both guests and hosts face challenges, allowing them to optimize the experience at every stage, from:

 A **Signing Up Online**:

 • Analyse how many customers successfully create an account, identify where users drop off, and optimize the sign-up flow to improve user acquisition.

 B **Making Reservations**:

 • Track how many users successfully complete the booking process. Identify stages with high abandonment rates (e.g., payment) and streamline the flow to reduce drop-offs.

C **Sharing Experiences on Social Media:**

- Measure social media mentions, reviews, and shares to understand how users feel about the service. Use insights to enhance word-of-mouth marketing.

D **Getting Help from Support:**

- Monitor support requests to understand where users face challenges. Provide proactive solutions, such as knowledge-based articles, to minimize friction and support dependency.

By mapping the **entire customer journey**, QuikDrive identifies opportunities for improvement at each touchpoint. This approach ensures a cohesive and engaging experience, turning occasional users into loyal customers. For example, if the analytics show a high drop-off rate during payment, product managers can prioritize streamlining the payment gateway for a more user-friendly and efficient experience.

2 **Customer POV**: Analysing what users think, feel, and experience at each touchpoint helps identify friction points that affect the journey.

What Customers Are Saying:

A **"I need a car-sharing service."**

- The customer wants a seamless way to rent a car for their needs. They start their journey by searching for available cars in their vicinity.

B **"I want to find the nearest available car."**

- Customers are looking for convenience and accessibility when choosing a car. They value accurate information regarding the nearest available cars.

C **"The app keeps crashing!"**

- Customers experience frustration when the app isn't stable or user-friendly, which hinders their ability to make bookings or manage rentals.

D **"My car broke down, and I need help!"**

- When issues arise, customers expect swift support, such as roadside assistance or guidance, for resolving any technical problems.

E **"I got someone on the first ring."**

- Customers are pleased when support is accessible and responsive. Quick access to customer support is a key determinant of satisfaction.

F **"I don't understand my bill!"**
- Customers may have difficulty understanding their billing details, which can create confusion and dissatisfaction if not properly addressed.

For **QuikDrive**, the **Customer POV** provides valuable insights into what users are saying and experiencing throughout their journey. Whether customers are looking for a car-sharing service, facing technical difficulties with the app, or needing roadside assistance, understanding their needs and frustrations is crucial. This customer-centric perspective allows **QuikDrive's** product managers to emphasize empathy – understanding the exact moments that delight or cause friction, and implementing solutions that enhance each user's overall experience, from booking to car return.

3 **Operational POV**: Analysing what processes or workflows may be causing friction, such as booking issues or availability challenges. This perspective focuses on metrics that help the business understand and improve customer experience, product efficiency, and support quality.

  1 **Interaction Metrics**

  - **Call Duration**:
    - Measure the average time taken to resolve customer issues or answer queries during support calls. Shorter durations often indicate more efficient support.
  - **Call Volume**:
    - Understand the number of calls received over a given period, especially during peak times, to identify patterns in support needs.
  - **First Contact Resolution (FCR)**:
    - Measure the percentage of issues resolved during the initial interaction with the customer. High **FCR** is a positive indicator of support effectiveness.
  - **Channel Utilization**:
    - Analyse the number of interactions per channel (e.g., app chat, phone support, social media) to determine where most customers seek assistance.

2 **Customer Metrics**
  - **Customer Lifetime Value (CLTV)**:
    - Evaluate how much revenue a customer is likely to generate over their entire relationship with the platform, allowing the prioritization of high-value customers.
  - **Customer Segmentation**:
    - Identify different segments of customers, such as frequent renters, occasional users, and first-time customers, to better understand customer behaviour and preferences.

- **Customer Satisfaction (CSAT):**
  - Use surveys or **NPS** scores after support interactions to assess customer satisfaction levels and identify areas for improvement.
- **Demographics:**
  - Analyse customer data such as age, location, and gender to customize marketing strategies or refine user experiences for specific demographics.

3 **Product Metrics**
- **App Performance:**
  - Monitor app stability metrics such as crash frequency, load times, and response times to identify and address technical issues that impact the user experience.
- **Feature Usage:**
  - Track how often certain features are used, such as "Find Nearest Available Car" or "Roadside Assistance." Understanding which features are popular helps prioritize future feature enhancements.
- **Problem Resolution Rate:**
  - Determine how many reported issues (e.g., app crashes or billing problems) are successfully resolved, and how long it takes to resolve them.
- **Booking Conversion Rate:**
  - Measure how many users who searched for a car successfully completed a booking, helping to identify any drop-offs or barriers in the booking process.

The **Operational POV** provides an in-depth look at metrics related to interaction, customer behaviour, and product performance. For **QuikDrive**, this means understanding the duration of support calls, analysing call volumes during peak times, identifying customer segments by demographics, and assessing car usage metrics. Such operational insights enable the **QuikDrive** team to measure the effectiveness of their services, streamline processes, and optimize resource allocation to meet customer needs more efficiently.

10.5 Conclusion

In this chapter, we delved into the critical importance of customer retention and the various analytics tools available to measure and improve it. By understanding and analysing customer behaviour through techniques such as **Cohort Retention Analysis, RFM analysis**, and **Customer Journey Mapping**, product managers can pinpoint the key drivers of customer loyalty and reduce churn. Retaining customers is essential to product success, and the insights gained from analysing the customer journey can shape how we enhance the user experience and optimize long-term engagement.

As we look ahead, retention is only part of the broader picture. **Product Adoption** is equally crucial, especially when it comes to ensuring that new features and improvements resonate with users. In the next chapter, we will build on the concepts of retention by exploring how product analytics can drive feature adoption and how tools can help product teams enhance their offerings.

11

DRIVING PRODUCT ADOPTION WITH ANALYTICS TOOLS

11.1 Introduction

Product adoption is a vital metric that indicates whether users are finding value in a product and engaging with its key features. In the digital product management landscape, leveraging analytics tools is essential for tracking, measuring, and improving this adoption. This chapter delves into how product managers can harness analytics tools to not only observe user behaviour but also inform decisions about feature development, prioritization, and optimization.

With the right set of tools, product teams can gain granular insights into how users interact with features, which features are driving value, and where there may be opportunities for improvement. From user research to product management tools, understanding the broad range of analytics available is key to driving better outcomes.

Additionally, this chapter will explore the categorization of analytics tools and how different roles within the product and extended teams can collaborate to extract value from them. Whether through real-time data on feature adoption or prioritization of future developments, product analytics is at the heart of modern digital product management, enabling teams to stay competitive and user-focused throughout the product lifecycle.

11.2 Feature Adoption

Feature Adoption refers to the process through which customers begin using and integrating new product features into their daily routines or workflows. Understanding feature adoption is critical for product managers, as it provides

DOI: 10.1201/9781003614180-11

insights into how effective a feature is, how well it resonates with users, and whether it aligns with user needs and expectations. Product managers can leverage product analytics to encourage feature adoption and refine their offerings effectively.

11.2.1 Techniques for Leveraging Product Analytics to Drive Feature Adoption

Leveraging product analytics is crucial for driving feature adoption, enabling product managers to understand user engagement, identify friction points, and optimize feature usage. By employing techniques like behaviour tracking, A/B testing, segmentation analysis, and targeted in-app messaging, product teams can boost feature adoption, ensure alignment with user needs, and enhance the overall product experience.

1 **User Segmentation and Targeting**

- Product managers can segment users based on their behaviours, demographics, or usage patterns to target the right audience for feature adoption. For example,
- **Example: Spotify** uses user segmentation to identify specific users who are likely to be interested in a new feature, such as playlist sharing. This way, they can focus their marketing and in-app messages on the right group.

2 **In-App Messaging and Notifications**

- In-app messages, pop-ups, or push notifications are effective techniques for driving feature discovery and engagement. These messages can be used to introduce a new feature and encourage users to try it out by highlighting its benefits or demonstrating how it can solve a specific problem for them.
- **Example: Instagram** introduced the "Reels" feature by showing an in-app tutorial to users who frequently created stories or watched video content. These notifications prompted users to create short videos, leading to a significant boost in feature adoption.

3 **A/B Testing and Optimization**

- Product managers can use **A/B** testing to evaluate how different variations of a feature or its introduction impact user adoption. By testing different UI elements, copy, or calls to action (**CTAs**), they can determine which approach works best in promoting the feature.
- **Example: LinkedIn** used A/B testing to refine its "Skill Endorsement" feature. By testing different ways to encourage users to endorse

connections' skills, they found the optimal approach to increase the adoption of this feature.

4 Guided Onboarding and Tutorials

- Providing guided onboarding experiences and interactive tutorials for new features can help users understand the value of the feature quickly. Users who receive step-by-step guidance are more likely to adopt the feature compared to those who have to figure it out on their own.
- **Example: Dropbox** uses interactive walkthroughs to demonstrate how to use collaboration features like "Dropbox Paper." By guiding users through the initial steps, they ensure that users feel comfortable using the feature right from the start.

5 Behavioural Triggers

- Behavioural triggers, such as sending an email or in-app message when a user performs a specific action, can be used to promote new features relevant to the user's recent activities. This personalization helps increase the likelihood of feature adoption.
- **Example: Slack** uses behavioural triggers to promote features like "Huddle." For example, when a user frequently sends messages in a specific channel, they receive a prompt to initiate a Huddle, highlighting the benefit of instant audio discussions.

6 Product Tours and Feature Highlights

- Creating product tours that highlight the benefits of a newly launched feature allows users to understand what the feature does and why it might be beneficial for them. This is especially useful for features that might not be immediately visible.
- **Example: Microsoft Teams** introduced "Together Mode" by displaying an optional product tour when users entered video meetings. This tour explained how the feature could improve meeting experiences, leading to higher adoption rates.

7 Incentivization and Rewards

- Offering incentives or rewards for users to try out a new feature is another effective technique to drive adoption. These incentives could be in the form of discounts, exclusive access, or even loyalty points.
- **Example: Airbnb** incentivizes hosts to adopt new features by offering discounts on booking fees or access to premium services. This strategy helps boost the adoption of features like "Smart Pricing" among hosts.

8 Analysing Drop-off Points and Bottlenecks

- By analysing product analytics, product managers can identify drop-off points where users abandon a feature. Understanding where and why users stop engaging with the feature provides valuable insights for optimizing the user experience and improving adoption rates.

- **Example: Netflix** tracks where users abandon a feature, such as adding a movie to a watchlist. They identified that users would often drop off when recommendations became repetitive. **Netflix** addressed this by improving the recommendation algorithm to provide more personalized suggestions, which resulted in increased watchlist feature adoption.

9 **Measuring Feature Adoption Metrics**

- Product managers can use product analytics to measure key metrics related to feature adoption, such as **Feature Usage Frequency, Time to First Use,** and **Engagement Depth**. These metrics provide a comprehensive view of how a feature is being adopted and its overall impact.
- **Example: Trello** tracks the frequency of "Power-Up" activations to understand how often users engage with its integrations. This helps **Trello** prioritize which Power-Ups are valuable and should be expanded upon, vs. those that need improvements.

11.2.2   Types of Product Features to Focus On

When evaluating product features using product analytics, it's important for product managers to understand the variety of features that contribute to a product's appeal and success. Different types of features serve different user needs, and effective product analytics should consider each type in relation to the overall user experience, adoption, and retention. Below are several types of product features that product managers should focus on in their analytics efforts:

1. Core Features

Core features are the foundational functionalities of a product. These features solve the primary problem that the product addresses or provide the essential tasks that users need to complete. They are non-negotiable and form the backbone of the product. Understanding how users interact with core features helps product managers determine if the product is delivering its core value and if users are deriving the expected benefits.

- **Analytics Focus:** Track feature usage frequency, engagement depth, and time to first use to assess whether core features are meeting user needs.
- **Example:** For **Slack**, core features include instant messaging and file sharing. Without these, **Slack** would not be considered a collaboration app. Product managers at **Slack** would focus heavily on analysing how often users send messages, share files, or make calls, to ensure these foundational features are used effectively.

2. Usability Features

Usability features enhance the product's ease of use and overall user experience. These are the features that provide users with a smooth, intuitive journey through the product, such as in-app guides, navigation elements, and customizable settings. While they aren't strictly necessary for delivering the core functionality, they play a crucial role in user satisfaction and conversion.

- **Analytics Focus**: Analyse drop-off points, user flow metrics, and customer satisfaction (**CSAT**) to determine how usability features impact the overall user experience.
- **Example:** Trello includes usability features like drag-and-drop cards and customizable labels. Analysing these features allows product managers to understand how they influence productivity and user satisfaction, leading to improvements in user retention.

3. Power Features

Power features are intended for more advanced or experienced users who need greater customization, control, or complex functionality. These features are not needed by all users but are essential for power users who want to maximize the potential of the product. Analysing power feature usage helps identify which users are the most engaged and how these features impact long-term retention.

- **Analytics Focus**: Monitor feature adoption among advanced users, frequency of use, and impact on retention to understand the value these features provide to your power users.
- **Example:** Userpilot offers detailed analytics dashboards for tracking user behaviour in SaaS products. Analysing which users engage with these advanced dashboards and how frequently provides insights into which customers derive the most value from them, helping the product team identify and nurture power users.

4. Niche Features

Niche features are designed to cater to the specific needs or preferences of certain user segments. These features often serve as powerful differentiators and help build loyalty within a particular audience. Analysing niche feature usage helps product managers understand how different segments interact with the product and what features are most valuable to them.

- **Analytics Focus**: Segment user analytics by audience type to determine which features are most valuable to specific segments. Assess retention and loyalty metrics for users who engage with niche features.
- **Example:** Xero, the online accounting software, offers a feature to automate tax calculations based on the user's region. Analysing the

adoption of this feature among customers in different regions helps **Xero** understand which markets are benefiting most and tailor their marketing strategies accordingly.

5. Engagement Features

Engagement features are designed to keep users active within the product. These features might include gamification elements, reminders, social interactions, or rewards. Analysing these features helps product managers understand how well the product is keeping users engaged and what motivates users to return.

- **Analytics Focus:** Measure engagement rates, session frequency, and user actions prompted by these features to evaluate their impact on overall engagement and retention.
- **Example: Duolingo** uses gamification to keep users coming back through streaks, badges, and leaderboards. By analysing user behaviour around these engagement features, **Duolingo's** product managers can determine how these features impact user motivation and language-learning consistency.

6. Retention Features

Retention features are intended to bring users back to the product and reduce churn. Examples include personalized content, loyalty programmes, and notifications that remind users of product value. Analysing retention features helps determine whether the implemented strategies are effective in keeping users engaged over time.

- **Analytics Focus:** Track metrics such as user churn rate, notification click-through rates, and loyalty programme enrolment to assess the effectiveness of retention features.
- **Example: Netflix** uses personalized recommendations to retain users. By analysing click-through rates on personalized content and viewing patterns, **Netflix** determines how well these features work in keeping users subscribed.

7. Monetization Features

Monetization features are those that directly drive revenue, such as premium upgrades, in-app purchases, and subscription plans. Understanding how users interact with monetization features helps product managers develop pricing strategies, optimize revenue generation, and determine when and how to upsell or cross-sell.

- **Analytics Focus:** Monitor conversion rates for premium upgrades, revenue from in-app purchases, and user segments that generate the most revenue.

- **Example:** Spotify offers a premium subscription with additional features like ad-free listening and offline playback. Analysing how free users interact with ads and upgrade offers provides insights into what drives subscription conversions.

Focusing on the different types of product features through product analytics helps product managers make informed decisions to improve user experience, drive feature adoption, and maximize product success. By categorizing features as core, usability, power, niche, engagement, retention, and monetization, product managers can effectively prioritize their efforts and deliver greater value to their users. Analysing how different segments interact with each type of feature provides a comprehensive understanding of user needs and behaviour, ultimately leading to a more successful and well-rounded product.

11.2.3   Best Practices for Product Feature Adoption Analysis

To effectively analyse product feature adoption, product managers should leverage specific best practices that provide a comprehensive understanding of user interactions, improve decision-making, and ultimately enhance the product experience.

Below are some best practices for performing a product feature adoption analysis, as shown in Figure 11.1.

1. Analyse Your Competitors
Conducting a **Strengths, Weaknesses, Opportunities,** and **Threats (SWOT)** analysis of your competitors provides valuable insights into market positioning and user expectations. By analysing your competitors' features, product managers can identify opportunities to differentiate their products and fill the gaps in the market.

- **Approach:** Assess the strengths that make your competitors successful, such as well-adopted features or unique offerings. Likewise, analyse where they fall short or where user complaints occur, as these weaknesses can be opportunities to deliver a superior experience.
- **Example:** Consider a wellness platform competing with other health and fitness apps. Performing a **SWOT** analysis could reveal that a competitor's app lacks social features, which can become an opportunity for you to introduce more engaging social tools, such as community challenges or virtual coaching.

2. Encourage Users to Share Feedback
User feedback is an invaluable resource for analysing product feature adoption. It provides direct insights into how users interact with your product

FIGURE 11.1 Feature Adoption Analysis.

and what they expect from it, allowing product managers to prioritize and improve features accordingly.

- **Approach**: Set up in-app surveys, feedback prompts, or dedicated customer service channels to gather user insights. Encourage users to be specific in their feedback to get a better understanding of what needs improvement.
- **Example**: For instance, **Microsoft Teams** regularly prompts users to rate their experience after video calls, asking them to provide additional feedback. This feedback is then analysed to improve usability features and address common pain points.

3. Use Segmentation to Improve Personalization

Segmenting users based on roles, industry, usage frequency, or any other relevant attribute helps product managers understand how different segments interact with product features. Different user groups may have distinct expectations, and analysing their feature usage helps improve personalization.

- **Approach**: Identify different user segments (e.g., power users, occasional users, or industry-specific users) and analyse their feature usage data separately. This helps in determining which features are particularly valued by different segments and how to personalize the experience for each group.
- **Example**: Suppose you have a **B2B SaaS** platform used by both small businesses and enterprises. Segmenting by company size can reveal that enterprise users use advanced analytics features more extensively, while small businesses prioritize ease of use. This insight can drive targeted product improvements and marketing strategies.

4. Involve Cross-Functional Teams

Collaboration across teams is essential for gaining well-rounded insights during feature adoption analysis. Each department brings unique perspectives to the table, helping ensure a comprehensive analysis.

- **Approach**: Involve stakeholders from different teams, such as engineering, sales, marketing, and customer support. They can provide valuable insights regarding user challenges, technical feasibility, sales challenges, and customer needs.
- **Example**: Product managers at **Shopify** involve engineering, customer support, and marketing teams when analysing feature adoption data. The engineering team provides insights into technical feasibility, customer support provides feedback on customer pain points, and marketing contributes to understanding how specific features align with user expectations.

5. Measure Key Metrics Related to Feature Usage

Analysing product feature adoption involves measuring specific metrics to determine how successfully a feature has been integrated into the user experience. These metrics include frequency of feature usage, average time spent on features, and engagement rates.

- **Approach**: Use analytics tools like **Amplitude** or **Mixpanel** to measure key feature adoption metrics, such as feature engagement rates, frequency of use, and drop-off points. Analyse which features drive the most engagement and identify areas where users may be struggling.
- **Example**: A video conferencing tool such as **Zoom** might track how often the "screen sharing" feature is used in meetings, as well as how long participants stay engaged while using this feature. These insights are then used to enhance the screen-sharing experience.

6. Identify the Aha! Moment for Each Feature

The "Aha! Moment" is the point at which a user realizes the value of a feature. Identifying this moment allows product managers to optimize the onboarding experience to help users reach it faster.

- **Approach**: Track which actions or behaviours lead users to become fully engaged with a feature. The quicker users experience the "Aha! Moment," the more likely they are to continue using the feature and derive value from it.
- **Example**: In a project management tool like **Trello**, the "Aha! Moment" might be when users create their first board and add cards to it. Analysing the onboarding flow and improving the steps that lead users to create boards can help increase feature adoption rates.

7. Prioritize Features Based on User Needs

Not all features will be of equal importance to every user, and prioritizing features based on user needs is key to improving product adoption. Understanding which features are critical helps the team allocate resources efficiently.

- **Approach**: Analyse user data to determine which features are most critical for achieving user goals. This helps in allocating resources towards enhancing features that drive the most value.
- **Example**: A fintech app like **Revolut** might discover that users value security features the most. As a result, the product team might prioritize enhancing multi-factor authentication and security alerts to increase user trust and retention.

8. Set Up A/B Testing to Validate Feature Effectiveness

A/B testing allows product managers to validate the effectiveness of new features and understand their impact on user behaviour. This helps determine whether a particular feature is driving adoption as intended or needs further refinement.

- **Approach**: Create two versions of a feature and randomly assign them to different user groups. Analyse user behaviour to determine which version performs better in terms of engagement and retention.
- **Example**: Spotify might **A/B** test different ways of displaying playlists to users – one group might see curated recommendations, while the other sees playlists created by friends. Analysing engagement rates helps **Spotify** determine which approach leads to higher feature adoption.

9. Review Feature Adoption Data Regularly

Product managers should review feature adoption data on a regular basis to identify trends, measure the impact of product changes, and refine the product roadmap. This practice ensures that product development is data-driven and in line with user needs.

- **Approach**: Set up a regular cadence for reviewing analytics dashboards to understand how feature adoption is progressing. Use this data to refine the product strategy and prioritize features for further development.
- **Example**: Netflix regularly reviews feature usage data, such as how often users engage with the "Skip Intro" feature, to determine if similar features should be introduced for different types of content.

Feature Adoption Analysis is a critical practice for product managers to understand user engagement and improve the overall user experience. By following these best practices – such as analysing competitors, gathering user feedback, segmenting users, collaborating across teams, and regularly reviewing data – product managers can effectively drive feature adoption, improve product-market fit, and create products that resonate with their users. An effective feature adoption strategy not only enhances the user experience but also improves customer satisfaction and retention, contributing to the long-term success of the product.

11.2.4 Summary: Feature Adoption

Feature Adoption is a critical aspect of product success, providing insights into how well a new capability resonates with users. By leveraging product analytics through segmentation, behavioural triggers, **A/B** testing, guided onboarding, and other data-driven techniques, product managers can maximize feature adoption and ensure that customers are deriving the intended value from their product. Using examples from companies like **Slack, Dropbox,** and **Airbnb** illustrates how these strategies are applied in practice, leading to improved user experiences and overall product success.

11.3 Product Analytics Tools

Product analytics tools are indispensable for the entire product team, providing insights across the product lifecycle – from initial development to continuous improvement. To gain a more detailed understanding, it is essential to look at how these tools are categorized, the different users within the product ecosystem who leverage these tools, and the metrics they generate.

11.3.1 Categorization of Product Analytics Tools

Product analytics tools can be categorized into four primary groups, each tailored for different stages of product development and different roles in the product lifecycle:

1. User Research Tools
User research tools help gather data about customer preferences, pain points, and behaviour. These tools are crucial during the discovery phase and help product managers and UX researchers validate assumptions and better understand customer needs.

- **Examples:**

    - **SurveyMonkey:** Enables conducting surveys for understanding customer needs and gathering quantitative feedback.
    - **UserTesting:** Provides video recordings of real users interacting with your product to understand the user experience.

2. Product Design Software
These tools assist in creating the overall product design, including visual layout, interface elements, and user journeys.

- **Examples:**

    - **Figma:** A powerful collaborative interface design tool used by product designers to create interactive prototypes and visual mockups.
    - **Sketch:** A vector graphics editor for UI and UX design, commonly used by designers to iterate on the product's look and feel.

3. Prototyping Tools
Prototyping tools help create interactive versions of products or features to get a feel of the end-user experience before actual development.

- **Examples**:
  - **InVision**: An industry standard for prototyping, enabling designers to create clickable mockups and share them with stakeholders for feedback.
  - **Axure**: A tool used for creating more complex, interactive prototypes and flow diagrams, often used by UX designers to iterate on feature sets.

4. Product Management Tools
These tools provide features for managing the product lifecycle, including planning, tracking, collaboration, and analysis.

- **Examples**:
  - **Jira**: An agile project management tool used to manage product backlogs, sprints, and development milestones.
  - **Trello**: A visual project management tool that helps product managers keep track of tasks, workflows, and team progress.
  - **Heap/Amplitude**: Product analytics tools that provide actionable insights to help optimize feature adoption and measure success metrics.

11.3.2 Users of Product Analytics Tools

Product analytics tools are used by different members of the product team, as well as extended core team members like Sales, MarCom, and Support. The roles of these different users and how they use the tools are explained below:

1 Product Team Members
- **Product Managers**: Use tools like **Jira**, **Heap**, and **Amplitude** to define features, prioritize development, track progress, and measure performance. Metrics like feature adoption, retention rates, and user behaviour help product managers make data-driven decisions.
- **UX/UI Designers**: Tools like **Figma** and **Sketch** are used to design user interfaces and experiences. These tools provide mockups and prototypes to understand user flows and validate designs.
- **Product Analysts**: Use **Google Analytics**, **Amplitude**, and **Mixpanel** to collect and analyse user engagement and product performance metrics, helping the product team understand how features are being used.

- **Developers**: Use tools like **Jira** for tracking work, understanding requirements, and ensuring the features they develop align with user needs.

2 Extended Core Team Members

- **Sales Teams**: Use CRM tools such as **Salesforce** integrated with product analytics like **Amplitude** to track the journey of leads, qualify customer segments, and prioritize sales efforts based on product usage insights.
- **MarCom Teams (Marketing and Communication)**: Use tools like **Google Analytics** and **Hotjar** to understand user interaction, website behaviour, and campaign performance, informing marketing campaigns and messaging.
- **Support Teams**: Use customer support tools like **Zendesk** integrated with product analytics to understand customer issues, address pain points, and provide support based on user behaviours.

11.3.3   Metrics: How Tools Help across the Product Lifecycle

Product Analytics tools generate a variety of metrics to help the product and product ops teams in their roles and responsibilities across the entire product lifecycle, from development to continuous improvement. The key metrics and insights provided include:

1 Metrics for Discovery and Design

- **User Research**: Tools like **UserTesting** and **SurveyMonkey** help product managers collect qualitative and quantitative insights into customer needs.
- **Design Metrics**: Tools like **Figma** provide insights into user flows and visual engagement, allowing designers to validate interface designs and interactions.

2 Metrics for Development

- **Feature Prioritization**: **Jira** and **Trello** help product managers track feature backlog and sprints. Using metrics such as story points and velocity, development progress can be assessed.
- **Developer Productivity**: Metrics such as sprint completion rates and the number of stories completed are generated from **Jira**, helping product managers assess productivity.

3 Metrics for Product Launch and Activation

- **Customer Activation Metrics**: Tools like **Amplitude** and **Heap** provide metrics such as activation rates, onboarding completion rates, and drop-off points during onboarding. These metrics help product managers optimize the onboarding experience for users.

- **Example: Spotify** uses **Amplitude** to monitor activation rates when introducing new features like "Spotify Wrapped."

4 Metrics for Product Usage and Retention

- **Usage Analytics:** Metrics such as feature adoption, session duration, and engagement rate are provided by tools like **Mixpanel**. These metrics help product managers understand which features are popular and which need improvement.

  - **Example: Instagram** used **Mixpanel** to track the adoption of the "Stories" feature and refine it based on user engagement.

5 Metrics for Churn and Customer Satisfaction

- **Customer Retention Metrics: Google Analytics** and **Amplitude** provide cohort retention metrics to analyse the behaviour of retained vs. churned users.

  - **Example: Dropbox** uses **Amplitude** to understand which actions during onboarding correlate with higher retention, such as file uploads and link-sharing activity.

- **Customer Satisfaction (CSAT):** Tools like **Hotjar** and **Qualtrics** provide surveys and heatmaps, allowing product teams to measure user satisfaction with key features.

6 Metrics for Revenue Growth and Continuous Improvement

- **Conversion Rates:** Tools like **Adobe Analytics** and **Heap** provide data on how users move through the product funnel, identifying friction points that need to be optimized to increase conversion.

  - **Example: IKEA** uses **Adobe Analytics** to track conversion rates, optimize user engagement, and refine digital experiences, improving conversion points and reducing bounce rates for better customer interactions and increased sales.

- **CLV and RFM Analysis: Salesforce** integrated with analytics platforms like **Pendo** provides insights into Customer Lifetime Value (**CLV**) and segmentation based on Recency, Frequency, and Monetary value (**RFM**).

  - **Example: Singapore Airlines (SIA)** uses **Salesforce** integrated with its analytics system to identify loyal customers, helping craft personalized offers for high-value travellers.

11.4 Conclusion

In this chapter, we explored how analytics tools are integral to driving product adoption and optimizing the user experience. By focusing on data-driven insights, product managers can prioritize feature development, track how users interact with the product, and continuously improve the value delivered to customers. Analytics tools offer a powerful way to ensure that product decisions are based on real user behaviour rather than assumptions.

As we conclude this chapter, it's important to reflect on the broader role of product analytics, as covered in Chapters 9–11. In Chapter 9, we introduced product metrics and user experience insights, focusing on **Pirate Metrics (AARRR)** and key customer experience **KPIs** like **NPS, CSAT**, and **CES** to gauge how well products meet customer needs. Chapter 10 then highlighted the importance of understanding customer retention through cohort analysis, retention curves, and journey analytics to uncover key factors driving loyalty and churn.

Together, these chapters provide a comprehensive guide to leveraging product analytics throughout the entire product lifecycle – from acquisition and activation to retention, adoption, and continuous improvement. With the right tools and data-driven approach, product teams can create meaningful customer experiences and ensure long-term success by constantly refining their products based on real-world user insights. As we move forward to examine the broader operational framework in Chapter 12, we will shift focus to the **Product Operating Model**, which helps bring these insights into action through structured processes and organizational alignment.

12

BUILDING THE PRODUCT OPERATING MODEL

12.1 Introduction

The **Product Operating Model (POM)** is an essential framework that connects product management activities with an organization's broader strategic goals, enabling product teams to deliver value efficiently and consistently. In today's competitive landscape, a well-structured operating model ensures that product managers not only create successful products but also align their efforts with the company's long-term vision. This chapter explores the key components of a **POM** and how it helps product teams maintain agility, drive innovation, and foster collaboration across departments.

In this chapter, we will discuss how to build and manage a **POM** that enhances organizational alignment, optimizes technology usage, and effectively manages portfolios. You'll discover how the **POM** can be a tool for creating a scalable, repeatable process that supports growth and continuous improvement. We will also dive into performance management, capability development, and the importance of robust process governance. By the end of this chapter, you will have a clear understanding of how to structure a **POM** to drive product success and support long-term organizational growth.

12.2 POM in Digital Product Management Framework

The **POM** not only complements the **Digital Product Management (DPM)** Framework but also aligns with the organization's broader strategic and leadership oversight. From an organizational perspective, the **POM** serves as a bridge between the day-to-day operational aspects of product management and the high-level strategic objectives set by leadership. It provides a

DOI: 10.1201/9781003614180-12

structured framework that ensures the goals outlined in the **DPM**'s core process groups are fully aligned with the company's long-term vision, market positioning, and competitive strategy. Figure 12.1 shows the **POM** within the **DPM** Framework.

Leadership teams rely on the **POM** to maintain oversight of resource allocation, performance metrics, and cross-functional collaboration, allowing them to make informed decisions that drive sustainable growth. By offering a clear structure for innovation management, portfolio management, and capability development, the **POM** supports leadership in steering product initiatives that align with the organization's strategic goals. This ensures that product managers not only focus on executing their tasks but also operate within a system that encourages continuous alignment with the company's mission, values, and long-term market positioning. In essence, the **POM** enables leadership to maintain the balance between strategic direction and operational execution, fostering innovation and ensuring market responsiveness across the product lifecycle.

12.3 Components in the Product Operating Model

12.3.1 Organizational Alignment

Organizational Alignment ensures that all parts of a business – from leadership to product teams – are working together towards common goals. For product management, alignment is essential to ensuring that products are developed, launched, and supported in ways that reflect the overall strategic objectives of the company.

Two types of alignment are critical: **Vertical Alignment**, which connects the product strategy to the company's overarching goals, and **Horizontal Alignment**, which ensures collaboration between different teams across the organization.

1 **Vertical Alignment: Company-Level vs. Product-Level Strategy**
   Vertical Alignment refers to ensuring that the product strategy is consistent with the company's broader mission and goals. The product's vision should directly support the company's mission, and the product roadmap should be designed to meet these high-level objectives.
   A typical strategic alignment looks like this:

   • **Company Mission:** Defines the overarching purpose of the organization and what it aims to achieve.
   • **Product Vision:** Outlines the specific value a product will deliver to customers and how it will contribute to fulfilling the company's mission.

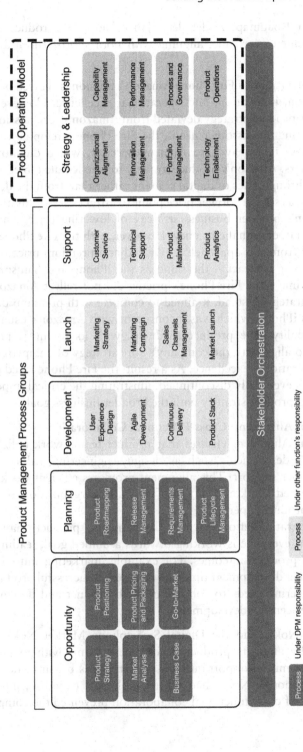

FIGURE 12.1 Product Operating Model in DPM Framework.

- **Product Roadmap:** A detailed plan of how the product vision will be executed over time, aligning with both short-term and long-term company goals.

  Example: Amazon Fire Phone Amazon's mission is centred on customer obsession, innovation, and operational excellence. However, the **Fire Phone's** product strategy deviated from **Amazon's** core mission. Instead of focusing on customer needs, the Fire Phone attempted to create an ecosystem tied heavily to **Amazon** services, which did not resonate with users. **Amazon's** product strategy for the **Kindle tablet** was clear – profit through sales of digital content rather than from the device itself, which was sold at a lower price point to attract users. This aligned with **Amazon's** broader business strategy of lowering prices and winning through operational efficiency. However, with the **Fire Phone,** Amazon strayed from this approach. Launched at a premium price of $199 on a two-year contract – the same as the **iPhone** and **Samsung Galaxy** at the time – the **Fire Phone's** pricing did not reflect **Amazon's** lower-price strategy. Instead, it aimed to compete with premium devices like **Apple's iPhone,** which was inconsistent with **Amazon's** usual focus on affordability. The product roadmap, with its premium positioning, failed to align with the company's core strategy of competitive pricing and operational excellence. As a result, the **Fire Phone** faced poor sales and was eventually discontinued, illustrating the critical importance of aligning product strategy with the broader business goals.

2 **Horizontal Alignment: Cross-Functional Collaboration**
Horizontal Alignment ensures that product teams work collaboratively with other departments such as design, engineering, sales, marketing, and customer support. This alignment promotes efficient workflows and reduces siloed thinking, allowing the entire organization to deliver a cohesive product experience.

By integrating efforts across departments, product managers can ensure that everyone is working towards a unified goal, leading to more successful product outcomes. For example, marketing must be aligned with product development timelines to ensure a successful product launch, and engineering needs to collaborate with product and design teams to ensure user-centred development.

Example: Nokia and the Digital Smartphone Market Nokia failed to horizontally align its product development teams with market trends, resulting in missed opportunities as smartphones began to dominate the market. Although Nokia had the technological expertise, internal silos and a lack of cross-functional collaboration prevented the company from responding swiftly to the growing competition from companies like **Apple** and **Samsung**.

Example: Kodak and Digital Photography Kodak's failure to embrace digital photography despite its own invention of the technology was another example of poor alignment. While Kodak's corporate mission was rooted in capturing moments and memories, it clung too long to its profitable film business. There was a lack of horizontal alignment between R&D, marketing, and leadership, which ultimately led to Kodak's downfall.

3 **Strategic Alignment Framework**

The importance of strategic alignment cannot be overstated, as it directly influences the success of products in the market. By following a clear framework – starting from the company mission and moving through product vision and road mapping – organizations can ensure alignment at all levels:

- **Company Mission**: Articulates the broader purpose and values of the organization.
- **Product Vision**: A forward-looking statement that describes how the product will solve customer problems and add value, while advancing the company's mission.
- **Product Roadmap**: A strategic tool that translates the product vision into actionable steps, detailing the features, timelines, and resources needed to achieve key milestones.

4 **OKRs and SMART Goals**

OKRs and **SMART** Goals are instrumental in aligning strategic objectives with day-to-day product activities.

OKRs (Objectives and Key Results) are a goal-setting framework used to define and track objectives and their outcomes. An **Objective** is a clear, qualitative goal that defines what you want to achieve, while **Key Results** are specific, measurable actions that indicate how you will achieve that objective. **OKRs** help organizations focus on outcomes rather than tasks, driving alignment and accountability across teams. They are typically set quarterly or annually, and the results are reviewed regularly to assess progress and make adjustments as necessary.

SMART Goals, on the other hand, are a more traditional goal-setting approach that ensures goals are **Specific, Measurable, Achievable, Relevant,** and **Time-bound**. This method provides clear criteria for what a successful goal looks like and when it should be achieved. **SMART** Goals focus on clarity and feasibility, ensuring that each goal is well-defined and realistic within a given timeframe.

While **OKRs** drive innovation and growth by pushing teams to stretch beyond comfort zones, **SMART** Goals provide structure to ensure that every objective is realistic and manageable. Both are essential tools for Strategic Alignment and performance tracking within organizations.

Examples of OKRs:

- **Increase Revenue**

  - **Objective:** Increase revenue from existing and new customer segments by expanding product offerings.
  - **Key Result 1:** Launch 3 new product features by Q3 that target untapped market segments.
  - **Key Result 2:** Achieve a 15% increase in average order value by offering premium subscription plans by year-end.
  - **Key Result 3:** Increase conversion rate from free trials to paid customers by 10% through improved onboarding and customer support by Q4.
  - **Example: Netflix's OKR** might involve launching new features or content to appeal to more audiences, increasing revenue through higher subscriptions.

- **Increase Customer Satisfaction**

  - **Objective:** Improve customer satisfaction by optimizing product performance and customer service.
  - **Key Result 1:** Reduce customer service response time by 20% through new self-service features and AI-driven chatbots by Q2.
  - **Key Result 2:** Achieve a Net Promoter Score (NPS) of 70+ by reducing product errors and improving reliability by the end of the year.
  - **Key Result 3:** Reduce the number of customer complaints by 30% by addressing top 3 recurring issues in the next product update.
  - **Example: Apple** could use **OKRs** to improve customer satisfaction with better support and faster software updates, ensuring fewer bugs and better product performance.

- **Great Customer Experience (CX)**

  - **Objective:** Create a world-class CX that increases customer retention and engagement.

    - **Key Result 1:** Redesign the customer onboarding process to improve ease of use, reducing customer drop-off rates by 25% by Q3.

- **Key Result 2**: Implement a personalized recommendation engine to increase customer engagement, boosting user interaction by 15% by Q4.
- **Key Result 3**: Reach a 90% customer satisfaction score in post-purchase surveys by improving the post-purchase experience, including follow-up communications and loyalty programmes.
- **Example: Amazon** might use **OKRs** to enhance CX by redesigning the checkout process to reduce cart abandonment rates and personalize product recommendations to keep customers engaged longer.

- **Increase Market Share in the Mobile App Sector**

  - **Objective**: Expand market share in the mobile app sector by launching new features and increasing user acquisition.
  - **Key Result 1**: Increase the number of active mobile app users by 25% through targeted marketing campaigns by Q3.
  - **Key Result 2**: Capture 15% of the target market by launching two new mobile-exclusive features by year-end.
  - **Key Result 3**: Improve mobile app store ratings to 4.5 stars or higher by addressing the top 5 user pain points by Q2.
  - **Example: Spotify** could set **OKRs** to increase its market share in the mobile app space by introducing unique in-app features, such as improved playlist curation and real-time sharing capabilities, while also addressing user experience (UX) issues to improve app store ratings.

- **Reach Profitability by March 2025**

  - **Objective**: Achieve company-wide profitability by March 2025 through cost reduction and revenue growth strategies.
  - **Key Result 1**: Reduce operational costs by 20% by optimizing cloud infrastructure and cutting non-essential expenses by Q4 2024.
  - **Key Result 2**: Increase monthly recurring revenue (**MRR**) by 30% by focusing on upselling existing customers and launching new pricing tiers by December 2024.
  - **Key Result 3**: Secure five new enterprise-level customers in key growth markets, contributing to a 15% increase in revenue by March 2025.
  - **Example: A SaaS** company, such as **Zoom**, could use these **OKRs** to balance cost control with strategic revenue growth, aiming for profitability through new pricing models, customer expansion, and operational efficiency improvements.

Organizational Alignment is crucial for maintaining a consistent and clear focus on delivering products that meet both customer expectations and company objectives. Through effective Vertical and Horizontal Alignment, product managers can create a cohesive strategy that resonates with customers and positions the organization for sustained success.

12.3.2 Innovation Management

Innovation is central to a company's ability to stay competitive and deliver value in a fast-evolving marketplace. In the context of the **POM**, Innovation Management involves ensuring that products and services are continuously improved or disrupted to meet emerging customer needs. This section will explore two types of innovation: **Sustaining** and **Disruptive**, followed by a deeper dive into four key approaches to product innovation.

1. Sustaining vs. Disruptive Innovation

Sustaining Innovation
Sustaining Innovation focuses on enhancing product performance based on feedback from existing customers. It's often about refining a product to reduce defects or improve efficiency. For instance, improving the battery life of smartphones or increasing the processing power of laptops are examples of Sustaining Innovations. These changes are driven by customer demand and are typically incremental but essential for maintaining competitiveness.

Disruptive Innovation
In contrast, Disruptive Innovation arises when a niche market, which is often overlooked by current market offerings, introduces simpler, less expensive products that initially don't meet mainstream customer expectations. However, as these products improve, they begin to displace traditional market leaders. For example, smartphones with poor camera capabilities initially catered to a small customer base, but as camera quality improved, they disrupted the standalone camera market. Other notable examples include Netflix replacing video rentals, and Airbnb disrupting the hotel industry.

Figure 12.2 shows the key differences between **Sustaining** and **Disruptive** Innovation across various aspects.

Example of Disruptive Innovation: Jet Skis Jet skis, initially developed as stand-up personal watercrafts (**PWCs**), were considered niche products catering to adventurous users. Over time, Kawasaki introduced sit-down jet skis, which expanded the market by making **PWCs** accessible to a broader audience. While sit-down jet skis are more expensive, they provided enhanced comfort and ease of use, representing a transformative innovation in the market.

2. Approaches to Product Innovation
Product Innovation can take multiple forms, depending on the goals and market positioning of a company. Four key approaches to Product Innovation

Sustaining Innovation		Disruptive Innovation	
	Focuses on improving existing products or services.	Addresses unmet or overlooked needs in a niche market.	
	Targets existing, well-established markets.	Often starts in niche markets with lower performance demands.	AirBnB
Customer Feedback	Driven by the needs and feedback of current mainstream customers.	Serves customers who are underserved by mainstream products.	
	Enhances existing technologies to improve performance and efficiency.	Introduces simpler, less expensive technology that evolves over time.	
Reduce Defects	Focuses on maintaining market leadership through incremental improvements.	Aims to disrupt incumbents by providing new value propositions or simpler solutions.	Netflix

FIGURE 12.2 Sustaining vs. Disruptive Innovation.

are **Product Platform Innovation, Crowdsourcing Innovation, Collaborative Innovation, and Customer Engagement Innovation**. Each approach offers unique ways to enhance a product's value, drive growth, and meet evolving customer needs. Whether through building a strong technological foundation, leveraging collective intelligence, fostering cross-functional collaboration, or creating deeper connections with customers, these methods play a pivotal role in keeping products relevant, competitive, and aligned with market demands.

A Product Platform Innovation

A **product platform** approach allows organizations to develop a suite of products using a common core or infrastructure. This is particularly effective for large-scale organizations aiming for scalability and consistency across multiple offerings.

- **Example 1: Singapore Government Tech Stack (SGTS)**
  The **SGTS** is a centralized platform developed by **GovTech** to enable Singapore's government agencies to build digital services quickly and efficiently. This platform streamlines and modernizes the development process by offering reusable components, such as deployment types (e.g., containers and serverless), **continuous integration and continuous delivery (CI/CD)** pipelines, API (Application Programming Interface) gateways, and orchestration tools.

  - **Core Concept:** SGTS acts as a product platform that supports the development of various government services. It eliminates the need for each agency to build its own tech stack from scratch, reducing development time and costs while improving the overall quality and security of applications.

- **Impact:** The platform has allowed agencies to develop applications that enhance public services like tax filing, citizen engagement, and healthcare systems. By using a common platform, the government has ensured consistency across services and improved interoperability.
- **Example Services:** OneService (for reporting municipal issues), digital tax services, and **SingPass** (national identity system) are examples of applications built using SGTS. These services enable seamless interaction between citizens and government, reducing "friction" in public service delivery.

- **Example 2: DBS Bank API Platform**
  DBS Bank in Singapore has transformed itself from a traditional bank into a digital-first institution, leveraging its API (Application Programming Interface) platform to build an ecosystem of financial and non-financial services.

  - **Core Concept:** DBS's API platform allows external developers to access a wide range of banking services, from payments to rewards programmes, via APIs. This enables the integration of **DBS** services into third-party applications, creating new products or improving existing ones.
  - **Impact:** This platform enables collaboration with partners like **McDonald's**, which uses **DBS's PayLah!** API for cashless payments in its delivery service. Another example is **Homage**, a startup that integrated **DBS's** rewards API to allow users to redeem points for home care services.
  - **Example Services:** In addition to traditional banking services, **DBS's** platform supports non-banking applications like food delivery, transportation, and even home care, creating a broader ecosystem that increases customer touchpoints.

- **Example 3: Amazon Web Services (AWS)**
  Amazon's AWS is one of the most famous examples of Product Platform Innovation. Originally built to serve **Amazon's** own infrastructure needs, **AWS** now provides cloud computing services to companies around the world.

  - **Core Concept:** AWS offers a range of cloud services (e.g., storage, computing power, databases) that companies can use to build and deploy their own applications without needing to maintain physical servers or data centers.
  - **Impact:** AWS transformed how businesses approach IT infrastructure by allowing them to scale easily, pay only for what they use, and innovate faster. Companies like **Netflix** and **Airbnb** use **AWS** to power their digital platforms.

- **Example Services**: AWS provides services like **EC2** (Elastic Compute Cloud), **S3** (Simple Storage Service), and **Lambda** (serverless computing), which have enabled thousands of startups and enterprises to build, launch, and scale their digital products efficiently.

B **Crowdsourcing Innovation**

Crowdsourcing taps into the collective intelligence of a community, allowing organizations to gather diverse ideas and solutions.

- **Example 1: Your Ideas for a Better Singapore**
  Singapore's government has crowdsourced ideas through various challenges, engaging citizens to solve national problems. This collaborative effort generates creative solutions and fosters civic engagement.
- **Example 2: My Starbucks Idea**
  Starbucks created a platform where customers could share ideas, vote on suggestions, and influence the company's Product Innovation process. This initiative enhanced customer loyalty and generated actionable ideas, such as new beverage flavours and store experiences.

C **Collaborative Innovation**

Collaborative Innovation emphasizes cross-functional teamwork, where different departments – design, engineering, and marketing – work together to develop solutions that meet both customer needs and business goals.

- **Tools for Collaboration**: Design and collaboration tools such as **Trello**, **Balsamiq**, and **Figma** enable cross-functional teams to share feedback in real time, co-develop products, and ensure alignment across teams.

D **Customer Engagement Innovation**

Customer Engagement Innovation focuses on creating meaningful and lasting interactions with customers. This could include improving product packaging, simplifying UXs, or leveraging social media to foster deeper customer relationships.

- **Example 1: SG Together Initiative**
  The **SG Together** initiative by the Singapore Government exemplifies how Customer Engagement Innovation can foster deeper civic participation and collaboration between citizens and the government.

  - **Core Concept**: Launched by the **Smart Nation and Digital Government Office (SNDGO)**, SG Together is designed to create a platform for Singaporean citizens to co-create, co-deliver, and shape policies, services, and initiatives with the government. It is aimed at enhancing citizen engagement by offering a participatory approach to governance, where individuals are actively involved in decision-making processes and the development of solutions for national issues.

- **Impact:** SG Together enables citizens to feel a sense of ownership over government projects and policies by engaging them through dialogues, town halls, and digital platforms. It emphasizes collaboration and collective problem-solving, allowing the government to better understand and respond to the needs and aspirations of its people. The initiative covers a wide range of activities, from feedback sessions to co-creating solutions in areas such as sustainability, urban planning, and community building.
- **Example Services:** Through SG Together, citizens are invited to participate in initiatives like the **OneService app**, which allows them to report municipal issues in real time and receive feedback directly from government agencies. The initiative also includes **hackathons and innovation challenges** where citizens can contribute ideas to solve national issues like digital inclusion, healthcare, and education. These activities encourage a culture of collaboration and trust between the public sector and citizens, ultimately improving policy outcomes and building a stronger sense of community engagement.

- **Example 2: NikePlus**
  Nike has continually innovated in how it engages with its customers by building a strong community through its **NikePlus** membership programme.

  - **Core Concept:** NikePlus combines physical products, digital services, and personal engagement to create a loyalty ecosystem that fosters deeper connections with its customers. It gives members access to exclusive products, personalized workouts, and special offers, making the Nike experience highly tailored to individual needs and preferences.
  - **Impact:** NikePlus isn't just about selling shoes and apparel – it's about creating a holistic lifestyle brand. Members can track their fitness goals through apps like **Nike Training Club** and **Nike Run Club**, receive curated product recommendations, and get early access to limited edition products. Nike also uses personalized push notifications, emails, and in-app content to keep users engaged, ensuring a seamless, ongoing customer relationship.
  - **Example Services:** NikePlus offers early access to product drops, personalized training plans, and invitations to exclusive events. Through mobile apps and in-store engagements, Nike has successfully combined physical and digital experiences, boosting both customer loyalty and brand advocacy. This innovation turns one-time buyers into long-term Nike brand advocates, constantly engaging users with relevant content and product experiences.

12.3.2.1 *Bringing Innovation into POM*

The **POM** ensures that innovation – whether sustaining or disruptive – is embedded into the company's DNA. By leveraging platforms, crowdsourcing ideas, collaborating across functions, and innovating customer engagement, companies can create products that are both market-leading and customer-centric. Through Innovation Management, the **POM** aligns product development with strategic goals, ensuring scalability, flexibility, and success in an evolving marketplace.

12.3.3 *Portfolio Management*

Portfolio management involves overseeing a company's entire product mix, which refers to the total number of product lines and individual products or services offered. Managing a product portfolio helps organizations make strategic decisions that maximize return on investment (**ROI**), identify areas for improvement, ensure alignment with overall business goals, and balance investments across different product initiatives. This approach is crucial for companies aiming to increase market share and revenue through a well-managed product portfolio.

1. Product Portfolio Management vs. Product Management

While a **Product Manager** focuses on overseeing one to three products, a **Product Portfolio Manager** takes a broader view, managing all products offered by the company. This includes making decisions about which products to invest in, which to phase out, and how to allocate resources across the portfolio.

For instance, **Microsoft** manages a wide product portfolio that includes its **Office Suite, Surface tablets,** and **Xbox consoles.** A Product Portfolio Manager at **Microsoft** would ensure that each product line aligns with the company's strategic goals, identifying areas of growth or improvement across the entire product range.

2. Tools for Portfolio Management

- **BCG Growth-Share Matrix**

  To make informed decisions, portfolio managers often rely on frameworks like the **BCG Growth-Share Matrix.** This tool helps assess the market performance of products by categorizing them into four quadrants: **Stars, Cash Cows, Question Marks,** and **Dogs.** Figure 12.3 shows the **BCG Growth-Share Matrix.**

A **Stars:**

- **Characteristics:** High growth, high market share.

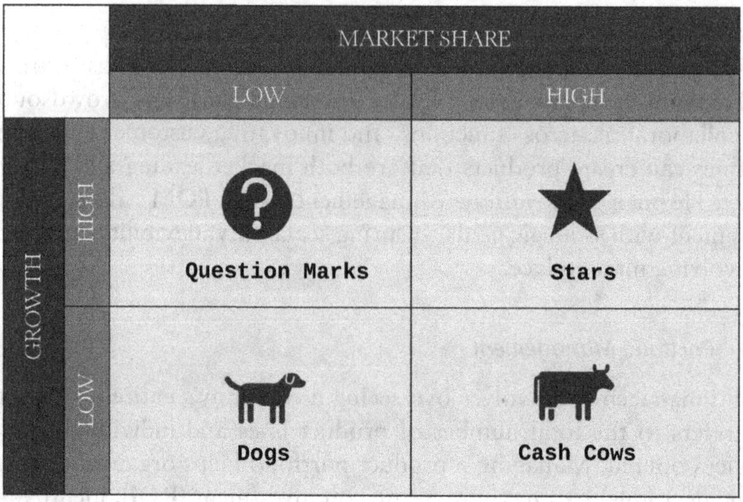

FIGURE 12.3 BCG Growth-Share Matrix.

- **Implications**: Stars are products in fast-growing markets that hold a strong market position. They require significant investment to maintain or grow market share, but they also have the potential to generate substantial revenue.
- **Example**: For **Apple**, the **iPhone** was initially a star, requiring heavy investment in marketing, innovation, and infrastructure but contributing significantly to revenue growth.

B **Cash Cows**:

- **Characteristics**: Low growth, high market share.
- **Implications**: Cash cows are established products with a large customer base in a mature market. They generate steady revenue with minimal investment, often funding other parts of the business.
- **Example**: **Microsoft Office** is a cash cow for **Microsoft**. Despite the software market maturing, it continues to dominate, providing substantial profits without requiring as much innovation or investment.

C **Question Marks** (also known as "Problem Children"):

- **Characteristics**: High growth, low market share.
- **Implications**: These are products in growing markets but with low market share. Companies must decide whether to invest in growing these products or phase them out. If nurtured correctly, they can become stars.

- **Example:** When **Netflix** began offering streaming services alongside DVD rentals, it was considered a question mark. The market was growing, but it was uncertain whether **Netflix** would become a leader in the space.

D **Dogs:**

- **Characteristics:** Low growth, low market share.
- **Implications:** Dogs are products that neither grow nor contribute significantly to the company's bottom line. They often use resources without providing much return, and companies should consider phasing them out.
- **Example:** **Google Glass** is an example of a product that became a dog. Although it had potential, it struggled to gain market traction and was eventually shelved.

The **BCG Matrix** helps businesses prioritize product investments. By focusing on stars and cash cows, they can sustain growth and profitability, while deciding whether to nurture question marks or eliminate dogs. This strategic insight is especially valuable in balancing portfolios, maximizing ROI, and guiding future investments.

- **Ansoff Matrix**
  Another helpful tool is the **Ansoff Matrix**, which helps product managers identify market growth opportunities. By analysing the relationship between existing and new products and markets, product managers can develop strategies to expand into new areas. Figure 12.4 shows the **Ansoff Matrix**.

A **Market Penetration:**

- **Strategy:** Focuses on increasing sales of existing products in existing markets. The goal is to grow market share by attracting competitors' customers or increasing usage among current customers.
- **Example:** **Coca-Cola** frequently uses promotional campaigns and loyalty programmes to increase market share in existing markets without changing its core product.

B **Market Development:**

- **Strategy:** Expanding existing products into new markets, either geographically or by targeting new customer segments.
- **Example:** **Netflix** originally offered streaming services in the U.S., but expanded into international markets like Europe, Asia, and Latin America to grow its customer base.

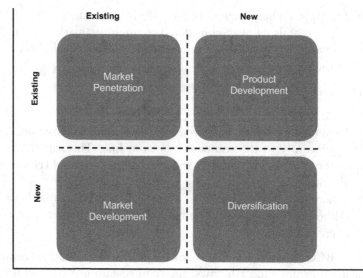

FIGURE 12.4 Ansoff Matrix.

C **Product Development**:

- **Strategy**: Introducing new products to existing markets. This strategy works well for companies that have a strong customer base and can leverage brand loyalty for new product offerings.
- **Example**: **Apple** constantly engages in product development by introducing new products like the **Apple Watch** to its existing customer base who already use iPhones, iPads, and Macs.

D **Diversification**:

- **Strategy**: Launching new products into new markets. This high-risk strategy is often pursued by companies seeking to reduce dependence on their core product lines.
- **Example**: **Amazon** diversified by launching **AWS**, entering the cloud computing market, which is entirely different from its original retail business.

3. Key Considerations for New Products

When introducing new products, product managers must evaluate the company's ability to take on new projects by asking key questions, such as:

- Is the business healthy enough to support a new product?

- Are there natural extensions to the existing product line?
- Does the company have the necessary expertise to design, build, and support the product?
- Will the new product cannibalize current offerings?
- Is there a growing market for the new product?
- Should we phase out underperforming products to focus on new opportunities?

4. Examples of Active Portfolio Management

- **Apple's Product Portfolio Management**
  Apple is well-known for its streamlined and focused approach to managing its product portfolio. Over the years, Apple has applied active portfolio management to ensure that its product lines align with market demand while delivering on its core brand promise of innovation, simplicity, and premium quality.

  - **Product Streamlining**: After Steve Jobs returned to Apple in the late 1990s, one of his key strategies was to simplify the product portfolio. At the time, Apple had dozens of different models of computers, which diluted the brand and confused customers. Jobs slashed the product range to just four categories: consumer and professional laptops, and consumer and professional desktops. This clear focus allowed Apple to concentrate its resources on developing high-quality products like the iMac and later the MacBook.
  - **New Product Development**: Active portfolio management also led to the creation of entirely new categories, such as the iPhone and the iPad, which became critical drivers of growth. Apple consistently reviews its portfolio and identifies gaps in both technology and customer needs, leveraging its brand to introduce new products that transform industries, such as the Apple Watch and AirPods.
  - **Portfolio Rationalization**: By discontinuing underperforming products, such as the iPod, and maintaining a core set of successful products, Apple ensures a high ROI across its portfolio while maintaining a unified brand experience.

- **Microsoft's Transition from Products to Platforms**
  Microsoft has evolved from a company primarily focused on software products to one that embraces platforms and ecosystems, particularly through Microsoft 365, Azure, and LinkedIn.

  - **Expanding the Portfolio with Azure**: Microsoft's active management of its product portfolio saw a strategic shift towards cloud services, particularly with the development and expansion of **Microsoft Azure**. Originally known for its dominance in operating systems with Windows and Office, **Microsoft** pivoted to include Azure, addressing the growing demand for cloud computing. This portfolio diversification helped the company remain competitive as businesses increasingly shifted from on-premise solutions to the cloud. Now, Azure accounts for a significant portion of **Microsoft's** revenue, alongside its traditional product lines.

- **Integration of Acquisitions:** **Microsoft's** acquisition of **LinkedIn** and **GitHub** shows how it manages its portfolio by integrating acquisitions that align with its strategic goals. **LinkedIn** complements **Microsoft's** existing productivity tools by giving it access to a social network that is heavily used by professionals. **GitHub** enhances **Microsoft's** developer ecosystem, fitting seamlessly into its broader cloud computing and developer tools portfolio.
- **Product Lifecycle Management (PLCM):** Active portfolio management also includes retiring older products that no longer fit into **Microsoft's** strategy. For example, **Microsoft** phased out **Windows Phone**, acknowledging that the smartphone market was dominated by iOS and Android. This allowed the company to redirect resources towards more promising areas, such as Surface devices and cloud services.

12.3.4 Technology Enablement

Technology is a crucial enabler in delivering products efficiently. A well-defined technology infrastructure ensures that product teams have access to the tools, platforms, and technical capabilities they need to build and deliver innovative products.

- **Scalability:** Ensuring that the technology stack supports growth as product usage scales.
- **Integration:** Providing seamless integration of different technology systems to streamline operations.
- **Tools and Platforms:** Empowering product teams with cutting-edge tools for collaboration, development, and deployment.

Here are key areas of Technology Enablement, along with examples of tools and platforms used by product teams, as shown in Figure 12.5.

1. Product Management Tools
Product management tools are essential for tracking product development, prioritizing features, and ensuring alignment between different teams.

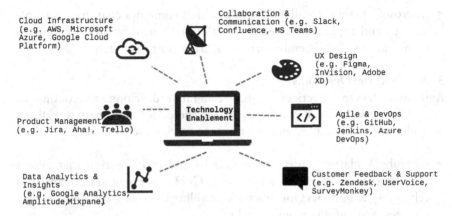

Cloud Infrastructure
(e.g. AWS, Microsoft
Azure, Google Cloud
Platform)

Collaboration &
Communication (e.g. Slack,
Confluence, MS Teams)

UX Design
(e.g. Figma,
InVision, Adobe
XD)

Technology
Enablement

Product Management
(e.g. Jira, Aha!, Trello)

Agile & DevOps
(e.g. GitHub,
Jenkins, Azure
DevOps)

Data Analytics &
Insights
(e.g. Google Analytics,
Amplitude,Mixpanel)

Customer Feedback & Support
(e.g. Zendesk, UserVoice,
SurveyMonkey)

FIGURE 12.5 Technology Enablement Tools.

These tools help product managers manage backlogs, create roadmaps, and collaborate across departments.

- **Jira**: A popular project management tool used to track issues, bugs, and development tasks, especially in teams practising **Agile** or **Scrum** methodologies. **Jira** enables teams to visualize workflows and prioritize tasks effectively.
- **Aha!**: A product roadmap software that helps teams plan strategies and capture ideas. **Aha!** is designed to integrate with tools like **Jira** and **Trello**, making it easier for product managers to align strategy with execution.
- **Trello**: A lightweight tool for visual project management that uses boards and cards to represent tasks. It's particularly useful for small product teams needing a flexible, easy-to-use solution for tracking progress.

2. Collaboration and Communication Platforms

Collaboration tools are vital for keeping teams in sync, especially when teams are distributed across different geographies or working remotely. These platforms provide seamless communication and support real-time collaboration on documents and projects.

- **Slack**: A widely used messaging platform that enables real-time communication within and between teams. **Slack's** integrations with tools like **Google Drive, Jira**, and **Zoom** make it a hub for collaboration across product, engineering, and marketing teams.
- **Confluence**: An **Atlassian** tool for team collaboration, documentation, and knowledge management. It integrates seamlessly with **Jira**, helping teams create and share product documentation, meeting notes, and requirements.

- **Microsoft Teams**: A collaboration tool that combines chat, meetings, file storage, and application integration. It's heavily used by product teams in organizations already embedded in the **Microsoft** ecosystem.

3. Agile and DevOps Tools

Agile and **DevOps** practices emphasize iterative development, continuous integration, and frequent product releases. These tools automate workflows and allow product and engineering teams to work closely together.

- **GitHub**: A platform for version control and collaboration that allows developers to manage code repositories. **GitHub** is essential for teams that rely on **Agile** and **DevOps** practices, enabling them to share code, review changes, and automate builds and releases.
- **Jenkins**: A CI/CD automation server that facilitates the automation of building, testing, and deploying code. Jenkins is crucial for teams practicing **DevOps**, ensuring frequent and reliable product releases.
- **Azure DevOps**: A set of tools for managing code repositories, pipelines, and artefacts. It integrates with **Azure** cloud services and enables teams to build, test, and deploy applications in an automated manner.

4. User Experience (UX) Design Tools

Product design is critical to delivering intuitive and user-friendly products. UX design tools help product teams create wireframes, prototypes, and user interfaces (UIs) that align with customer needs.

- **Figma**: A collaborative interface design tool that allows designers and product teams to create wireframes and prototypes. **Figma's** cloud-based platform makes it easy for teams to collaborate in real time, iterating on designs quickly.
- **InVision**: A prototyping tool that helps teams turn static designs into interactive prototypes. It's widely used by **UX/UI** designers to create mockups and gather feedback from stakeholders and users.
- **Adobe XD**: A tool for designing and prototyping UXs for web and mobile apps. **Adobe XD's** integrations with other **Adobe Creative Cloud** tools make it ideal for teams that require advanced design capabilities.

5. Data Analytics and Insights Platforms

Data is essential for making informed decisions throughout the product lifecycle. Analytics platforms provide insights into customer behaviour, product usage, and market trends, enabling teams to validate their strategies and make data-driven improvements.

- **Google Analytics**: A web analytics tool used to track website traffic, user behaviour, and engagement. **Google Analytics** provides insights into how users interact with a product, helping teams refine their designs and features based on real data.

- **Amplitude**: A product analytics platform that helps teams understand user behaviour and measure the impact of product changes. **Amplitude** provides deep insights into user journeys, feature adoption, and retention, making it easier for product managers to optimize the UX.
- **Mixpanel**: Another powerful product analytics tool that tracks user interactions with web and mobile applications. It provides insights into how users engage with specific features, helping product teams measure the effectiveness of new releases and identify areas for improvement.

6. Cloud Infrastructure and Scalability

Cloud platforms provide the infrastructure necessary to build, deploy, and scale digital products. These platforms enable product teams to manage resources efficiently, deploy applications globally, and ensure high availability.

- **AWS**: A leading cloud platform that offers a wide range of services, including computing power, storage, and databases. **AWS** enables product teams to build scalable applications and manage their infrastructure with ease.
- **Microsoft Azure**: A cloud platform that provides services for building, testing, deploying, and managing applications. **Azure's** integration with Microsoft tools makes it a popular choice for organizations that need scalable infrastructure and advanced analytics capabilities.
- **Google Cloud Platform (GCP)**: Google's cloud offering, which provides infrastructure and machine learning capabilities. **GCP's** powerful data analytics services enable teams to extract insights from large datasets and build artificial intelligence (AI)-driven products.

7. Customer Feedback and Support Tools

Customer feedback is a critical input for product development. These tools allow product teams to gather feedback, manage customer support, and track feature requests, ensuring they stay aligned with user needs.

- **Zendesk**: A customer service platform that allows product teams to manage support tickets, track issues, and gather feedback. **Zendesk** helps product managers prioritize feature requests and ensure customer concerns are addressed promptly.
- **UserVoice**: A feedback management tool that allows teams to gather feature requests, prioritize them based on user votes, and share roadmaps. It's particularly useful for product managers looking to align product development with customer needs.

- **SurveyMonkey**: A survey tool that helps teams collect feedback from customers, users, and stakeholders. Product teams can use **SurveyMonkey** to gauge satisfaction, gather insights on new features, and prioritize development efforts based on real-world data.

12.3.4.1 Summary: Technology Enablement

Technology Enablement provides the foundation for modern product management by equipping teams with the tools, platforms, and capabilities they need to collaborate effectively, make data-driven decisions, and deliver high-quality products at scale. Whether it's managing backlogs with **Jira**, conducting user research with **Figma**, or scaling infrastructure with **AWS**, technology plays a vital role in streamlining processes and driving product success. By adopting the right technology stack, product teams can increase efficiency, enhance collaboration, and continuously improve their product offerings.

12.3.5 Capability Management

Capability Management focuses on building and developing the core competencies required for product managers to navigate the intersection of business, customer needs, and technology. In the dynamic world of digital products, successful product managers must possess a blend of business acumen, customer empathy, and technological understanding, along with strong soft skills that foster collaboration, adaptability, and leadership.

Product managers must balance these competencies to guide products through the entire lifecycle – from conception to market launch and beyond – ensuring that products meet business objectives, address customer needs, and leverage technological advancements.

1. Intersection of Business, Customer, and Technology

At the heart of DPM is the ability to operate effectively at the intersection of **Business, Customer,** and **Technology**. This intersection requires product managers to make strategic decisions that align with business goals, deliver a compelling CX, and integrate technical feasibility.

- **Business**: Product managers must ensure that their products align with organizational goals, market trends, and financial targets.
- **Customer**: Understanding the customer journey, needs, and behaviour is critical for creating a product that not only solves a problem but delivers a delightful experience.

- **Technology**: Product managers need to possess sufficient technical knowledge to collaborate effectively with engineering teams and ensure that the product leverages modern tools and innovations.

Additionally, product managers must be adept at **soft skills** such as communication, leadership, and adaptability. These skills are critical for aligning cross-functional teams and driving a product's success across its lifecycle.

2. Digital Product Management Capability Matrix
The **DPM Capability Matrix** in Table 12.1 outlines the core competencies across four key areas: Business, Customer, Technology, and Soft Skills.

1 Business Competencies

- **PLCM**: Product managers must oversee the entire lifecycle of a product, from ideation and development through to launch, scaling, and eventual product retirement. This requires strategic planning and continuous monitoring.
- **Business Acumen**: A strong understanding of financial metrics, profit and loss, and strategic goals is essential. Product managers need to align their product initiatives with business goals and ensure optimal **ROI**.
- **Market Orientation**: Awareness of market dynamics and competition is key. Product managers must understand market demands and keep pace with changing trends to maintain product relevance.
- **Go-to-Market Strategy**: Product managers must craft robust go-to-market strategies that align marketing, sales, and support to deliver a product successfully to its intended audience.
- **Pricing Strategy**: Defining the right pricing structure to maximize profitability while delivering value to customers is another core business competency.

2 Customer Competencies

- **CX**: Designing a product with CX in mind means considering every touchpoint and interaction a customer has with the product.
- **User Research and Feedback**: Gathering data from customers through surveys, interviews, and usage analytics helps inform product decisions and prioritize features.
- **Product Design**: Working closely with **UX/UI** designers, product managers must ensure that the product is not only functional but also easy and delightful to use.

TABLE 12.1 Digital Product Management Capability Matrix

Key Area	Core Skills/Knowledge
Business	1. Product Lifecycle Management (PLCM): Overseeing products from development to retirement. 2. Business Acumen: Understanding financials, ROI, and business strategy. 3. Market Orientation: Awareness of market trends and competitors. 4. Go-to-Market Strategy: Planning product launches and marketing strategies. 5. Pricing Strategy: Setting prices to meet business goals while providing customer value.
Customer	6. Customer Experience (CX): Designing products with customer touchpoints in mind. 7. User Research and Feedback: Gathering insights through surveys, interviews, and analytics. 8. Product Design: Collaborating with UX/UI designers to create intuitive, user-friendly products. 9. Customer-Centric Innovation: Leveraging customer insights to drive Product Innovation. 10. Customer Retention Strategies: Developing strategies to retain and engage users.
Technology	11. Technical Knowledge: Understanding the technical feasibility and challenges of product features. 12. Agile Methodologies: Leveraging Scrum and Agile frameworks for efficient product development. 13. Product Stack: Familiarity with the tools and technologies used to build and maintain digital products. 14. Data Analytics: Utilizing analytics tools to track product performance and user behaviour. 15. DevOps Awareness: Understanding continuous integration, deployment, and product scalability.
Soft Skills	16. Leadership: Inspiring and leading cross-functional teams. 17. Communication: Effectively communicating with stakeholders at all levels. 18. Collaboration: Working across departments (engineering, design, marketing) to achieve common goals. 19. Problem-Solving: Addressing complex challenges creatively. 20. Adaptability: Adjusting to changes in market trends, customer needs, or technology shifts.

- **Customer-Centric Innovation:** Product managers must continuously innovate by leveraging customer insights, ensuring the product remains relevant and valuable to the customer base.
- **Customer Retention Strategies:** Developing strategies to keep customers engaged and using the product, such as introducing new features or personalized services, is critical for long-term success.

3 Technology Competencies

- **Technical Knowledge**: While product managers do not need to be engineers, they must have a foundational understanding of the technologies used in product development to collaborate effectively with the engineering team.
- **Agile Methodologies**: Agile frameworks such as Scrum enable product managers to manage product development iteratively, delivering value to customers quickly and incorporating feedback throughout the process.
- **Product Stack**: Knowledge of the tools, applications, and infrastructure used to build and manage digital products is crucial for understanding how the product is developed and maintained.
- **Data Analytics**: Product managers must use data analytics tools to track product performance, user engagement, and key performance indicators (**KPIs**).
- **DevOps Awareness**: An understanding of **DevOps** practices, such as CI/CD, ensures that the product is built efficiently and scales smoothly.

4 Soft Skills

- **Leadership**: Product managers are responsible for guiding cross-functional teams, ensuring alignment, and driving a product towards successful outcomes.
- **Communication**: Effectively communicating the product vision, progress, and changes to various stakeholders (such as executives, developers, and customers) is essential for transparency and collaboration.
- **Collaboration**: Product managers must work closely with engineering, design, marketing, and sales teams to ensure product development is aligned with the company's objectives.
- **Problem-Solving**: Product managers face numerous challenges throughout the product lifecycle, and strong problem-solving skills are needed to navigate these effectively.
- **Adaptability**: Markets, technologies, and customer needs are constantly evolving. Product managers must be adaptable and open to revising their strategies to respond to these changes.

12.3.5.1 Summary: Capability Management

Capability management in DPM is about building the right mix of business, customer, technology, and soft skills. Product managers must navigate these areas simultaneously, balancing strategic goals with customer needs, technological feasibility, and team collaboration. By mastering these competencies, product managers can drive innovation, deliver value, and maintain a competitive edge in the digital marketplace. The **DPM Capability**

Matrix provides a structured approach to understanding and developing the skills needed to excel in this dynamic field.

12.3.6 Performance Management

Performance management ensures that both products and teams are meeting the expectations set by leadership. This component involves setting clear KPIs, tracking performance, and making adjustments to ensure that both product and business goals are achieved.

- **Setting KPIs:** Defining clear performance metrics for products, such as customer satisfaction, revenue growth, and time to market.
- **Continuous Improvement:** Regularly reviewing performance data to identify areas for improvement.
- **Feedback Mechanisms:** Implementing structured feedback loops to gather input from customers and stakeholders.

Performance Management within Product Operations is a structured approach to evaluate and improve the efficiency, effectiveness, and overall performance of product management teams and processes. It ensures that the teams and systems in place are aligned with both short-term objectives and long-term strategic goals. Performance management in this context involves continuous assessment, identification of gaps in capabilities, and the implementation of improvement initiatives to raise product management maturity across the organization.

This section covers two crucial tools for effective performance management: **Gap Analysis in Product Management Capabilities** and the **Product Management Maturity Model**. These tools enable organizations to assess their current capabilities, identify areas for improvement, and plan steps to reach higher levels of product management maturity.

1. Gap Analysis in Product Management Capabilities

Gap analysis is a method used to compare an organization's current state with its desired future state, identifying any gaps in product management capabilities. In the context of product management, gap analysis helps organizations evaluate their competencies, processes, and tools to uncover deficiencies that may hinder product development, market success, and overall performance. By understanding these gaps, product managers can create targeted strategies to close them and improve the organization's product management capabilities.

Key steps in conducting a gap analysis for product management:

1 **Define the Ideal State:** Determine what success looks like for your product management function. This includes defining goals, the necessary

competencies, best practices, and the required tools for managing the entire product lifecycle. For instance, an ideal product management team might have deep expertise in market analysis, customer journey mapping, and agile methodologies.

2 **Assess the Current State**: Evaluate the current capabilities of the product management team. Look at their skill sets, existing processes, and the tools they are using. Surveys, interviews, performance reviews, and audits can be used to gather this information. Identify whether teams lack technical knowledge, customer insights, or efficient collaboration tools.

3 **Identify the Gaps**: Compare the ideal state with the current state to identify gaps. These could be competency gaps (e.g., insufficient market research skills), process gaps (e.g., lack of agile adoption), or tool gaps (e.g., absence of analytics platforms). An example of a gap could be an organization's inability to effectively use customer data to inform product decisions.

4 **Develop an Action Plan**: Based on the gaps identified, create a roadmap to close them. This may involve training initiatives, implementing new tools, or improving collaboration across departments. For example, if a gap exists in data analytics capabilities, the team could invest in training programmes for product managers or adopt more advanced analytics tools like Amplitude or Mixpanel.

5 **Monitor Progress**: Continuously track the organization's progress in closing the identified gaps. This ensures accountability and allows for adjustments to the action plan as necessary.

2. Product Management Maturity Model

The **Product Management Maturity Model** is a framework used to assess the maturity of an organization's product management practices. It helps organizations understand where they currently stand in terms of product management capabilities and processes and what steps they need to take to reach a higher level of maturity. A mature product management organization is one where product development is customer-focused, data-driven, agile, and well-integrated with the business strategy.

The maturity model typically consists of five levels:

Level 1: Initial

- **Characteristics**: Product management practices are ad hoc and chaotic. There is little to no formal process for developing or managing products. Success depends on individual efforts rather than systematic approaches.
- **Challenges**: Lack of alignment with business goals, inconsistent product development, reactive problem-solving.
- **Example**: Startups or small businesses where there is no dedicated product management function, and decisions are made by founders or ad-hoc teams.

Level 2: Managed

- **Characteristics**: Basic processes for product management are established. There are some formal roles and responsibilities, but product development may still be siloed or disconnected from broader business goals.
- **Challenges**: Inconsistent collaboration across teams, minimal use of data to inform product decisions, limited customer insights.
- **Example**: A company that has defined product management roles but lacks robust tools and consistent processes, relying heavily on intuition.

Level 3: Defined

- **Characteristics**: Product management processes are clearly defined, repeatable, and aligned with business strategy. Product managers collaborate effectively with other departments such as marketing, sales, and engineering.
- **Challenges**: Difficulty in scaling product management practices and maintaining alignment as the organization grows.
- **Example**: Medium-sized companies with established product management teams using customer feedback and basic analytics tools to inform decisions.

Level 4: Quantitatively Managed

- **Characteristics**: Product management is data-driven, with clear KPIs and performance metrics guiding decisions. Customer feedback is integrated into the product development process, and advanced tools like customer journey analytics and cohort analysis are used to understand behaviour and inform strategy.
- **Challenges**: Continuous improvement is required to stay competitive, and there may be challenges in implementing advanced tools across all teams.
- **Example**: A technology company that uses data analytics tools like Heap or Mixpanel to optimize product performance, ensuring that product decisions are based on customer insights and business goals.

Level 5: Optimizing

- **Characteristics**: Product management is a core strategic function, deeply integrated with the organization's overall vision. Continuous improvement and innovation are at the heart of the product management process, with sophisticated data and customer feedback loops.
- **Challenges**: Staying ahead of market trends and technology while managing product portfolio complexity.

- **Example:** Large organizations like Google or Apple, where product management drives innovation, market leadership, and operational excellence.

Using the Maturity Model in Practice

Organizations can use the Product Management Maturity Model to conduct regular assessments of their product management practices. By identifying where they fall on the maturity scale, they can take proactive steps to improve their practices, close capability gaps, and elevate their product management function.

For example:

- A **Level 1** startup may focus on formalizing roles and establishing basic processes for product development.
- A **Level 3** organization may focus on adopting advanced analytics tools and embedding customer feedback more effectively into the development process.
- A **Level 5** company may focus on maintaining a culture of innovation and continuous improvement to sustain its competitive edge.

12.3.6.1 Summary: Performance Management

Performance management is a critical aspect of Product Operations. Through tools like **gap analysis** and the **Product Management Maturity Model**, organizations can assess their current capabilities, identify areas for improvement, and continuously develop their product management function. A mature, high-performing product management team is one that operates efficiently, makes data-driven decisions, and aligns with the broader business strategy. By striving for higher levels of maturity, product teams can deliver better products, faster, and with greater alignment to customer needs and market trends.

12.3.7 Process and Governance

Process and Governance is the backbone of a well-functioning product management system. It ensures that there are clear, repeatable processes in place and well-established governance structures that guide decision-making, accountability, and alignment with strategic objectives. This section delves into how **Process and Governance** operates within the context of Product Operations, ensuring that product teams work efficiently, product goals are met, and resources are optimally utilized. In addition, this section explores how Process and Governance interlink with the **DPM Framework's core**

process groups, enabling streamlined product development, launch, and support.

1. Defining Process and Governance

Process and Governance refers to the established procedures, policies, and accountability structures that guide how product management activities are carried out. It involves creating clear workflows, defining roles and responsibilities, and ensuring compliance with organizational standards. Effective governance ensures that product teams have a structured approach to decision-making and execution, reducing ambiguity, streamlining operations, and aligning product initiatives with broader business goals.

Key components of Process and Governance include:

- **Clear Workflows**: Documented and repeatable processes that define how key product management tasks are performed, from ideation to post-launch support.
- **Role Clarity**: Clearly defined roles and responsibilities, ensuring everyone on the product team knows their duties and how they fit into the bigger picture.
- **Decision-Making Protocols**: Established governance frameworks for how product decisions are made, approved, and executed.
- **Compliance**: Ensuring that all processes adhere to internal policies, regulatory requirements, and industry standards.

For example, in a well-governed product team, when a product update is ready for release, there's a clear process for finalizing, testing, approving, and launching the update. Governance ensures that product decisions aren't made in silos but are aligned with company-wide objectives.

2. Governance in the Digital Product Management Framework

The **DPM Framework** consists of five core process groups: **Product Opportunity, Product Planning, Product Development, Product Launch,** and **Product Support**. Governance plays a vital role in each of these stages, ensuring that processes are followed and that product management efforts are aligned with business goals.

Here's how **Process and Governance** integrates with each process group:

1 Product Opportunity:

- In this group, governance ensures that market analysis, product strategy, and business cases are built on sound data and decision-making processes. It establishes approval protocols to ensure that opportunities align with the organization's overall goals before resources are committed.

2 **Product Planning:**

- During product planning, governance ensures that product roadmaps and release plans are reviewed and approved by key stakeholders. It helps prioritize product requirements effectively, ensuring alignment with the broader product vision.

3 **Product Development:**

- Governance ensures that agile methodologies and development practices are adhered to while maintaining flexibility. It also sets the processes for quality control and UX standards, so that products are developed in a way that consistently meets customer expectations.

4 **Product Launch:**

- In the product launch phase, governance helps in crafting a coordinated launch strategy that aligns with marketing, sales, and product teams. It ensures that timelines, budgets, and resources are properly managed, with structured sign-offs from stakeholders before the product hits the market.

5 **Product Support:**

- Governance in product support includes setting up structured feedback loops, and ensuring that customer service and technical support processes are followed efficiently. It also establishes metrics for measuring product performance and customer satisfaction, providing accountability post-launch.

3. Establishing Effective Governance Frameworks

To implement strong processes and governance within Product Operations, product teams need to establish frameworks that provide structure while allowing flexibility for innovation and responsiveness. These frameworks help standardize workflows, align teams, and ensure accountability at every stage of product management.

Key Elements of an Effective Governance Framework:

1 **Standardized Product Management Processes:** Formal processes for product ideation, development, testing, release, and support. These processes should be adaptable and evolve as needed, particularly in agile environments.
2 **Cross-Functional Collaboration:** Governance frameworks should facilitate collaboration across teams such as marketing, engineering, sales, and support. Ensuring alignment between departments is crucial to avoid silos and inefficiencies.

3 **Decision-Making Authorities**: Clearly defined decision-makers for each stage of the product lifecycle. This can include governance committees or councils that oversee strategic product decisions to ensure alignment with business priorities.
4 **Risk Management**: Established processes to identify, assess, and mitigate risks in product development and launch. This includes compliance with legal, security, and regulatory standards.
5 **Performance Metrics and Accountability**: Set up clear KPIs to track product performance throughout its lifecycle, ensuring that each stage aligns with broader business goals. Governance ensures that accountability is enforced when targets are not met.

4. Tools and Platforms for Process and Governance
Technology plays a crucial role in implementing and maintaining effective processes and governance. There are several tools and platforms that product teams can use to ensure that processes are streamlined, collaboration is optimized, and governance structures are adhered to.

Examples of tools that support Process and Governance in Product Operations include:

- **JIRA**: For managing product development workflows, tracking progress, and ensuring compliance with governance protocols.
- **Trello**: A visual project management tool that helps teams track product management tasks, collaboration, and deliverables.
- **Confluence**: For documentation management and sharing governance policies and standard operating procedures (SOPs) across teams.
- **OKR Software (e.g., Ally.io, 15Five)**: Tools that help product teams align their objectives with business goals and ensure strategic oversight.
- **Project Management Platforms (e.g., Monday.com, Asana)**: Used for task tracking, role assignments, and workflow standardization across product teams.

These tools ensure that governance is not only enforced but also flexible enough to adapt to evolving business needs and product lifecycles.

5. Aligning Governance with Product Success Metrics
One of the most critical functions of governance is linking decision-making processes to product success metrics. Governance frameworks should ensure that decisions made in the planning and development phases are linked directly to KPIs such as customer satisfaction, time to market, and product revenue.

For example, governance processes that enforce continuous integration and testing during development can reduce defects and improve product quality, directly contributing to higher customer satisfaction post-launch.

Similarly, governance protocols that require cross-functional collaboration during launch planning can lead to better alignment between marketing and product teams, ensuring that products are released on time and with appropriate customer engagement strategies.

6. Governance and Product Operations Maturity

As product teams mature, so too must their governance processes. **Governance maturity** evolves alongside the organization's overall product management maturity. A well-established product governance framework is a key indicator of a mature Product Operation, where decision-making is not reactive but proactive, and processes are continually refined for efficiency.

Organizations at lower maturity levels might rely on informal processes, whereas more mature organizations have formalized governance structures that integrate with their PLCM strategies.

At the highest level of maturity, governance becomes embedded in the culture of the organization, allowing teams to operate with both autonomy and accountability, while adhering to best practices and strategic objectives.

12.3.7.1 Summary: Process and Governance

Process and Governance form the foundation of successful Product Operations by providing structured workflows, clear accountability, and streamlined decision-making processes. Governance ensures that product management activities align with the organization's broader business goals, while also allowing for flexibility and innovation.

When aligned with the **DPM Framework's core process groups,** governance enhances every phase of product management – from identifying market opportunities to supporting products post-launch. By implementing effective governance frameworks and leveraging the right tools, organizations can manage risk, improve product outcomes, and ensure long-term success in an increasingly competitive market.

12.3.8 Product Operations

Product Operations is an emerging discipline that focuses on enabling product teams, ensuring alignment with strategic objectives, and fostering collaboration. Product Operations Managers handle tasks like data analysis, process optimization, and cross-functional coordination.

Product Operations (**Product Ops**) is an integral function within a **POM** in an organization, ensuring that product teams operate efficiently and are aligned with the business, customer, and technology objectives. Product Operations supports various aspects of product development, from managing data and insights to overseeing processes and governance, all while facilitating customer and market research. A well-defined **POM**, which includes Product

Operations as a core function, helps ensure the seamless functioning of the product management ecosystem and enables the successful launch, adoption, and scaling of products.

Product Operations plays an essential role at the intersection of business, customer, and technology. Its responsibility is to provide alignment, transparency, and efficiency throughout the product lifecycle. It ensures that products are developed with business objectives in mind, customer needs are well understood and addressed, and the technology being utilized is leveraged effectively.

The primary function of Product Operations is to serve as the connective tissue within the product organization, ensuring efficiency, strategic alignment, and cross-functional collaboration, as shown in Figure 12.6. The key functions of Product Operations are:

1 **Ensuring Efficiency**: Product Operations provides consistent processes, frameworks, and best practices to ensure product teams operate efficiently.
2 **Facilitating Data-Driven Decision-Making**: Product Operations consolidates data and insights that enable Product Managers to make informed and strategic decisions.
3 **Orchestrating Product Lifecycle Events**: Product Operations is responsible for overseeing key events, such as product launches, by coordinating all cross-functional teams.

In this section, we've introduced the foundational role that **Product Operations** plays within the **POM**, ensuring coordination, data-driven decision-making, and cross-functional alignment across teams. Product Operations provides consistent processes, frameworks, and best practices,

Product Operations		
⚙	ᴵᴵᴵ	♻
Ensuring Efficiency	Facilitating Data-Driven Decision-Making	Orchestrating Product Lifecycle Events
Consistent processes, frameworks, and best practices	Data and insights consolidation	Product launches, by coordinating all cross-functional teams

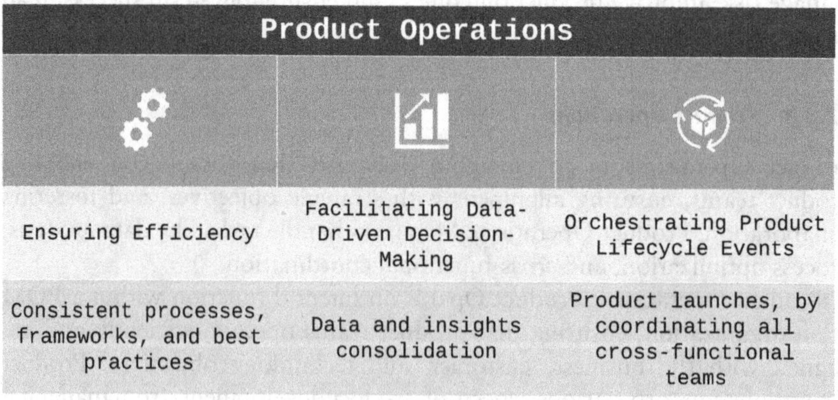

FIGURE 12.6 Functions of Product Operations.

which enable product teams to operate efficiently. It also consolidates data and insights that support Product Managers in making strategic, informed decisions. Moreover, Product Operations oversees key product lifecycle events, such as product launches, orchestrating efforts across multiple teams to ensure smooth execution.

Chapter 13, *Scaling Product Operations*, delves deeper into the team model of Product Operations, breaking down roles and responsibilities within a Product Ops team. This includes understanding how Product Operations Managers differ from Product Managers, with a focus on their distinct responsibilities in ensuring operational excellence. Additionally, we will explore the maturity levels of Product Operations and how organizations can progressively scale this function to optimize efficiency and product success as they grow.

12.4 Conclusion

This chapter has outlined the critical components of a **POM** that contribute to a robust and scalable product management infrastructure. By exploring key areas such as Organizational Alignment, Innovation Management, Portfolio Management, Technology Enablement, and Process & Governance, this chapter has demonstrated how each element plays a crucial role in ensuring strategic success and operational efficiency. The **POM** acts as a guiding framework that aligns product teams with broader business objectives while driving innovation, managing resources, and optimizing performance.

As companies scale, the need for a structured yet flexible operating model becomes increasingly important. The chapter underscores the significance of having a clear vision and processes in place to foster cross-functional collaboration and continuous improvement. Finally, we introduced the pivotal role of Product Operations, which not only enhances efficiency but also orchestrates key product lifecycle events.

The next chapter, *Scaling Product Operations*, will further explore how to implement and scale Product Operations effectively, providing insights into team structures, maturity levels, and the vital role they play in the long-term success of digital products.

13
SCALING PRODUCT OPERATIONS

13.1 Introduction

In any growing organization, the complexity of managing multiple products and teams requires an approach that ensures smooth operations, alignment, and efficiency. This is where **Product Operations (Product Ops)** come into play. **Product Ops** acts as the connective tissue between product management, engineering, marketing, sales, and other cross-functional teams, ensuring that processes run smoothly and efficiently. As companies scale, the role of **Product Ops** becomes even more essential in orchestrating product lifecycle events, optimizing workflows, and enabling data-driven decision-making.

This chapter will delve into the key aspects of scaling **Product Operations**, discussing team structures, the roles and responsibilities of **Product Ops**, and how **Product Ops** maturity evolves within an organization. We will also highlight the distinction between a **Product Ops** Manager and a **Product Manager,** and explore how **Product Ops** integrates into a scaling product team.

13.2 The Role of Product Operations in Scaling

Product Operations ensures that the strategic goals of product management are effectively translated into operational success. The three primary functions of Product Ops are:

- **Ensuring Efficiency:** Product Ops creates consistent processes, frameworks, and best practices that enhance team efficiency. By standardizing workflows

DOI: 10.1201/9781003614180-13

and providing operational support, they allow product managers to focus on strategy and execution rather than administrative tasks.

- **Facilitating Data-Driven Decision-Making:** One of the key roles of Product Ops is to collect, consolidate, and analyse data from various sources, such as customer feedback, product usage metrics, and market insights. By providing product managers with accurate and actionable data, Product Ops ensures that decisions are informed and aligned with the overall business strategy.
- **Orchestrating Product Lifecycle Events:** From product launches to key updates, Product Ops ensures that all teams involved in the product lifecycle are aligned and working cohesively. By coordinating efforts between engineering, sales, marketing, and support, they help streamline product launches, scale product features, and maintain a seamless customer experience.

13.3 The Product Operations Team Model: Roles and Responsibilities

As organizations grow, scaling **Product Operations** requires building out a specialized team with defined roles and responsibilities. A typical Product Ops team may include the following key roles:

- **Product Operations Manager:** This role focuses on building and maintaining operational frameworks that support product teams. The Product Ops Manager ensures that best practices are followed, processes are streamlined, and product teams have the necessary tools to succeed. They act as the key liaison between product managers and cross-functional teams, ensuring alignment.
- **Product Operations Analyst:** The analyst gathers and interprets data to drive insights. This role is crucial in creating reports on product performance, customer feedback, and operational metrics. By providing data-backed insights, Product Operations Analysts empower product managers to make informed, strategic decisions.
- **Process Improvement Specialist:** This individual is responsible for identifying inefficiencies and bottlenecks in existing workflows and proposing solutions to enhance productivity. By continuously optimizing internal processes, the Process Improvement Specialist ensures that the organization remains agile and responsive to changes.
- **Product Launch Coordinator:** A critical role in orchestrating product lifecycle events, the Product Launch Coordinator manages the logistical aspects of bringing a product to market. This includes coordinating

cross-functional teams, managing timelines, and ensuring all aspects of the launch are on track and aligned with the overall strategy.

13.4 Product Ops vs. Product Teams

To understand how Product Ops contributes to the product organization, we need to dive into the various functions, roles, and responsibilities that Product Ops covers.

Product Operations (Product Ops) and Product Teams have distinct but complementary roles within an organization. While Product Teams focus on defining, building, and enhancing the product itself, Product Ops ensure that the processes, tools, and insights necessary for efficient product development and scaling are in place. Product Ops act as the backbone of the product function, facilitating operational excellence, removing roadblocks, and creating standardized approaches that help Product Teams stay focused on innovation and customer value. Understanding these roles and how they interconnect enables the organization to create a cohesive strategy for delivering high-quality products to the market efficiently.

1 **Aligning Product Goals with Business Objectives:**

- **Product Ops Team:** The Product Ops team ensures that product initiatives align with the company's overall business goals. This includes creating frameworks to evaluate how each product contributes to the company's growth and revenue.
- **Product Teams:** Product Managers and development teams focus on defining features, prioritizing user needs, and delivering products that achieve business goals.

2 **Addressing Customer Needs through Insights:**

- **Product Ops Team:** The Product Ops team is responsible for collecting, analysing, and synthesizing customer insights through market research and Voice of Customer (VOC) programmes. It provides this data to product teams to ensure that customer needs drive the product strategy.
- **Product Teams:** Product Managers utilize insights provided by Product Ops to shape the roadmap, design new features, and improve customer satisfaction.

3 **Ensuring Technological Feasibility:**

- **Product Ops Team:** Product Ops collaborates with engineering to evaluate the technological feasibility of product initiatives. This includes assessing whether features can be delivered on time and within budget.

- **Product Teams**: Product Managers work with development teams to explore potential solutions and iterate on features based on user feedback.

13.5 Product Ops Manager vs. Product Manager Roles

The roles of a Product Operations (Product Ops) Manager and a Product Manager are complementary yet distinct, both being crucial in ensuring that a product is designed, developed, and delivered successfully. Each role focuses on different aspects of product development and operations, with the Product Manager acting as the strategic visionary and the Product Ops Manager providing operational support and efficiency, as shown in Figure 13.1.

1 Product Manager's Role: The Visionary and Customer Advocate

The Product Manager's primary role is to define the product vision and strategy, ensuring that the product meets customer needs and delivers value. They bridge the gap between the business, market, and engineering teams, ensuring that the product aligns with the company's objectives. Key responsibilities of a Product Manager include the following:

- **Defining Product Vision and Strategy**: Product Managers are responsible for crafting the long-term vision of the product, understanding customer needs, and ensuring that the product meets these needs.

Example: At **Spotify**, Product Managers set the direction for features like "Discover Weekly" to improve user engagement and enhance the experience of personalized music recommendations.

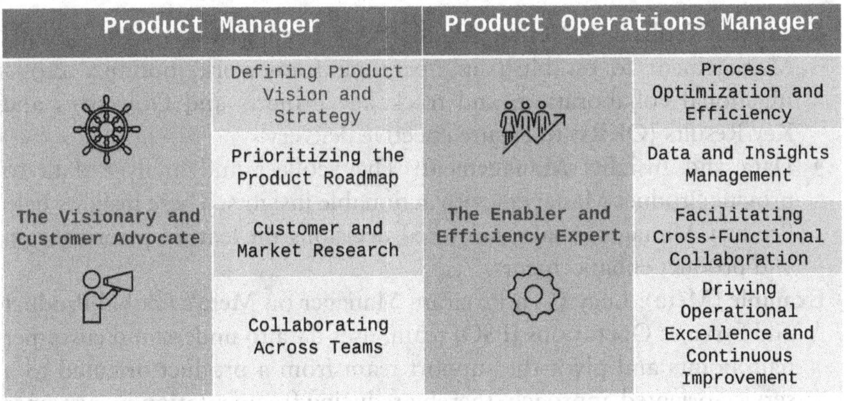

Product Manager		Product Operations Manager	
	Defining Product Vision and Strategy		Process Optimization and Efficiency
	Prioritizing the Product Roadmap		Data and Insights Management
The Visionary and Customer Advocate	Customer and Market Research	The Enabler and Efficiency Expert	Facilitating Cross-Functional Collaboration
	Collaborating Across Teams		Driving Operational Excellence and Continuous Improvement

FIGURE 13.1 Product Manager vs. Product Operations Manager.

- **Prioritizing the Product Roadmap**: They create and manage the product roadmap, determining what features or improvements should be developed, and in which order.

Example: At **Tesla**, Product Managers prioritize features for Autopilot improvements based on customer feedback and the competitive landscape in autonomous driving.

- **Customer and Market Research**: Product Managers gather customer insights through direct interviews, surveys, and data analysis to translate customer needs into product requirements.

Example: **Airbnb** Product Managers interact with hosts and guests to gather insights, translating them into initiatives like the "Superhost" programme.

- **Collaborating Across Teams**: Product Managers work closely with engineering, design, sales, and marketing teams to ensure that the product is built according to requirements and launched successfully.

Example: At **Slack**, Product Managers work with design and engineering teams to improve messaging features, ensuring they remain intuitive and cater to user needs.

2 Product Ops Manager's Role: The Enabler and Efficiency Expert

The Product Ops Manager is responsible for optimizing the operational aspects of product management. They help ensure efficiency in the product development lifecycle and streamline processes to reduce friction, allowing Product Managers to focus on strategic initiatives. Key responsibilities of a Product Ops Manager include the following:

- **Process Optimization and Efficiency**: The Product Ops Manager streamlines processes, implements best practices, and removes bottlenecks to maximize efficiency in product development.

Example (Netflix): A **Netflix** Product Ops Lead partners with Product Management to establish an operating framework, optimize cross-functional collaboration, and track key projects and Objectives and Key Results (**OKRs**) to ensure effective delivery.

- **Data and Insights Management**: They collect and analyse data to provide Product Managers with actionable insights. These insights help Product Managers make informed decisions on feature prioritization and product enhancements.

Example (Meta): Lucy C., a Program Manager on **Meta's** Global Product and Services Operations (**PSO**) team, uses data to understand customer pain points and pivot the support team from a product-oriented to a service-oriented approach, thereby reducing fragmentation in customer support.

- **Facilitating Cross-Functional Collaboration**: Product Ops Managers coordinate between different teams – such as engineering, marketing, and support – to ensure alignment and effective collaboration.

Example (Spotify): The Product Ops Manager at **Spotify** acts as a community manager, connecting the product function across the organization, promoting product learning programmes, and ensuring smooth communication.

- **Driving Operational Excellence and Continuous Improvement**: They lead process improvement initiatives and create an operational framework to support the product lifecycle.

Example (Netflix): At **Netflix**, Product Ops Managers lead operational activities and improve processes to maximize efficiency, ensuring that cross-functional teams are working towards common goals.

13.5.1 *Key Differences between Product Manager and Product Ops Manager*

The fundamental difference between a Product Manager and a Product Ops Manager lies in their focus areas: the Product Manager is responsible for defining **what** the product should be and **why** it should exist, while the Product Ops Manager is focused on **how** to bring that product to life efficiently. Product Ops Managers ensure the processes and workflows are optimized so that Product Managers can concentrate on delivering value to customers.

- **Meta**: At Meta, the Global PSO team is responsible for supporting customer experience and ensuring product scalability. While Product Managers define features for new business solutions, Product Ops Managers like Lucy C. drive operational changes to streamline service delivery and improve customer support experiences.
- **Netflix**: The Product Ops Lead at Netflix partners with the Product Management Lead to ensure that all operational activities are conducted efficiently, aligning teams with OKRs and leading cross-functional collaboration to deliver the product's objectives. This role ensures the success of initiatives, allowing Product Managers to focus on innovation and feature prioritization.
- **Spotify**: At Spotify, the Product Ops Manager facilitates the product team's community, connects product functions across the organization, and manages onboarding, ensuring Product Managers can focus on building a creative and impactful product environment.

Product Managers and Product Ops Managers play essential but distinct roles in the product development process. While Product Managers are primarily focused on creating the right product that solves user problems and meets market needs, Product Ops Managers focus on supporting the product teams by optimizing processes, enabling collaboration, and ensuring operational excellence. Together, they create a well-functioning product development environment, with Product Managers driving the **why** and **what**, and Product Ops Managers driving the **how**, leading to better customer experiences and more successful products in the market.

13.6 Product Operations Maturity Model

Product Operations capability can be developed at different levels of maturity to ensure optimal efficiency, alignment, and collaboration. The levels of maturity can be categorized as follows, with three key areas of focus: **Operational Foundations**, **Strategic Synergy**, and **Cross-Functional Alignment**. Figure 13.2 depicts the Product Operations Maturity Model.

1 **Foundational Practices Level of Maturity**
    This level is focused on establishing foundational structures such as operational foundations, strategic cohesion, and stakeholder alignment.

- **Operational Foundations – PDLC, Governance, Delivery Cadences:**

    Product Ops establishes the Product Development Life Cycle (PDLC), providing structure and delivery cadences to ensure smooth and consistent execution.

    Example: Airbnb used foundational practices to align their product teams by establishing standardized delivery cadences, enabling them to efficiently roll out updates to the platform.

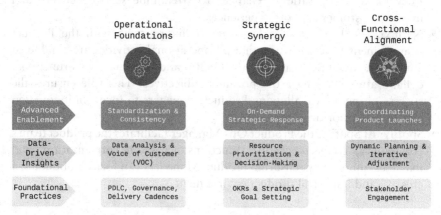

FIGURE 13.2 Product Operations Maturity Model.

- **Strategic Synergy – OKRs and Strategic Goal Setting:**

  Product Ops facilitates the establishment of OKRs to link team initiatives with strategic organizational goals.

  Example: Google has successfully implemented OKRs across teams to ensure alignment between individual product initiatives and overall company strategy.

- **Cross-Functional Alignment – Stakeholder Engagement:**

  Product Ops ensures that stakeholders across different functions are engaged, aligned and have visibility into product timelines, updates, and milestones.

  Example: Netflix improved cross-functional alignment by providing stakeholders with dashboards that detail the status of each product initiative, improving collaboration between marketing, engineering, and operations.

2 **Data-Driven Insights Level of Maturity**
   The next level of maturity emphasizes data-driven insights and informed decision-making to optimize processes and outcomes.

- **Operational Foundations – Data Analysis and Voice of Customer (VOC):**

  Product Ops uses data and customer feedback to drive prioritization, validate product features, and ensure that product decisions are customer-centric.

  Example: Amazon uses customer data analysis to continuously refine product features and improve the customer experience.

- **Strategic Synergy – Resource Prioritization and Decision-Making:**

  Product Ops plays a role in strategic decision-making, helping allocate resources to initiatives with the greatest potential impact and making informed tradeoff decisions.

  Example: Spotify applies data-driven resource prioritization to allocate resources to features that enhance user engagement, such as personalized playlists.

- **Cross-Functional Alignment – Dynamic Planning and Iterative Adjustment:**

  Product Ops supports dynamic and iterative planning to ensure that product teams remain agile and responsive to evolving customer and market needs.

  Example: Meta (Facebook) employs dynamic planning to adjust features and rollout strategies based on real-time user feedback and engagement metrics.

3 Advanced Enablement Level of Maturity

Advanced enablement focuses on achieving consistency, agility, and full-scale product launch orchestration.

- **Operational Foundations – Standardization and Consistency:**

  Product Ops ensures standardization across teams by implementing frameworks and best practices that streamline product operations.

  Example: **Tesla** has established standardized operational practices to maintain consistency across product updates and manufacturing processes.

- **Strategic Synergy – On-Demand Strategic Response:**

  Product Ops provides support for on-demand strategic planning, enabling teams to pivot quickly based on new insights or market dynamics.

  Example: **Slack** leveraged on-demand strategic planning to quickly adapt its product offerings to cater to the remote working surge during the pandemic.

- **Cross-Functional Alignment – Coordinating Product Launches:**

  Product Ops oversees product launches, ensuring collaboration across functions to execute successful launches that meet both market and customer needs.

  Example: **Samsung** effectively coordinates cross-functional teams during new Galaxy product launches to ensure a smooth rollout in multiple regions.

13.7 Embarking on the Product Operations Journey

Embarking on the Product Operations journey requires a well-structured approach to building the capability within the Product Portfolio function. This journey involves gradually increasing the level of maturity, from basic to advanced, to establish a high-performing Product Ops function. Each level of maturity represents a different set of capabilities, with key areas such as operational efficiency, strategic synergy, and cross-functional alignment as the pillars.

1 Start with Foundational Practices:

- Establish PDLC processes, governance models, and delivery cadences. Align product teams with organizational objectives using OKRs and ensure stakeholders are aligned, engaged and have visibility into key initiatives. At this stage, organizations focus on establishing predictability and transparency.

2 **Evolve Towards Data-Driven Decision-Making:**

- Incorporate data analysis and the VOC (Voice of Customer) to make decisions. Product Ops should begin facilitating the reallocation of resources based on strategic priorities and dynamically adjusting plans. Teams need to be flexible in adapting to changing market conditions while leveraging data for continuous improvement.

3 **Advance to Consistent, Standardized Practices:**

- Standardize processes across the product portfolio, making consistent practices the norm. Provide on-demand access to strategic insights, allowing teams to plan and pivot based on market changes. Product Ops takes an active role in orchestrating launches, focusing on efficient and impactful market introductions.

13.8 Conclusion

Product Operations (Product Ops) is a vital enabler for achieving product success, ensuring the alignment of teams, processes, and customer needs within an organization. It plays an essential role in supporting product managers and other cross-functional stakeholders, driving strategic alignment, operational efficiency, and collaboration across the product lifecycle. By establishing foundational practices, leveraging data-driven insights, and ultimately enabling advanced coordination, Product Ops enhances productivity and creates a consistent, customer-focused approach that fosters successful product development and market growth.

As organizations progress through different levels of maturity – from foundational to advanced enablement – they benefit from increased alignment between their strategic goals, operational foundations, and cross-functional collaboration. This journey is critical for creating an environment that supports scalability, informed decision-making, and agility in response to changing market conditions and customer needs.

Product Ops also differentiates itself from Product Management by focusing on operational excellence rather than product-specific features, ultimately complementing the work of Product Managers. Whether it's enabling better decision-making through data insights or managing processes for product launches, **Product Ops** empowers teams to work effectively and achieve long-term success.

By embedding **Product Ops** deeply into the **Product Operating Model**, companies can ensure that their products consistently meet market demands, create exceptional customer experiences, and sustain competitive differentiation. It is not just about building products – it's about building them right, and at the right time, while efficiently orchestrating every part of the product journey.

14

INTEGRATING THE DPM PROCESS GROUPS

14.1 Introduction

In the increasingly complex and competitive digital landscape, integrating different aspects of product management into a cohesive strategy is essential. The **Digital Product Management (DPM) Framework** outlines five core process groups: **Product Opportunity, Product Planning, Product Development, Product Launch,** and **Product Support.** Each process group addresses different phases of the product lifecycle, but to drive successful product outcomes, these groups must function seamlessly together.

In this chapter, we will explore how product managers and organizations can integrate these process groups to ensure a smooth product lifecycle and how effective alignment across teams can lead to stronger product execution, faster time to market, and higher customer satisfaction.

14.2 The Need for Integration in Product Management

The **DPM** framework is not a set of isolated processes, but rather a holistic approach to managing the product lifecycle. For digital product managers, understanding how these five core groups interact is crucial to ensuring that product initiatives are aligned with business goals, customer needs, and market opportunities.

Integration involves more than just following each process in sequence; it's about understanding where overlaps exist and how information flows between stages. A well-integrated product management process connects strategic planning with execution, customer feedback with product iterations, and cross-functional teams with shared objectives.

DOI: 10.1201/9781003614180-14

When these processes are integrated, organizations can:

- **Avoid Silos:** Product teams and other departments such as marketing, engineering, and customer support will work cohesively, eliminating communication breakdowns.
- **Improve Agility:** Decisions can be made faster, and changes can be implemented more efficiently across the product lifecycle.
- **Increase Accountability:** When processes are connected, it's easier to track responsibility for each phase of product development and ensure transparency in decision-making.

14.3   Mapping the Core Process Groups for Integration

1 Product Opportunity

At the start of the product lifecycle, **Product Opportunity** is focused on identifying and validating market gaps and crafting a product vision. This phase sets the foundation for all future stages. To integrate this process with the others:

- Ensure that the insights and data gathered in the opportunity phase flow directly into **Product Planning** to create a roadmap that aligns with market needs.
- The vision and objectives should also serve as guidelines for **Product Development**, ensuring that the product team builds something with a validated market fit.
- **Go-to-Market Strategy** formed here must be aligned with both the **Product Launch** and **Product Support** teams, creating a cohesive path to customer acquisition and ongoing support.

2 Product Planning

In this phase, product managers define the product roadmap, prioritize features, and plan the release strategy. Effective integration in this stage involves the following:

- Ensuring that **Product Development** teams have the resources, timelines, and specifications needed to execute the roadmap efficiently.
- Collaborating closely with **Marketing and Sales** teams to integrate the **Go-to-Market Strategy** into the release plan, ensuring that timelines for development and launch are aligned.
- Coordinating with the **Product Support** team to ensure that post-launch processes, such as customer service and technical support, are anticipated in advance.

3 **Product Development**

During **Product Development,** the product takes shape. Here, integration with the other process groups is crucial for ensuring that what gets built aligns with market demand and customer expectations:

- Continuous communication with the **Product Opportunity** and **Product Planning** teams ensures that market shifts or feature priorities are accounted for.
- Feedback loops must be established with **Product Support** teams to incorporate real-time customer insights into product iterations.
- Collaboration with **Sales and Marketing** teams during development ensures the product is aligned with customer messaging and ready for launch.

4 **Product Launch**

A successful **Product Launch** is not just about unveiling a product; it's about executing a well-coordinated strategy across departments. To ensure successful integration during the launch phase:

- Align **Marketing Campaigns** with the launch roadmap to ensure that promotional materials, messaging, and target audiences are ready.
- Work closely with **Sales Channels** to ensure product availability and provide sales teams with the resources needed for customer engagement.
- Pre-emptively involve **Product Support** teams so they are equipped to handle potential customer inquiries and issues upon launch.

5 **Product Support**

Product Support is often an overlooked but critical part of the product lifecycle. For effective integration:

- Establish feedback loops with the **Product Development** team, so that customer feedback and product usage data can drive future improvements.
- Collaborate with the **Product Opportunity** team to identify emerging market trends or customer needs that may lead to new opportunities.
- Coordinate with the **Marketing** team to maintain consistent messaging post-launch, especially when addressing customer issues or rolling out product updates.

14.4 Cross-Functional Alignment

One of the primary challenges in product management is ensuring cross-functional alignment between different teams – product managers, designers, developers, marketers, and support staff. Integration between the **DPM** process groups requires breaking down silos and fostering a collaborative culture where information is freely shared and decisions are made collectively.

1 **Cross-Team Collaboration Tools**
   To facilitate integration, tools such as project management software (e.g., **JIRA, Monday.com**) and collaboration platforms (e.g., **Slack, Trello**) can play a key role. These tools allow different teams to work together, track progress, and maintain visibility across all stages of the product lifecycle.
2 **Alignment Meetings and Processes**
   Regular cross-functional alignment meetings – such as **stand-ups, sprint reviews**, and **product roadmap meetings** – ensure that all teams are on the same page regarding product development progress, market needs, and upcoming milestones.

14.5   The Role of Leadership in Integration

Product managers play a pivotal role in ensuring that the integration between these process groups is seamless. However, leadership and executive oversight are equally important to set the tone for collaboration and ensure that product teams have the resources and support they need to integrate effectively. Leaders must ensure the following:

- **Strategic Alignment**: Ensuring that the product vision remains aligned with business goals throughout the product lifecycle.
- **Resource Allocation**: Providing the necessary tools, personnel, and budget to integrate the product process groups effectively.
- **Cultural Encouragement**: Fostering a culture of transparency and accountability where cross-functional teams work towards shared objectives.

14.6   Continuous Integration for Continuous Improvement

The product lifecycle doesn't end with the launch; integration continues as a cyclical process. By establishing systems for continuous feedback between the core process groups, product managers can ensure that products are improved iteratively based on customer feedback, performance data, and evolving market trends.
This cyclical integration leads to the following:

- Faster product iterations and refinements.
- Enhanced customer satisfaction by addressing issues or improvements promptly.

- Stronger alignment between business strategy, product vision, and market execution.

14.7 Conclusion

Integrating the core process groups of the DPM framework is key to ensuring product success. By connecting **Product Opportunity**, **Product Planning**, **Product Development**, **Product Launch**, and **Product Support**, product managers can ensure that their products are developed and delivered in alignment with customer needs and business objectives.

15

LEADING ETHICAL PRACTICES IN DIGITAL PRODUCT MANAGEMENT

15.1 Introduction

In the rapidly evolving world of digital product management (DPM), product managers are not just responsible for the commercial success of their products – they are also stewards of ethical practices. As data privacy concerns, artificial intelligence (AI) adoption, and automation accelerate, product managers must consider the ethical ramifications of their decisions. Building products that enhance user experience, ensure privacy, and uphold trust requires an understanding of both the ethical landscape and the leadership role that product managers play. This chapter delves into the importance of ethical leadership in DPM, outlining strategies for embedding ethical principles into every phase of the product lifecycle.

15.2 The Role of Ethical Leadership in Digital Product Management

Ethical leadership in product management is about more than simply adhering to laws and regulations. It involves proactively addressing issues such as data privacy, inclusivity, bias in AI, and the potential societal impacts of technology. Product managers are uniquely positioned to lead ethical initiatives because they interact with multiple stakeholders, including customers, engineers, and business leaders.

DOI: 10.1201/9781003614180-15

Key elements of ethical leadership include the following:

- **Trust**: Building and maintaining trust with users is essential. Trustworthy products are those that protect user data, respect privacy, and offer transparency about how personal information is used.
- **Inclusivity**: Ensuring that digital products serve diverse groups of users is another ethical obligation. Ethical leaders prioritize accessibility and inclusivity in product design and development.
- **Social Responsibility**: Products, particularly in industries like AI, fintech, and healthcare, can have wide-reaching social impacts. Ethical product managers must weigh these effects and create products that contribute positively to society.

15.3 Data Privacy and Security

With the rise of data-driven products, ensuring privacy and security has become one of the most critical ethical challenges for product managers. Data is often referred to as the new oil, but mishandling it can erode trust and lead to significant legal and reputational risks. Ethical product leaders must implement data privacy principles such as **data minimization, user consent,** and **secure data storage**.

Key Questions for Product Managers:

- How is user data being collected, and is it necessary?
- Are users clearly informed about how their data is used?
- What safeguards are in place to protect data from breaches?

Example: GDPR Compliance and the Role of Product Managers. The General Data Protection Regulation (**GDPR**) serves as a benchmark for data privacy laws globally. Product managers must ensure that their products comply with such regulations, particularly when handling personal data. **Facebook's** data scandals, for instance, have underscored the importance of robust data privacy measures and transparency.

15.4 Ethical Use of Artificial Intelligence and Automation

AI and automation offer immense benefits, but they also present ethical challenges, such as algorithmic bias and job displacement. Ethical product managers need to ensure that AI systems are built and deployed responsibly. This includes examining biases in datasets, ensuring transparency in decision-making, and considering the impact of automation on jobs and communities.

Key Questions for Product Managers:

- Is the AI system designed to avoid bias?
- How transparent are the AI-driven decisions to users?
- What are the broader societal impacts of implementing automation in this product?

Example: Google's Ethical AI Guidelines. Google has adopted ethical AI guidelines to ensure that its AI-driven products respect user privacy, avoid bias, and maintain transparency. For example, when developing facial recognition technologies, ethical concerns about surveillance and discrimination have forced companies to halt or adjust their product roadmaps to mitigate risks.

15.5 Accessibility and Inclusivity in Product Design

Ensuring inclusivity and accessibility is not just a design choice – it's an ethical obligation. Digital products must cater to a wide range of users, including those with disabilities. Ethical product managers incorporate inclusive design principles, ensuring that everyone can access and benefit from the product.
Key Questions for Product Managers:

- Have the diverse needs of all user groups been considered?
- Is the product accessible to users with disabilities?
- How is the product serving underrepresented communities?

Example: Microsoft's Inclusive Design Approach. Microsoft has adopted inclusive design principles, ensuring that its products are accessible to users with a range of abilities. The company's **Xbox** Adaptive Controller, for example, was designed to accommodate gamers with limited mobility, demonstrating how inclusivity can drive innovation.

15.6 Transparency and Communication

One of the core tenets of ethical leadership in DPM is transparency. Customers increasingly demand to know how decisions are made and how products work, particularly when it comes to data handling and AI-driven systems. Ethical product managers communicate openly and honestly with their users, providing clear information about product features, limitations, and data usage.

Key Questions for Product Managers:

- Are users informed about the potential risks or limitations of the product?

- How transparent are the product's data usage policies?
- What steps are being taken to ensure accountability?

Example: Apple's Privacy Policies. Apple's privacy campaigns highlight the company's focus on transparency. By emphasizing user control over personal data and promoting features like privacy labels on apps, **Apple** has built trust with its customers, differentiating itself in an industry where privacy concerns are growing.

15.7   Ethical Considerations in Product Support

Ethical leadership extends beyond product development and launch – it also includes product support. This involves handling customer issues with empathy, providing transparent processes for problem resolution, and ensuring technical support is aligned with ethical standards, such as not exploiting user data.

Key Questions for Product Managers:

- Are customer support teams trained in ethical problem-solving?
- Is customer data treated with respect during support interactions?
- How are support practices contributing to overall trust in the product?

15.8   Ethical Frameworks in Digital Product Management

In the ever-evolving field of **DPM**, where innovation and rapid technological advancement can often overshadow other considerations, ethics remains a critical component. Ethical frameworks provide guidelines to help product managers make decisions that respect user rights, maintain trust, and contribute positively to society. This section explores three broad ethics frameworks – **Consequentialist, Duty, and Virtue ethics** – and how they apply to DPM through real-world examples.

1   Consequentialist Ethics

The **Consequentialist** framework evaluates actions based on their outcomes. In **DPM**, product managers using this approach focus on creating digital products that maximize positive outcomes for users, stakeholders, and society. If a product feature improves user experience or accessibility for a larger portion of the market, a Consequentialist might argue that the benefits outweigh the negative effects, even if some groups are disadvantaged.

Example: A social media platform considering data collection to personalize user experiences must balance this against the potential loss of user privacy. Consequentialist ethics would weigh the positive outcomes, such as enhanced user engagement, against the risk of users feeling violated by the lack of privacy.

2 Duty Ethics

Duty ethics, also known as deontological ethics, focuses on adherence to rules, principles, or duties, regardless of the outcome. A product manager guided by duty ethics would prioritize following regulations and ethical standards over potential gains. In this framework, user privacy, transparency, and fairness are fundamental duties that must be respected.

Example: Duty ethics would dictate that a mobile app handling sensitive health data must prioritize privacy and security – even if there is a compelling business case for data-sharing partnerships. In 2021, the period-tracking app **Flo** was accused of misleading users about data privacy, sharing sensitive information with **Facebook** and **Google** without user consent. From a duty ethics perspective, this breach of trust was ethically impermissible, regardless of the business benefits.

3 Virtue Ethics

Virtue ethics emphasizes the character and moral virtues of the individuals making decisions. In **DPM**, this framework encourages product managers to focus on fostering virtuous traits like honesty, empathy, and integrity. Product managers adopting virtue ethics would make decisions that align with these virtues, aiming to build products that reflect ethical excellence.

Example: A product manager faced with introducing advertising to a children's app might avoid manipulating kids' attention for profit, opting instead for transparent and ethical marketing. In this case, the virtue of honesty and responsibility towards vulnerable users, like children, guides decision-making.

15.9 Self-Driving Cars

Self-driving cars, also known as autonomous vehicles (**AVs**), are one of the most groundbreaking innovations in transportation technology. Companies like **Google's Waymo**, **Tesla**, and **Uber** have been leading the charge in the development and deployment of self-driving technology. Below are detailed examples of how these companies are navigating the challenges and advancements of autonomous driving technology, along with ethical considerations related to their development:

1 Google's Waymo

Waymo, a subsidiary of **Alphabet** (**Google's** parent company), is widely considered a pioneer in the AV industry. Starting as **Google's** self-driving car project, **Waymo** has since evolved into a leader in **AV** technology, focusing heavily on safety and transparency.

- **Key Features:**

  - **Rigorous Testing**: **Waymo's** self-driving cars have logged over 20 million miles on public roads and billions of simulated miles in diverse conditions. The company emphasizes safety and has shared detailed reports on how its technology makes decisions on the road, which includes avoiding collisions, navigating complex intersections, and predicting the behaviour of other road users.
  - **Ethical Transparency**: **Waymo** has set a standard for transparency in AV testing, regularly releasing safety reports to the public. These reports detail the decision-making processes of the car, outlining how the vehicle reacts to pedestrians, cyclists, and other vehicles, even in unpredictable scenarios.
  - **Deployment**: **Waymo's** autonomous taxis have been operating in Phoenix, Los Angeles, and San Francisco, offering driverless rides to customers. This real-world deployment demonstrates their confidence in the technology's safety and reliability.

- **Ethical Considerations:**

  - **Decision-making Transparency**: **Waymo** places a significant focus on ensuring that its ethical decision-making processes, especially in split-second situations like potential accidents, are clear to the public.
  - **Public Safety**: The company's heavy emphasis on safety protocols addresses public concerns regarding the reliability of autonomous cars.

2 Tesla's Autopilot

Tesla's Autopilot is one of the most well-known examples of semi-autonomous driving technology, providing advanced driver assistance features like lane keeping, adaptive cruise control, and limited self-driving capabilities. **Tesla** continues to push towards full self-driving (FSD), with the goal of enabling its vehicles to operate completely autonomously.

- **Key Features:**

  - **Autopilot**: **Tesla's Autopilot** system allows for a high level of automation in specific driving conditions. While drivers are still required to monitor the system, **Tesla's** vision is to move towards full autonomy. **Autopilot** can change lanes, maintain speed, and avoid obstacles with minimal driver input.
  - **Full-Self Driving (FSD) Beta**: **Tesla** has been rolling out **FSD** beta versions, which aim to offer fully autonomous capabilities. FSD

includes features such as automatic navigation on highways, self-parking, and the ability to recognize and respond to traffic lights and stop signs.

- **Human Override:** Tesla incorporates the option for human intervention, which allows the driver to take control in emergency situations. This is critical in maintaining a balance between safety and innovation.

- **Ethical Considerations:**

  - **Human-in-the-Loop:** Tesla's system allows drivers to override the self-driving system, ensuring that human judgement can still intervene during critical moments. This is an ethical safeguard, giving users control in case the system makes a questionable decision.
  - **Data Collection and Privacy:** Tesla gathers vast amounts of driving data from its customers to improve its autonomous systems. While this enhances the technology, it also raises concerns around data privacy and consent, as customers are not always fully aware of the extent to which their data is being used.

3 Uber's Self-Driving Cars

Uber was one of the most high-profile companies attempting to deploy self-driving cars until it sold its AV division in 2020. The company's self-driving car project encountered significant challenges, particularly regarding safety after a fatal accident involving one of its AVs in 2018.

- **Key Features:**

  - **Ambitious Deployment Plans:** Uber aimed to integrate self-driving cars into its rideshare network to reduce costs by eliminating drivers. It conducted trials in multiple cities, including Pittsburgh and Phoenix.
  - **Collaboration with Volvo:** Uber partnered with Volvo to equip their vehicles with self-driving technology. The collaboration aimed to combine Volvo's hardware with Uber's autonomous software to create a scalable self-driving fleet.

- **Ethical Considerations:**

  - **Safety and Public Trust:** In 2018, one of Uber's self-driving cars struck and killed a pedestrian in Tempe, Arizona. This incident led to intense scrutiny over the company's safety protocols, the vehicle's inability to identify and avoid the pedestrian, and the role of the safety driver in the car. Uber temporarily halted its AV testing following the accident, raising questions about the technology's readiness for real-world deployment.

- **Accountability and Responsibility**: The ethical dilemma of assigning responsibility – whether to the car's software developers, Uber, or the safety driver – highlighted the importance of having clear ethical frameworks in place for AVs.

15.10 The Trolley Problem

The **Trolley Problem**, a classic ethical dilemma, can be applied to the development of self-driving cars, which are now increasingly present on the roads. In the original **Trolley Problem**, a runaway trolley threatens to kill five people on the tracks unless a lever is pulled to divert it, killing one person on another track. In DPM, this dilemma is reflected in how self-driving cars are programmed to make life-or-death decisions.

15.10.1 Application of Ethical Frameworks

Let's apply the three Ethical Frameworks to the following dilemma of self-driving cars.

<u>Self-Driving Car Dilemma:</u>
You are a software engineer working for a company that develops autonomous driving software. You're currently working on an update to the decision-making algorithms for emergency scenarios.
A recently surfaced issue is the "Trolley Problem," a hypothetical situation where the autonomous vehicle must choose between two harmful outcomes:

- The car, to avoid a group of five pedestrians who suddenly appear in its path, could swerve into a wall, likely seriously injuring the single passenger inside.
- The car could continue on its path, likely injuring or even killing the five pedestrians.

<u>Question:</u> Should you modify the algorithm to always prioritize the lives of multiple people over one, even if that one is the passenger?
The following options are based on the use of the three common ethical frameworks:

1 **Consequentialist**: Implement the change, as protecting multiple lives over one is ethically permissible, even if it harms the passenger. A consequentialist would support self-driving car software that prioritizes minimizing overall harm, even if it means sacrificing the passenger to save more lives.

2 **Duty**: Reject the change, as it's not ethically permissible to directly harm the passenger, regardless of the potential benefits. From a duty ethics standpoint, the self-driving car must respect its duty to the passenger, protecting their safety at all costs.

3 **Virtue**: Implement the change but also inform all potential customers about this feature, allowing them to make an informed decision. A virtue ethicist would value transparency and fairness, giving users the choice to opt into such ethical decision-making systems. An alternative option using the Virtue framework is to reject the change and seek a third solution that doesn't risk harming either the passenger or pedestrians. This option embodies a commitment to continual ethical innovation, where the company seeks safer, more ethical alternatives.

15.10.2   Human Override and Control in Self-Driving Cars

In the case of self-driving cars, applying the three ethical frameworks – Consequentialist, Duty, and Virtue – can guide product managers in deciding how these vehicles should respond to complex, life-and-death situations. But what about giving humans a role in these decisions? That's where follow-up considerations, like human override and stakeholder engagement, come into play.

While programming self-driving cars with ethical decision-making algorithms is crucial, product managers should also consider giving passengers or operators a say in those moments. Imagine being in a car when it faces an unavoidable accident. Wouldn't you want some form of control?

- **Human-in-the-Loop**: This approach allows human intervention during critical decision-making moments. For instance, if the car detects an impending accident, it could alert the passenger or operator, giving them the option to take control and override the automated system. This feature ensures that a human presence is still part of the decision-making process when an ethical dilemma arises.
- **Manual Override**: Another safeguard is a manual override system, where passengers can regain control of the vehicle in emergencies. This offers peace of mind, knowing that even though the car is driving itself, they can step in if something goes wrong.

By building in these options, product managers can balance the benefits of automation with the need for human decision-making, especially in ethically challenging situations.

15.10.3 Stakeholder Engagement in Ethical Decisions

The decisions made by self-driving cars don't just affect the passengers inside; they have broader societal implications. That's why it's crucial for companies developing this technology to involve stakeholders in shaping its ethical frameworks.

- **Public Consultation**: Engaging the public in ethical discussions about how self-driving cars should behave in certain situations ensures that the systems align with societal values. Should a car prioritize the lives of pedestrians over passengers, or vice versa? By gathering input from a diverse range of people, companies can better reflect societal preferences in the ethical decisions programmed into these vehicles.
- **Collaboration with Ethicists**: In addition to public input, working with ethicists and philosophers can help address complex moral questions. These experts can provide insights on how to tackle ethical dilemmas, such as the Trolley Problem, in ways that balance technological innovation with moral responsibility.

15.11 The Principle of Double Effect (PDE)

The **Principle of Double Effect** (**PDE**) states that an action with both positive and negative effects is permissible if the negative outcome is not the direct intention and the positive outcome is significant. In DPM, **PDE** can apply when introducing features that have unintended side effects.

Example: In the case of the **Flo app**, the positive intention was to provide women with useful health tracking, but the unintended negative effect was the misleading of users regarding data privacy. The data-sharing scandal affected millions of users, violating the trust and transparency expected of ethical digital products. Applying **PDE**, the app developers should have ensured that the positive benefits of health tracking did not come at the cost of users' privacy.

15.12 Conclusion

In an age where digital products have a profound impact on individuals and society, ethical leadership in product management is not just a differentiator – it's a necessity. From ensuring data privacy and security to fostering inclusivity and promoting transparency, ethical product managers play a vital role in building products that not only succeed in the market but also contribute positively to society.

Ethical leadership in DPM requires product managers to consider the broader consequences of their actions, beyond business objectives. By understanding and applying the three ethical frameworks – **Consequentialist, Duty,** and **Virtue** ethics – product managers can make decisions that protect user privacy, ensure fairness, and foster trust. From handling data privacy in apps like **Flo** to programming self-driving cars, ethical decision-making remains central to building products that serve users and society responsibly. The use of ethical frameworks, the **Principle of Double Effect,** and real-world examples like **Google's Waymo** and **Tesla's Autopilot** highlight the importance of maintaining integrity in the development and management of digital products.

As product managers navigate the complex challenges of the digital age, integrating ethical considerations into every decision is crucial for long-term success and trust.

16

DRIVING CONTINUOUS IMPROVEMENT AND INNOVATION

16.1 Introduction

In the digital age, standing still is akin to moving backward. Products that thrive today can quickly become obsolete tomorrow if not continuously enhanced and evolved. As customer needs change, technologies advance, and competitors emerge, digital product managers are responsible for ensuring that their products remain relevant, valuable, and innovative. This chapter is dedicated to understanding how continuous improvement and innovation intersect and how they can be applied in the context of digital product management to achieve sustained growth and competitive advantage.

By integrating agile methods, customer feedback loops, and a culture of constant experimentation, product managers can keep their teams adaptive and responsive to the changing market landscape. The concepts covered in this chapter aim to equip digital product managers with the skills, tools, and mindset needed to drive consistent progress and embrace bold, game-changing innovations.

16.2 The Importance of Continuous Improvement

Continuous improvement in product management requires a constant cycle of learning, iteration, and optimization. Continuous improvement is the practice of making incremental enhancements to a product, process, or service over time. For digital product managers, this concept is critical because it allows them to identify inefficiencies, solve pain points, and optimize customer experiences in a structured and iterative manner.

DOI: 10.1201/9781003614180-16

Chapter 9 sets the foundation for how data plays a critical role in understanding customer behaviour and preferences. In this chapter, we extend this concept to include how data drives improvements in both product development and operational efficiency.

By integrating tools for product analytics, customer insights, and real-time feedback, product teams can identify areas where their products fall short and make informed adjustments. Building on the metrics discussed in Chapter 9, the data that helps improve retention, engagement, and product adoption becomes the foundation for long-term success.

Key questions that product managers should ask in the continuous improvement process include the following:

- Where are users experiencing friction in the product?
- What features are driving the highest levels of engagement?
- How can operational efficiency be improved to allow faster iterations?

Chapter 13 highlights the importance of standardized processes and frameworks to support product teams. In this chapter, we build upon that by introducing additional tools and frameworks that support continuous improvement and innovation:

- **PDCA** (Plan-Do-Check-Act): A cyclical framework that allows teams to plan new features, test them, analyse outcomes, and refine them based on results.
- **OKRs** (Objectives and Key Results): This goal-setting framework ensures that product teams remain aligned with broader business objectives while focusing on key performance metrics.
- **Retrospectives**: Regular team reflections to assess what went well, what didn't, and how to improve.
- **Customer Feedback Loops**: Gathering and analysing user feedback to inform small, iterative changes.
- **Process Optimization**: Refining workflows and development processes to reduce waste and improve efficiency.

Example: Spotify regularly updates its app based on user feedback, tweaking the user interface, improving playlist suggestions, and refining search capabilities, all to improve the overall user experience.

By using these tools, product managers can set clear goals, track progress, and make data-informed decisions that drive continuous product enhancements.

16.3 Balancing Incremental Innovation with Disruptive Innovation

Innovation often focuses on disruptive ideas, but successful product management balances this with operational excellence. As discussed in Chapter 12, product managers must ensure that innovations are aligned with organizational goals and strategies. Product managers must be able to balance both types of innovation to ensure long-term success.

There are two main types of innovation:

- **Incremental Innovation**: Small, continuous improvements to existing products.
- **Disruptive Innovation**: Transformative changes that create entirely new market opportunities.

Product managers must evaluate which approach to pursue based on the maturity of the product and market conditions. In fast-evolving industries like tech, a combination of both is essential to maintain relevance while exploring new opportunities. Innovation frameworks like **Design Thinking** and **Lean Startup**, which were referenced in earlier chapters, can be applied to fuel both types of innovation.

16.3.1 Incremental Innovation

Incremental Innovation focuses on making small, continuous improvements to existing products, processes, or services. Unlike disruptive innovation, which seeks to fundamentally alter markets, incremental innovation refines and enhances what already exists, often through minor adjustments that accumulate over time to create significant value. This type of innovation allows businesses to stay competitive by meeting evolving customer needs, optimizing internal processes, and incorporating new technologies without drastically changing their business model. It is a safer, more stable approach to innovation, aimed at sustaining growth and maintaining operational excellence while steadily improving the customer experience and product performance.

Here are some examples of Incremental Innovation, as shown in Figure 16.1:

- **Enhancing Existing Products**: Improving the performance, features, or quality of existing products to meet evolving customer needs and stay competitive in the market.
  - *Example*: **Apple's** regular updates to its **iPhone**, adding better cameras, processors, or new software features while retaining its core product identity.

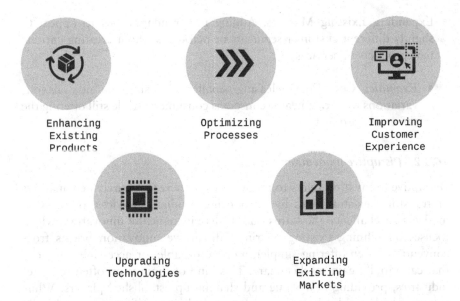

FIGURE 16.1   Examples of Incremental Innovation.

- **Optimizing Processes**: Streamlining internal operations, improving efficiency, and reducing costs without significantly altering the product or business model.

  - *Example*: **Toyota's** introduction of lean manufacturing practices, improving production efficiency while maintaining its core product lineup.

- **Improving Customer Experience**: Making small but meaningful improvements in how customers interact with the product or service, aiming to enhance user satisfaction and loyalty.

  - *Example*: **Netflix** refining its recommendation algorithm over time to make content suggestions more relevant to users, resulting in a better viewing experience.

- **Upgrading Technologies**: Incorporating gradual technological advancements such as better materials, refined software, or improved usability to keep up with market standards and customer expectations.

  - *Example*: **Microsoft's** continuous improvements to its Office suite with added collaboration tools and cloud integration, keeping it relevant to modern business needs.

- **Expanding Existing Markets**: Adding minor adaptations to appeal to slightly different customer segments or markets without creating entirely new products or services.

  - *Example*: **Coca-Cola** releasing smaller can sizes or new flavour variations to attract health-conscious consumers, while still offering the same core product.

16.3.2 Disruptive Innovation

Disruptive Innovation refers to innovations that create entirely new markets or transform existing ones by introducing products, services, or business models that challenge the status quo. Unlike incremental innovation, which focuses on refining existing offerings, disruptive innovation breaks from convention, often offering simpler, more affordable, or accessible solutions that can rapidly gain market share. This kind of innovation often redefines industries, providing new value and shaking up established players. While it carries higher risk, the potential for rewards is significant, as it typically opens up new opportunities and reshapes the competitive landscape.

Here are some examples of Disruptive Innovation, as shown in Figure 16.2:

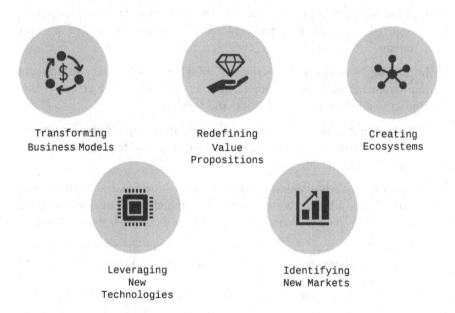

FIGURE 16.2 Examples of Disruptive Innovation.

1 **Identifying New Markets**: Disruptive innovation often targets underserved or unserved market segments.

- *Example*: **Uber**, for instance, disrupted the taxi industry by creating a new market for ride-sharing services, making transportation more accessible and affordable for a broader audience.

2 **Leveraging New Technologies**: Disruptive innovations frequently emerge by taking advantage of emerging technologies that can radically improve efficiency or customer experience.

- *Example*: AI-powered virtual assistants, like **Amazon's Alexa**, changed how consumers interact with technology by making voice control a key interface for smart devices.

3 **Transforming Business Models**: Companies adopting disruptive innovation often change how products or services are delivered, transitioning from traditional models to platforms or subscriptions.

- *Example*: **Spotify** revolutionized the music industry by offering unlimited music streaming via a subscription model, shifting away from individual music purchases.

4 **Redefining Value Propositions**: Disruptive innovations change how customers perceive value by offering benefits that were previously unavailable or considered unimportant.

- *Example*: **Tesla** redefined the electric vehicle market by offering not just eco-friendliness but also high performance, making electric cars desirable for a wider audience beyond environmentally conscious consumers.

5 **Creating Ecosystems**: Successful disruptive innovations often result in the creation of ecosystems that combine hardware, software, and services into integrated experiences.

- **Example: Apple's iPhone** not only revolutionized mobile phones but also built an ecosystem around its App Store, iOS platform, and services like iCloud, redefining mobile computing.

6 **Lowering Barriers to Entry**: Disruptive innovations tend to democratize access, making previously expensive or complex products available to a broader audience.

- **Example: Airbnb** disrupted the traditional hotel industry by allowing anyone with a spare room to become a host, lowering the barriers to entering the accommodation market.

16.4 Agile Methods for Driving Iterative Innovation

As referenced in Chapters 2 and 3, modern product management often leverages Agile and Lean methodologies to foster iterative development and continuous learning. Agile methods enable teams to quickly adapt to changes, while Lean principles focus on maximizing value and reducing waste.

Agile sprints, for example, allow product teams to break down large goals into smaller, manageable tasks. This fosters both innovation and efficiency by enabling regular feedback and quick adjustments. This chapter delves into how product managers can use these methodologies to foster a culture of continuous improvement, focusing on:

- Short, iterative cycles to improve speed-to-market
- Constant customer feedback to validate improvements
- Reducing bottlenecks through cross-functional collaboration (as discussed in Chapter 5)
- Embedding Innovation into the Product Lifecycle

Innovation should be embedded into every stage of the product lifecycle – from ideation and development to market launch and post-launch support. Drawing from earlier chapters like Chapters 5 and 8, this section focuses on how product managers can integrate innovative practices into each phase.

For example,

- During product development, encourage cross-team collaboration to explore new solutions and technical capabilities, as referenced in Chapter 2.
- During market launch, foster experimentation by testing new go-to-market strategies discussed in Chapter 4.
- After launch, integrate continuous feedback loops from customer service teams to refine and enhance product offerings, as explained in Chapter 8.

16.5 Customer-Centric Innovation

Innovation that focuses on solving real customer problems or enhancing customer experiences is often the most impactful. By adopting a customer-first mindset, product managers can drive product evolution in ways that meet unmet needs and exceed customer expectations. Customer-centric innovation not only improves user satisfaction but also opens opportunities for disruptive innovations.

Key techniques include the following:

- **Innovation Sprints:** Time-boxed periods where teams focus on brainstorming and developing innovative ideas that address customer pain points.

- **User Testing:** Gathering feedback from real customers to validate new features or product ideas before full-scale rollout.
- **Co-Creation with Customers:** Involving users directly in the development process through workshops, focus groups, or crowdsourcing.

Example: Airbnb's early success was driven by listening closely to hosts and travellers, adapting its platform to make it easier to use, and introducing features that significantly improved both the booking and hosting experiences.

16.6   Fostering a Culture of Innovation

Encouraging innovation requires fostering an organizational culture that supports creativity, experimentation, and risk-taking. Product managers play a key role in promoting this culture by advocating for the exploration of new ideas, encouraging cross-functional collaboration, and supporting teams in challenging the status quo. Referencing lessons from Chapter 7, product managers should foster a workplace where employees feel empowered to contribute innovative ideas and take ownership of product improvements.

Key strategies include the following:

- **Encouraging Experimentation:** Allowing teams the freedom to test new ideas and fail fast without fear of punishment.
- **Celebrating Wins and Failures:** Recognizing both successful innovations and the learnings gained from failed experiments.
- **Cross-Functional Collaboration:** Bringing together diverse teams from product, design, engineering, and marketing to foster a broad range of ideas and perspectives.

Example: Google famously allows employees to spend 20% of their time on personal projects, which has led to the development of several successful innovations, including **Gmail** and **Google News**.

16.7   Data-Driven Innovation

In today's digital world, data is the foundation of informed decision-making. Product managers need to utilize data analytics tools to track user behaviour, measure product performance, and identify opportunities for improvement. Data-driven innovation helps teams focus on what works, pivot away from what doesn't, and optimize product offerings based on real-world usage. Key tools and techniques for data-driven innovation:

- **A/B Testing:** Running experiments with different product versions to determine which performs better.

- **Product Analytics:** Using tools like Amplitude, Mixpanel, or Google Analytics to measure how users interact with a product.
- **Predictive Analytics:** Leveraging machine learning to anticipate user needs and improve product features.

Example: Netflix uses **A/B** testing to experiment with various user interface layouts and recommendation algorithms to enhance the user experience and increase engagement.

16.8   Conclusion

Continuous improvement and innovation are the twin engines that power digital product management in today's competitive landscape. By adopting an agile mindset, leveraging customer insights, and fostering a culture of creativity and experimentation, product managers can drive both incremental enhancements and groundbreaking innovations. Whether refining existing features or exploring disruptive technologies, product managers must always strive to push boundaries, ensuring that their products evolve and thrive in an ever-changing market.

In the journey of digital product management, continuous improvement and innovation are not just about adding new features or improving efficiencies. They're about creating a sustainable, forward-thinking mindset that fuels long-term product success. As covered in previous chapters, from *Leading Product Development* to *Building the Product Operating Model*, the road to product innovation requires collaboration, data-driven insights, and a culture that fosters creativity. This chapter ties it all together, reminding product managers that innovation and improvement should be embedded into the DNA of every product, every process, and every team.

INDEX